A Liberal Tool Kit

A Liberal Tool Kit

PROGRESSIVE RESPONSES TO CONSERVATIVE ARGUMENTS

David Coates

Westport, Connecticut
London

Library of Congress Cataloging-in-Publication Data

Coates, David.
   A liberal took kit : progressive responses to conservative arguments / David Coates.
      p. cm.
Includes index.
ISBN 978-0-275-99866-0 (alk. paper)
   1. Conservatism—United States. 2. Liberalism—United States. 3. Right and left
(Political Science). 4. Political parties—United States. 5. United States—Politics
and government—2001 I. Title.
   JC573.2.U6C63 2007
   320.51'30973—dc22   2007014266

British Library Cataloguing in Publication Data is available.

Library of Congress Catalog Card Number: 2007014266
ISBN-13: 978-0-275-99866-0
ISBN-10: 0-275-99866-5

First published in 2007

Praeger Publishers, 88 Post Road West, Westport, CT 06881
An imprint of Greenwood Publishing Group, Inc.
www.praeger.com

Printed in the United States of America

∞™

The paper used in this book complies with the
Permanent Paper Standard issued by the National
Information Standards Organization (Z39.48–1984).

10   9   8   7   6   5   4   3   2   1

For Shannon, Grace, Kristin, and Nate.
Each in their different ways, America's best hope for a better future.

Contents

Acknowledgments

It is not just the American economy that has moved further into debt as this book has been written. I have, too. In preparing what follows, I've gathered debts to a very special set of research assistants and friends. It was only through the dedicated efforts of Shannon Philmon, Grace Johnson, Kristin Olson, and Nate Reister that the writing of this book was even possible. I'm indebted to all four of them both for the quality of their research and for their willingness to tolerate lines of argument that so often diverged from their own. In addition to gathering much of the material upon which the manuscript was constructed, Shannon, Grace, Kristin, and Nate also read and commented on parts of the argument as it emerged. So, too, did family and friends: Eileen, Tom, and Ed; Peter Siavelis, Joel Krieger, Mark Miller, Michele Gillespie, Kevin Pittard, Neal Walls, Kathy Smith, and Greg Pollock. None of them are responsible for what follows, but all of them in their different ways helped to make what follows stronger. I thank them all.

For more detail than the notes can provide on the sources underpinning the arguments surveyed here, and for suggestions on further reading, please visit the blogsite associated with this book. You'll find it at http://www.liberaltoolkit.blogspot.com.

1

A Call to Arms

Democratic politics is largely a spectator sport. The crowd gets to play every now and then but, between elections, it's largely a matter of watching and listening. Most of us tire of that more quickly than we should, probably because—in a world of 24-hour news coverage—words flow in huge numbers, washing over us like summer rain. We get wet, and depending on the color of the rain, we either like it or we don't. Between 1994 and 2006, given the predominant color of the water then falling in political America, those of a liberal persuasion didn't enjoy the rain much at all.

Political parties are the great rainmakers of the modern age. They package ideas. They put together programs. They organize blocs of voters. They tell us what's happening—what's going right and what's going wrong. They point a way forward, and they provide us with protection against the rain coming from the other side. When they're effective, they provide a narrative linking the private hopes of their supporters to some great national program of reform. They keep their own people dry by the quality of that narrative—by the ability of the arguments and images they deploy to act as an effective umbrella against narratives coming from the other side. For at least 30 years after the New Deal, the biggest umbrella in American politics was a liberal one, constructed and held up by the Democrats. But not any more: that umbrella broke long ago, great holes torn in its canvas by the disintegration of the New Deal coalition and the rise of the Christian Right. These days—in one branch of government after another—a conservative

umbrella holds sway, and it's Republicans who are the normal political beneficiaries of its canopy.

The common sense of the age currently drips with the language and preoccupations of American conservatism. There was a time when the economic agenda of politics was dominated by full employment and the
minimum wage, and the social agenda by affirmative action and the war on
poverty. But not any more: In 2006, economic policy was preoccupied with
tax cuts and deregulation, and the top items on the social agenda were gay
marriage and the rights of the unborn child. Since 1980 at least, the entire
center of political gravity in the United States has shifted significantly to the
right, pulling the programs and arguments of even the liberal wing of
the Democrats after it. If unopposed, that rightward pull will be unstoppable
and self-sustaining, permanently closing the space for progressive politics by
establishing the dominance of entirely conservative political terminologies,
agendas, policies, values, and world views. Tom DeLay, in resigning from the
House of Representatives in June 2006, defended his record by asserting the
democratic importance of partisanship; and he was right. There is a *democratic* as well as a progressive need to roll that conservative orthodoxy back—
to challenge it in each of its dimensions—so that the Republic can enjoy again
a real debate on political language, policy agendas, social values, and organizing
philosophies.

Creating that debate is not easy, however, because the structures generating and sustaining this conservative orthodoxy are already extensive and
firmly in place. The conservative bloc is a strong and well-organized one.
Think of it for the moment like a great circle, cut pizza-like into overlapping
triangular slices. Fiscal conservatives, social conservatives, neocons in the
foreign policy community, the Christian Coalition, Buchananites, and even
the occasional liberal Republican. Or think of it as a pebble dropped in a
pond, releasing ever wider ripples across the surface of the water as it sinks.
Politicians at the center, libertarian think tanks and conservative newspapers
in the middle, the shock jocks of right-wing radio and television at the edge
of the pond itself. Either way, the political forces of the American Right
are huge, well-financed, and remarkably disciplined: a veritable conservative
army that at the peak of its power between 2004 and 2006 controlled all the
branches of the federal government.

The wonderful thing about armies, however, is that they contain divisions. The wonderful thing about peaks is that they are always followed by
troughs. For the American Right, the 2006 midterm election was one such
trough. It was also one that brought to the surface deep divisions on policies
and priorities among the various slices of the conservative pizza, on topics
as disparate as immigration and the war in Iraq. The preachers and the plu-
tocrats fell out publicly in 2006,[1] which is why now is precisely the moment
for liberals to answer back, letting the voice of the other America be heard
loud and clear again. For there is another America, and there is another

voice. It's another America that currently is scattered—as pockets of blue in a sea of red—weakened by that very dispersal and by its lack of a deep and complex support structure to match the Republicans' own. And there is another voice—lots of voices, actually—voices informed by gentler and nobler sets of values than those prevalent in the American Right. But those voices are also scattered and often hidden—lost in a hundred think tanks, buried in newsrooms, and tucked away in the staff rooms and union offices of working America. To pull those voices together, and to turn a midterm protest vote into support that will last and grow, is the most vital task currently facing the Democratic Party. But it is not a task that will be completed successfully until and unless liberals can match conservatives in the quality of their arguments, the confidence of their position, and the strength of the overarching narrative that they tell. This book has been prepared in the hope that it can contribute to the reawakening of that liberal confidence.

ANSWERING BACK

If we are to answer back effectively against conservative orthodoxies that are as strongly held and widely disseminated as those we now face, our liberal rebuttal will have to be powerful in both what it says and how it is delivered. Creating arguments stronger than those we face requires that we learn from the way our political opponents build and disseminate their arguments, and that we set standards for ourselves that are higher than those common in conservative circles. To that end, the following guidelines seem appropriate and will be followed in all the material developed here.

We need to deal with the alternative point of view in all its complexity

The first guideline is this. It's no good deluding ourselves about the potency of our case by testing our arguments only against easy targets or straw men. What we have to do instead is build the conservative case in all its faces—putting its weak and strong components in their appropriate slots—and then respond to the case in its totality. We have to summarize conservative arguments with as much care as we can manage—leaving out as little as possible—and actually guide people to the places in which they can read those arguments more fully themselves. To do anything less would be intellectually dishonest and politically self-defeating.

We need to balance complexity in argument with clarity in presentation

Second, we have to put the liberal response together in ways that make it accessible to the people who will use it. We have to make that response as strong and all-encompassing as it can be—and that means also making it as complex and internally coherent as it needs to be—but complexity in argument must not be matched by complexity in presentation and language. On the contrary, the prime skill we need to develop is one of saying complicated things in simple ways. Effective arguments are those that people can own. They can't own what they can't understand—and we won't persuade others if we can't first persuade ourselves.

We need to design arguments that can run the gamut from sound bites to theses

Third, the liberal response needs to be constructed in such a way that it can be used differently for different audiences. Some audiences need long and complex conversations. In others, the long and complex would fall like concrete rain. All arguments are built out of separate parts, and all good arguments move from the specific to the general, the simple to the complex, the visible to the underlying, the empirical to the theoretical, and so on. Our answers have to be of that sophisticated kind, but they also have to be built from stand-alone parts that can be extracted for use in each specific case. We have to put the rebuttal together, that is, in such a way that people wanting to use it can easily cherry-pick the parts that are appropriate for the audience with which they happen to be dealing.

We have to anchor our case in solid and reliable evidence

Fourth, if the exercise in which we're engaged is to be more than one of assertion and counterassertion, we also have to make sure that what we say is anchored in systematically gathered and high-quality data. That means that our case has to be firmly rooted in the best scholarship that's currently available. Conservative advocates tend not to read widely outside their comfort zone, but we have to; and as we do so, we have to make it possible for others to take the same journey themselves. Extensive footnotes (and in this case, also an *academic blogsite*[2]) are therefore vital to this purpose. People don't need to read the footnotes or visit the site if they don't want to. Their existence might be reassurance enough. But the underpinnings of what we say have to be part of how we answer back, because only by showing that the underpinnings of our arguments exist (and are accessible) can we legitimately ask of our conservative opponents that they too demonstrate the foundations of theirs.

The problem specification has to be superior

Fifth, in addition to the quality of evidence, we will need to focus on the way problems are framed and premises followed through. The Republican Right has long recognized the importance of how issues are "framed," and so too must we. Someone on welfare can be a "casualty," a "victim," or the "agent" of his or her own poverty, and which of those three notions prevails effectively fix the political responses thought appropriate. If welfare recipients are victims, they need help. If they're agents, they need strictures. So the policy implications of each problem specification have to be made clear, as does the evidence justifying the specification chosen. If the poor are victims, it has to be demonstrated. Equally, if they're not, their responsibility for their own plight has to be shown; and we need to do the showing.

... and the logic has to be tight

Sixth, if that demonstration is to be effective, there can be no leaps in the logic that carries us from problem specification to solution, and no treating of one issue in isolation from the rest. In the triangle of wages, employment, and global competition, for example, the conservative argument we face is that raising the first (wages) in the context of the third (global competition) must adversely affect the second (jobs). If we don't like the low-wage policy which that argument generates, we either have to challenge the logic of the conservative linkages or change one of the variables in play. In this case, we're going to find that one of the variables has to go. We're going to find that we can't have a viable wages policy without designing a trade policy that's consistent with it. If we don't get those two things into some coherent and logical line, moderate and sensible people just aren't going to be persuaded that our liberal alternative is even credible, let alone desirable. Our arguments, therefore, will only persuade if they are genuinely superior and complete.

REACHING OUT

So there are standards here that we have to meet as we answer back. If we do so, two things should follow. The first is that the democratic character and quality of the debate should go up. We might not win every argument, but win or lose, knowledge of the issues and their solutions should be significantly enhanced. And anyway, more likely than not, if we hit these standards, we will win many of those arguments, and minds will slowly and imperceptibly change. Not the minds of the totally committed, of course. Those are already hermetically sealed by a catechism of clichés and half-truths that no dialogue can loosen. But if our arguments are strong and our procedures rigorous, we might reach other minds—more open minds, minds more liberal with a lowercase "l"—minds of more independent voters still keen to get to the bottom of the international and local ills that befall us.

To reach them, a book like this has no choice but to engage openly and honestly with problem specifications and policy solutions from across the aisle. If conservative commentators point to genuine problems, those problems must be conceded. If conservative answers have merit, that merit must be recognized. The whole premise on which this book is written is that moderate opinion will not be won over by denigrating positions with which we disagree, or by denouncing people whose politics are not our own. Moderate opinion will be won over only through the superiority of the arguments and solutions with which we respond to those positions and those people. Liberal arguments and solutions of that superior kind are readily available—and in some quantity—if you know where to look for them. The task of this book is to bring them together for easy use, in a structured conversation with the inferior ones currently being canvassed by the Republicans in Washington.

THE GREAT MOVING LEFT SHOW

Robert Reich once wrote a wonderful essay describing how the Republican Party had captured and colonized what he called the four great narratives of American political life—two hopeful, two fearful—that once had been the bedrock of support for progressive causes: "the triumphant individual," "the benevolent community," "the mobs at the gate," and "the rot at the top."[3] Twenty-five years earlier, in a different but related country, Margaret Thatcher had done the same thing to the Democratic Party's equivalent there—the British Labour Party. She'd stolen their best tunes, drained them of their center-left content, and filled them with a conservatism of her own. She took their vocabulary—a vocabulary of freedom, justice, and equality— and replaced its progressive content with a conservative one. She took the Left's main policy weapons and turned them upside down: telling the British people to think of the democratic management of a private economy as the main cause of that economy's poor performance. She effected what was known at the time as "the great moving right show."[4]

But in the end, that theft of all that was best and progressive in the politics of the United Kingdom failed, because even she couldn't create a unified and civilized society by advocating a politics that sets individuals against each other in an unregulated struggle for survival. Margaret Thatcher couldn't do it in the United Kingdom and the Republicans won't be able to do it here either. There's already a gap between the grand visions of their rhetoric and the realities within which we all live, a gap between promise and performance that holds out the possibility that we might yet trigger "a great moving left show," pulling the center of gravity of American politics back into the civilized center. But shows of that kind don't happen unless somebody puts them on, which is why it's now time for us to get the narratives back, time for us to sing our tunes again. To sing well and to sing together, we all have to learn the same words.[5] Here, in the chapters that follow, culled from the work of the finest think tanks of the Democratic Left, are some of those words. Let's hope they help us to perform a little better in the immediate future than we have in the immediate past.

2

Clearing the Decks

There are powerful conservative arguments out there that liberals need to think about with considerable care: arguments put forward with conviction by people of genuine integrity and by institutions of high academic repute. Debating with them is a serious and important endeavor. But there are other arguments out there too—arguments of less force and value—that need to be cleared away first. These other arguments have a different purpose. They exist less to stimulate debate than to close it down, and they are disseminated less by intellectuals within the conservative movement than by their more populist outriders, who collectively make up a kind of right-wing "heavy brigade." We eventually will have to compete with the pedigree conservatives, but first we need to deal with their rottweilers.

DOGS OF WAR

Republican rottweilers come in a number of forms. They come as private bloggers—in increasing numbers, indeed. They come as right-wing shock jocks—now so plentiful as to have their own hierarchy of popularity. And they come as journalists with their own weekly columns, newsletters, books, and regular media appearances. As is to be expected in such a host, quality varies, but the best of them are very good indeed at what they do. Liberals may not care much for the Ann Coulters, Sean Hannitys, Michael Savages, Bill O'Reillys, and Rush Limbaughs of this world, but these people are not to be ignored. They see themselves as active warriors in a vital culture war, collectively orchestrating a powerful offensive against progressive positions and the individuals who articulate them.[1] It's an offensive that seeks not so much dialogue as closure. Its effect—and presumably also part of its purpose—is the construction in conservative ranks of a deep-rooted refusal even to listen to progressive arguments, let alone to be swayed by them: a refusal created mainly by the systematic denigration of all things liberal. We live in our own version of McCarthyite times.[2]

This jamming and blocking offensive has a set of standard components that we need to recognize and refute. Invariably, the first move in much of the blocking literature is the creation of a "composite" liberal of extreme and unpalatable views, who is then used as shorthand for liberals of all varieties. That composite and crazy liberal is labeled as profoundly un-American, and indeed anti-American, in impact and even in intention. He or she is often presented as in league with hostile foreigners and, as such, is positioned as a direct threat to the stability of core American values and institutions. The liberal message, we are told, is not to be argued with. It's to be defined out of court. Never go for the message. Go for the messenger. The message isn't to be taken seriously. It's to be labeled and dismissed as the prime cause of the very social ills about which liberals so regularly complain: ills that would then quickly disappear if liberals would also do the same.

Let's see how this works out in practice. Here's how to write like a conservative rottweiler.[3]

Straw men and Trojan horses

First you put together a composite liberal—a genuine straw person. You find one little-known radical, a Ward Churchill or the like, and you condemn him for believing something particularly outlandish. A few pages later, you find a different radical, and condemn him (or her) for believing something else equally bizarre.[4] Because the two named individuals are both labeled by you as liberals, you're quickly able to treat every liberal as though he or she believed both those outlandish things—although in reality the views you've chosen are extreme ones and, indeed, are held as core opinions by very few liberals. If anyone is indelicate enough to point that out, you allow the lack of fit between the claim and the data to make no difference whatsoever. Instead you treat liberalism as a political tendency that's idea-prone to extreme radicalism, whether its adherents realize it or not, thus enabling you to insist that, even when your readers are only moderate liberals, they're still in bed with radicals and—like every Trojan horse—must stand condemned accordingly.

Patriots and traitors

The next trick is to go "nativist," by wrapping your conservative views in the American flag. There are a number of ways of doing this: the more of them you use, the more effective the tactic becomes. Start by talking lovingly of an

America of suburban peace and family values—a golden age of 1950s calm[5]—and then imply that one generation of liberal policies destroyed that calm and a second one now threatens the survival of the values on which it was based. Scan foreign experiences, cherry-pick some failures, and imply that liberal policies have foreign roots in exactly those same failures. Don't mention the positive European impact on the Founding Fathers. Talk only of America escaping the European yoke: Describe a unique city on a hill imperiled by liberal (foreign-inspired) policies that weaken security, run counter to American individualism, and erode the Protestant work ethic. And, if in doubt, throw in a dash of anti-intellectualism too: comparing good American conservative common sense with the "soft Marxism" of Scandinavian social democracy or the arrogance of French statism.[6] That way, even when conservative administrations malfunction in Washington, the critique can be turned—not into one against conservatism (with its obvious liberal solution)—but into yet more antistatism. Not even conservative government works, you should imply, so let's keep the government out of things altogether!

Label the message, shoot the messenger

Make sure next that any policy or political position with which you disagree is labeled pejoratively, with as many "bad" tags as you can find. Do as much negative labeling as possible. Don't just disagree with a judicial ruling. Make sure that that ruling came from an "activist" judge.[7] Never miss the opportunity to characterize any federal initiative with which you disagree as, at best, "a challenge to states' rights" and, at worst, as "socialist." Keep before the American people a stark choice between "freedom"—understood as no public policy disturbance of the status quo—and "socialism": with the latter understood as any proposal likely to redress inequality, increase taxation, or restrict the rights of the rich.[8] And never simply disagree with your liberal opponent. Always denigrate that opponent, and talk of him or her in medical or animal terms: as an infection, a cancer, or as vermin who need removing, cutting out, or putting down.[9] Always insist that "you don't have to compromise with depravity"[10] and, at the same time, always inflate the power and prestige that you attribute to those with whom you disagree. The less influential they are, the more you must label them as totally dominant in a set of institutions with which your readers are familiar but which they don't directly and intimately know: at the very least, in the media, higher education, the federal bureaucracy, the Democratic Party, and the trade unions. Always present yourself, that is, as an oppressed and persecuted minority, the better to obscure who exactly it is who is doing the persecution and setting the agenda these days.

Blame the victim, demonize the do-gooder

If that doesn't work, then turn reality entirely on its head. Ignore the vast body of evidence now available to us on how inherited inequalities are denying this generation of Americans the chance to begin their search for prosperity on a level playing field. Instead, build your arguments on a glorified and over-simplistic version of the American Dream, by insisting that rapid individual progress is still straightforwardly guaranteed to those who strive with sufficient individual zeal for its immediate attainment.[11] That approach will give you a series of huge advantages in the arguments stakes. It will enable you immediately to blame the victim, not the perpetrator, of any social ill that liberals bring up for policy debate. You'll be able to blame poverty on the poor and unemployment on the jobless, pregnancy on the feckless young, and divorce on lack of faith. That will then free you of any moral obligation to do anything about any of those things. It will also enable you to put the entire blame for the social ills now besetting contemporary America on previous liberal attempts to set those ills to right. Current levels of income inequality can be blamed on Johnson's "War on Poverty." High levels of welfare dependency and the rise of single-parent families can be similarly explained away, although activist judges of a liberal persuasion can also be blamed for part of that: namely, *Roe v. Wade*. Don't on any account give even an inch to any successful public welfare policy: not here, not in Europe, not even in the developing world. If you find one, don't discuss the reason for its success at all. Instead, focus the discussion immediately on its necessarily greater adverse side effects on all sorts of important economic and social institutions—the more the merrier, indeed—from economic growth and personal living standards to individual morality and the rise of the pornographic Internet.

Outflank the Republican Party on its right

And as one final element in your peroration, make sure that you present every member of the Republican leadership in Washington as some kind of closet liberal. Don't for a moment admit that present administration policy is in any sense genuinely conservative.[12] To do that would be to throw away the two great advantages that playing the "outflanking card from the right" always gives you: namely, (1) a base from which to continually pull the Republican Party further and further away from government-imposed solutions of any kind, and (2) iron-clad protection against liberal claims that conservative policies, when applied, invariably fail. For if you outflank George W. Bush on his right, every failure so listed can then quickly be redefined as a consequence, not of conservatism, but of its betrayal. Explaining inadequacies of Republican policy in that way—as the product of, at best, only a "flawed conservatism"—leaves wonderfully intact the unchallengeable status of your basic premises: that societies work best when governed least, that private charity is always superior to any form of public welfare provision, and that government regulation is by definition some form of creeping socialism. The great thing about unchallengeable premises of that kind is that you can recycle them forever, in that way giving them the appearance of truth simply by the power of regular repetition. Finally, as your parting shot, do make certain that some of the things you say about President Bush, or liberals, or Arabs are so outlandish that not even a conservative media outlet like *Fox News* will disseminate them, because that will give you yet more evidence of how deeply entrenched within apparently right-wing institutions is the covert liberal monopoly of the entire American cultural network.[13] Don't talk to liberals. Talk past them, by talking also past the conservative establishment.

A LIBERAL RESPONSE

The first thing to be said in response is that this form of argumentation is not only crude, distorting, and illegitimate—although it is all of those things—it's also profoundly undemocratic. It is crude and distorting. Arguments are caricatured and individuals are lampooned, and the misuse of data—the cherry-picking of examples and the unexamined nature of premises—robs the whole exercise of any serious intellectual integrity. But the biggest danger is none of that. The biggest danger is the antidemocratic one. This is a body of conservative argumentation that claims to be defending American freedoms and showing the superiority of freedom in the western hemisphere over freedom elsewhere. But its mode of argument—its tone, its vitriol, its intolerance of alternatives, its underlying fundamentalism—all these features jeopardize the very freedoms it claims to defend. At the very least, we have to say back to the Ann Coulters of this world that respect for opponents, and the give and take of points of view, is the very basis of a democratic culture: a basis that is clearly safer in our hands these days than it is in hers.

We will deal in the appropriate chapters with the individual claims made in the rottweiller literature about particular policy areas. Here we need to establish some broad responses that apply across the literature as a whole: guidelines on how best to respond to the general attack being made.[14]

Get the target right

The first thing we have to insist on is that the debate between conservatives and liberals be focused on actual arguments by actual people. There can be no space in any intelligent debate on the future of the United States for the construction and chasing of straw men. We mustn't do it ourselves, and we mustn't tolerate it in others. We must continually reassert the complexity of positions on both the left and the right. If conservative popularizers want to invent liberal monsters of their own imagination, the better to claim that they alone can slay them, they're free to do that; but they're not free then to claim that by so doing they have refuted real liberals with real policies. That political animal is far more difficult to kill—not least because it has more than one head. The liberal camp is a broad one, characterized by internal disagreements as well as by shared values, and although the center of gravity of liberal views is definitely to the left of conservative ones—that's not in dispute—there's also a considerable overlap between the ranges of opinion that cluster around those centers. Indeed, the most pressing responsibility on moderates in the face of this conservative onslaught is to seek out that common ground and to pull political discussion back and away from the agenda-setting of the people who *are* the true radicals, the true outliers, in contemporary U.S. politics—namely, sections of the Republican Right itself.

Locate the real Trojan horse

If there is a Trojan horse problem in U.S. politics right now, it's one for the conservative coalition far more than for the liberal one, and not in the way that Michael Savage and Pat Buchanan would have it. George W. Bush may be too liberal for their tastes on issues like immigration and foreign trade, but that's not the case we need to make. We need to ask instead just how many liberal Republicans voted for George Bush in 2000, expecting compassionate conservatism and global disengagement, only to get welfare retrenchment, tax breaks for the privileged, and the erosion of environmental controls, not to mention the Bush family's private war. We need to ask just how many liberal conservatives, even now, take comfort in the carefully constructed moderation of the president's State of the Union addresses—and find there a genuine desire to reach out across the aisle to the entirety of the American people—only to discover later that, in the pork barrel politics of Washington, well-placed Republican lobbyists effectively negate that outreach by slipping into law special privileges for the already overprivileged. We need constantly to remind moderate Republicans that a vote for George Bush was also a vote for the army of extreme conservatives who, between 2000 and 2006, slipped into positions of power and influence on the coattails of his claims about compassion, social justice, and the protection of the weak. We need constantly to remind them that, in a very genuine sense, the inmates took over the asylum and that we've just started to get it back.

Recapture the flag

"Nativism" is always the last refuge of the bankrupt, and we have to keep saying that. The flag is not just a Republican flag. There are many Americas and many Americans—some conservative, some liberal—all of them in their different ways passionate about this country and determined to see it prosperous and secure. The New Deal was not a foreign import, after all. On the contrary, it was just as home grown as the Pledge of Allegiance itself. In important and valuable ways the United States is a unique—and a uniquely free—society, but it is also one that shares many problems and processes with equivalent industrial democracies elsewhere. Given that commonality of situation and agenda, it is at the very least strange that a country so uniquely constructed by the migration to it of the brightest and the best should now choose to denigrate the contribution of foreign ideas—and even of foreign people—to its future internal development. National pride is an important virtue, but such pride often comes before a fall. The United States does some things well that others do not, and we should glory in that. But by the same token, there are economic and social dimensions of the United States that don't bear easy comparison with the best of the rest abroad. So it's always worth looking outward as well as inward, to see whether there are things to be learned with profit from the way they are performed elsewhere, and we must keep insisting on that intellectual and political openness. It might suit the Republican Right on occasion—for short-term political advantage—to ridicule everything French, but the Founding Fathers were not so indiscriminate in their reaction to the finest of European thought and practice. So who is our best guide in this—Jefferson or Limbaugh? You only have to pose the question to see the answer.

Fight the adjectival war

Because a key element in the framing of political agendas is the language in which that frame is built, any successful reestablishment of the liberal voice must include, as one of its first objectives, the recapturing of the language itself.[15] We need a war on adjectives.[16] Judging is always an "active" exercise. Conservative judges are activist judges, too. If they weren't, the composition of the bench wouldn't matter so much to conservatives and liberals alike. The choice is not between active and inactive judges. It's between progressive and conservative ones, and we should say so. By the same token, we should say, too, that a health care system to which everyone has access is not by that fact alone transformed into a socialist one. It would only be that if all the doctors inside it were turned into state employees. A health care system to which everyone has access is merely a "universal" one. Calling it "socialistic," and implying it has old-style Russian overtones, makes it unappealing. Calling it a universal health care system, and implying it would be like the systems in Germany or the United Kingdom, changes the overtones entirely. That relabeling doesn't remove the need to ask whether a foreign model has any relevance here, but at least it allows the question to be posed without the answer having been predetermined. We should always insist on neutral terminology and then ask of our conservative critics: What are you so afraid of that you have to wrap your chosen solutions in loaded adjectival cling-film? If your answers are so visibly superior, why do you need to build such a defensive linguistic wall around them?

Raise the standard of debate

Key, too, to the reestablishment of the liberal voice as an important presence in American politics must be the insistence on a more measured and civilized form of debate between those who would participate. The intensity and speed of denigration of opponents now common on the American Right has happened before. It happened in very similar ways in Germany and Italy in the 1920s, as they headed to fascism rather than toward FDR's New Deal. If the contemporary debate is to be productive of long-term democratic outcomes, it has to be pulled to a higher and a calmer standard than that currently prevalent in many populist right-wing circles. Intellectual closure is always dangerous for democracy—and fundamentalism, in whatever form, always threatens the enlightenment project in which the political freedoms of this country are embedded. Tolerance and dialogue, reason and reflection, the free exchange of ideas and information—these are the very lifeblood of an informed and democratic citizenry. One vital task of liberals in these troubled times is to keep that tolerance, reason, and untrammeled debate alive. The democratic patient is not dead yet, but its health is definitely in danger. We must set high standards for ourselves: standards that privilege criticism over castigation. And we must insist on similar standards in our political opponents: no replacement of civilized democratic discourse by the politics of the hustings.

Ridicule the nonsensical

Standards have to be about more than tone of voice or mode of address. They also have to be about the quality of evidence, and the testing of assertion against data. Is it really the case, as Ann Coulter would have it, that "nationally renowned liberal female journalists have been known to offer oral sex to elected officials just for keeping abortion on demand legal"?[17] Are we really to believe, with Michael Savage, that many of America's leading universities "are often nothing more than houses of porn and scorn"?[18] Some of the propositions common in the popular writings of the Conservative Right—these included—are simply nonsensical and have to be recognized as such. Try asking a Katrina victim whether trickle-down economics works when you're already up to your neck in water. See how many virgin "queens" you can find who decided to get pregnant because they wanted a welfare check. And see how many al-Qaeda terrorists you can name who supported a secular Baathist like Saddam Hussein before Dick Cheney decided that getting rid of him was the best way of blocking Osama bin Laden. Repetition of idiocy does not remove it. Self-deception is self-deception, no matter how many times it's practiced. Just because conservative critics insist that their view of the world is more realistic than ours—that we, not they, are the hopeless romantics—it does not remove from them the obligation to study that reality rigorously. After all, they're currently busy reshaping it in line with their fantasies. Bulls in china shops tend to do damage—they certainly are doing it now. We need to remember that the next time a right-wing Republican asks us for our vote.

Insist on the use of evidence

A lot of the disagreements between liberals and conservatives are open to resolution by the examination of appropriate evidence, so we must insist on the presence and use of carefully researched facts throughout the policy-debating process. Facts should not frighten us. If they frighten others, then that would suggest that much of what is now argued as axiomatic is in fact special pleading by the privileged. A free exchange of ideas and arguments should make that clear. Of course, in politics as in life, facts are not in the end the determining factor. Choices will still have to be made. But in an informed democracy, those choices are made all the better when the data in which they're set are secure. So what have we to lose? If we're wrong—if the data suggest things that we don't want to hear—then conservatives are entirely correct to insist that we surrender the field to them. But if we are not so in error—if the evidence, when examined, leaves holes in our opponents' proposals and underlying philosophies—then they, too, will need to respond in kind. This is not a matter of partisanship. It's a question of the quality of the research on which important political decisions are made. If the rush to war in 2003 told us anything, it told us that bad data make for bad policy. The systematic exploration of the facts can only improve the policy debate at home and abroad. And so we should insist, on both sides of the aisle, *out* with cliché, *down* with half-truths, *in* with hard and systematic data, and *in* all the time, and not just when the evidence happens to fit our already entrenched preconceptions.

Slow down the discussion

Moreover, and for all its stridency, this new conservative orthodoxy is extremely insecure. Indeed the stridency appears to be, as much as anything, a reaction to the dangerously thin foundations on which so much of the right-wing case now rests. A more firmly grounded and self-confident orthodoxy would not need to move with such speed to close down debate, fall back on clichés, or denigrate the foreign and the different. Insisting that French fries be renamed freedom fries tells us nothing about the quality of the fries, but it does tell us a lot about the insecurities of those who would rename them. The penchant of so much of the right-wing media for rapid dialogue has two great advantages for them that we need to expose. It enables them to keep the discussion at the level of the superficial and the slick, privileging quick clichés over longer and more reflective forms of analysis. And it enables them quickly to circumvent data they dislike, arguments they can't answer, and problems they wish not to discuss. We need to challenge these right-wing "scream-fests,"[19] insisting instead that major political issues receive the full historical and analytical treatment they deserve. Gossip and trivia from inside the Beltway make for easy television, but at best they constitute poor political education. Chris Matthews may call his program *Hardball*, but actually it's not hard at all.

Expose the underlying hypocrisy

It was Anatole France who once pointed out that both the rich and the poor had the right to sleep under the bridges of Paris, but that oddly enough, the rich didn't choose to do so. So often these days, the language of universal individual rights is used by conservative advocates to block off public policy that might strengthen collective rights, in the process reinforcing and protecting the positions of the privileged. Offering tax cuts to the rich as *the* one effective policy to help the poor really requires strong ideological balls, and we have to admit that the members of the Republican Right are well endowed in that particular part of their political anatomy. Programmatic castration seems essential here. It's up to us to show, over and over again, the self-serving nature of many right-wing policies. If conservative opponents of the liberalization of immigration rules suddenly develop a deep concern for the impact of immigration on the wages of the working poor, then we need to ask them how they voted on the raising of the national minimum wage. If conservative opponents of gay marriage argue that homosexuality offends the laws of God and undermines the sanctity of the family, we have to ask them why divorce rates are highest in the states of the Bible Belt. And if George W. Bush belatedly declares his concern with the adverse effects of global warming, we have to ask him why he won't support a carbon tax or ratify the Kyoto Protocol. It's up to liberals to raise time and time again the central question facing the whole compassionate conservatism project: compassion for exactly whom? Is it for the rich or for the poor, the privileged or the downtrodden? That's the issue. Too often on the Republican Right these days, the rhetoric is morally pretentious while the practice is sordidly self-serving. And we need to say as much.

Clarify the value choice

In the end, we can't avoid issues of value. No one can. Bill O'Reilly is right. There is a culture war going on in the United States right now, one rooted in different value systems. The Republican Right might claim that its voice is less ideological than that of its progressive opponents, but that claim is ludicrous. If ideas were not important, Ann Coulter would not write her books. But she does, and no doubt she will go on writing, and she should. But what's good for the goose must also be good for the gander. It's now our turn to do exactly the same thing. We have to ask our political opponents: What are your values? What offends you most? Are you more offended by the presence of widespread poverty amid affluence in the richest country on earth, or do you react with greater venom to the arrival of the Internal Revenue Service (IRS) to take from you some of your private wealth in order to apply it to the greater good? Is it more important to you that an employer can hire and fire at will than it is to see labor laws that give American citizens strong and dependable rights at work? Are you prepared to pay more for imported goods produced by overseas workers who are paid decent wages, or don't you care about the conditions of the foreign poor if any easing of their conditions would corrode your capacity to consume? How wide does your commitment to individual rights stretch—out from you through your family to whom? Does it extend from the basic political right to vote to the wider social right of children to grow up in houses free of poverty and with access to adequate health care? Are you selfless just on Sunday, or does your Christian morality—your concern for your fellow man or woman—last all week?

We have to ask, and we need to know.

_____ 3 _____

The Wonders of "Trickle-Down Economics"

I f there are two general economic facts on which the entire American
Right appear to stand united, they are these: that taxation is a bad thing,
and that things improve the more that taxation declines. Not surprisingly,
therefore, the centerpiece of George W. Bush's entire domestic economic
program has been the reform of the American tax system. He's commissioned inquiries into it; he's used it as his main weapon of economic recovery; and he's now spending his last years in the White House working to
make permanent the temporary tax cuts introduced during his first term. In
2001, his administration oversaw the introduction of a $1.35 trillion pack-
age of tax cuts—the largest since 1981—a package phasing in reductions in
individual tax rates and estate taxes, and increases in child tax credit—the
whole package to last until 2010. In 2003, the president signed into law
legislation that lowered until 2008 the tax rates on capital gains, dividends,
and business investment, and brought into immediate effect the reductions
in individual income tax rates legislated in 2001. In 2006, the president
brought forward an additional $70 billion worth of tax cuts, extending the
main elements of the 2003 package until 2010.

Tax changes of this kind garnered for the Bush White House extensive
support within and beyond the Republican coalition, although none of
the packages legislated into existence so far have satisfied the party's right
wing—at least not entirely. Fiscal conservatives in particular remain convinced that the Bush administration, for all its orthodoxy on the importance

of tax reduction, spends far too much money on far too many programs and remains far too cautious in the reforms it advocates and in the changes it achieves. George Bush is still a "big government" president in the minds of many of those who voted for him, and their enthusiasm for him has been significantly diluted by that fact. The Republican Right has a bigger and more radical taxation agenda than any currently being pursued by the White House, an agenda built around propositions of the following kind.

Taxation in the United States is at historically high levels, and needs to be brought down as a matter of urgency

Western Europeans often recognize the existence of two kinds of wage—the private wage and the social wage—and then treat taxation as a legitimate payment for important forms of social provision.[1] But that's not the way taxes are understood and presented by the Republican Party and its conservative allies here in the United States. Here, it's the private wage that is uniquely privileged. It's your money. It's hard earned. Taxation is a burden on it, something from which any sane person automatically seeks maximum "relief." Nearly $4 in every $10—"an all-time high,"[2] conservative commentators regularly tell us—is now "taken" in taxes by various levels of government: taken in direct and in hidden ways. That tax "take" hurts us all. It hurts American businesses, burdening them with the administrative costs of complex tax codes that distort investment, and it hurts American families, whose wages are squeezed by ever-rising taxes. The entire tax code is said to be riddled with anomalies and a lack of fairness. Dividends are taxed twice and, through the estate tax, even death itself is taxed, imposing "an undue, unfair and frankly, un-American burden on families, farmers and entrepreneurs."[3] The tax code in the United States is said to have grown into such a monster that no one can now operate legally within it without the help of a growing army of tax specialists and without surrendering to the government ever-larger quantities of private information that no public agency should possess. "Working families are paying four times more in taxes today than they did in the 1950s," Sean Hannity has written, and "many are struggling just to make ends meet";[4] which is why good news in the world of taxation—according to President Bush at least—occurs only when "Americans keep more of their hard-earned dollars because of tax cuts."[5]

Tax cuts are the quickest and most effective way of generating economic growth and rising employment

"Our economy prospers," the president told us in April 2006, "when Americans like you make the decisions on how best to spend, save and invest."[6] The most effective way to generate output and employment is simultaneously to ease the tax burden on consumers and companies. The goal of tax policy should be "to minimize the impediments to the behaviors—work, saving, investment and entrepreneurship—that generate production and income. Fundamental tax reform is capable of generating growth."[7] Particularly in a recession marked by a slump in business investment, it makes sense to go for an "aggressive tax-cutting policy ... to get the capital investment engine running again."[8] Lowering corporate taxation frees companies to invest, in turn strengthening their competitive position. It frees them to add workers to their payroll, thus boosting demand. And, "when Americans have money to spend, everyone wins, because jobs are created by that spending."[9] The lower the tax burden on the employment of labor, the more jobs can be created. The less taxation discourages investment and innovation, the greater will be the rate of economic growth. In fact, tax cuts enhance the flows of revenue within the economy, on which taxation itself can then be levied. Cutting taxes, therefore, is paradoxically the best way to generate a virtuous cycle of company growth, private affluence, *and* taxation revenue. It contrasts favorably with the "tax rates/tax revenue downward spiral"[10] associated with liberal-inspired tax increases, which only suppress consumer demand, discourage investment and employment, and erode the tax base. "The message is clear. Republicans giveth, Democrats taketh away."[11]

Big government needs to be rolled back to stop it from crowding out the private enterprise on which long-term economic prosperity depends

That rising flow of taxable revenue is the part of the antitax argument that troubles many within the Republican coalition: the observable paradox that "starving the beast"[12] of tax revenues will not itself curb the growth of government. For fiscal conservatives, "deficits are a symptom" but "spending is the disease," because "government spending diverts resources from the productive sector of the economy."[13] Government borrowing pushes up interest rates, squeezing out marginal investment initiatives in the private sector. Heavy taxation discourages foreign investment, and government regulations pull the allocation of domestic resources away from what, in a perfectly competitive environment, would be optimally efficient. So if government has to be in the economy at all—and only pure Libertarians within the Republican coalition deny the existence of a limited list of vital public functions that have to be financed by taxation of some kind[14]—then conservative forces in the United States tend to favor as flat a tax as possible.[15] An ideal tax system, for the Republican Right, would tax all economic activity equally at one rate, would have that rate set at the lowest possible level, would eliminate all forms of double taxation, would levy taxes on purchases rather than on incomes, and would be so simple as to remove the need for the existing plethora of accountants and tax-return software.[16] As Bill O'Reilly put it in a press release to Edward Kennedy, "hard work and self-reliance leads to success on the job, Senator. Wise up and spread the word, and get your hand out of my pocket."[17]

Taxes need to be kept low because market solutions are always preferable to government ones

It's not simply that Republicans don't like paying taxes. In a very real sense, they don't like government either. There's a deeper premise at work inside this argument about lowering taxation: the belief that money spent by government is necessarily inferior—in the quality of what is provided and in the freedoms

that it brings—to money spent privately by citizens. Republicans habitually
treat markets as Adam Smith did: as the one place in which—as if by an invisible hand—people are led to serve the general interest by single-mindedly pursuing their own. Anything disturbing such market exchanges is then treated, at
best, as an interference with freedom and, at worst, as a challenge to liberty
itself. It's simply no use trying to buck the market. If you want the wages of
the poor to rise, for example, the last thing you must do is increase the minimum wage. That will only stop small firms from creating the jobs that pay the
wage and will inflate labor costs across the entire economy, creating unemployment in sectors that have to compete with cheap labor-based companies
abroad. And never, of course, give trade unions an inch. Labor market regulation actually makes worse the job loss and poverty that it pretends to make
better. For there's no "invisible hand" at work in the world of politics, pulling
everything into good order. That only occurs in unregulated markets. In a
political world free of market discipline, office-holders are always high on
promise and low on performance: so it's better not to give them any more
dollars than is absolutely necessary. Keeping your dollars, and using them
yourself, will always produce a better outcome, and not just for you, but for
everyone else as well.[18]

Rising tides raise all ships, so cutting the taxes of the rich is the most effective way to help the poor

The surest route out of poverty is through paid employment, and the only
route to paid employment is through job creation by the private sector. Liberal
taxation policies, dictated by outmoded class ideology—policies that take
money from the rich and give it to the poor—are exactly the kind of thing that
hurts the poor most. As Abraham Lincoln said, "you can't raise the wage
earner by holding down the wage giver." The only truly reliable route to a general rise in living standards is through a taxation system that rewards effort
and enterprise. Because it's successful entrepreneurs who pay by far the largest
slice of federal income tax, cutting the taxes of the successful makes the most
sense in the pursuit of economic growth. As Rush Limbaugh put it, "how in
the world can anyone with a brain come forth and say 'I am against tax cuts
for the rich. I'm only going to have a tax cut for the middle class.' If you give
a tax cut to people in the bottom 20 percent, you're not going to stimulate
anything."[19] The fastest way to reduce the number of the American poor is to
let the companies who can generate employment get on with the business of
doing so. Republicans understand that "government does not create prosperity,
and nobody in Washington can wave a wand and create jobs."[20] They know
that government works best by getting out of the way, by cutting unnecessary
regulation, by removing barriers to investment and job creation, and by allowing those who can make money to actually make it—and then keep and invest
it in their (and their country's) future. There's a powerful faith in *trickle-down
economics* at the core of the Republican Party's current conviction that "to
keep our economy strong and growing ... tax relief needs to be made permanent."[21] Money made by the rich, so the argument goes, will pull the poor up
behind it.

A LIBERAL RESPONSE

So what could possibly be wrong with that? The following things, at least.

Don't be so sure that it was the tax cuts that triggered economic growth

Because two things coincide in time, it doesn't automatically follow that they're in any way causally related. That's true no matter how many times the causal link between them is either stated or implied. The Bush administration will no doubt keep on saying that its tax cuts have triggered economic growth, but unfortunately for the case they're trying to make, the tax cuts to which they now attach such importance actually began to bite only *after* the recession, not during it.[22] The impression that's often given by advocates of sweeping tax cuts in the United States—of an economy so over-burdened by taxation that it will immediately leap into life once that burden is removed—is an entirely false one. The share of gross domestic product (GDP) passing through the hands of the federal and state governments is no larger than that passing through the hands of governments in most industrial democracies,[23] and it is not significantly different now to the share passing through the hands of the Clinton administration after 1992 when the U.S. economy boomed. In fact, in 2004, at 27.8 percent of national income, the tax take was actually the lowest in 37 years.

Even in the 1990s, the "burden of taxation" carried by companies and consumers in the United States was significantly lower than that carried by their Swedish equivalents, and yet Sweden was the other major industrial economy, alongside the American, that grew rapidly in that decade. There have even been times in postwar U.S. economic history during which the relationship between taxation levels and economic growth rates has been exactly the *reverse* of that canvassed by the Republicans, times during which rates of economic growth have been higher with capital gains taxes at 45 percent than at 20 percent.[24] And that shouldn't surprise us, because no matter what the Republicans now claim, there's just no simple one-to-one relationship between tax levels and growth spurts in modern economic systems. The factors triggering economic growth are far more complex than that. Politicians like to lay claim to economic success when it happens and to blame others for economic downturns when they come. But the truth is that they're always riding the tiger, and they're not in full control of the animal in any of the phases of its existence, no matter how often they tell us that they are.

The kind of tax cuts that might have triggered growth were precisely the kind of tax cuts that George Bush did *not* introduce

The more sophisticated advocates of tax cuts normally differentiate between the types of taxes to be done away with in the interest of economic growth, differentiating between tax cuts designed to placate the Republicans' political base and taxes cut to trigger economic performance. Increasing the child tax credit in 2001 is an example of the first. Lowering the taxation rates on dividends in 2003 is an example of the second. The claim normally made is that, over time, the Bush administration did refocus its taxation reforms properly, away from social engineering and toward the encouragement of saving and investment.[25] Yet ironically, just as it did so, in 2003—reducing taxes on capital to their lowest level since the 1930s—"personal savings as a percentage of after-tax income fell . . . for the first time since the Depression. Americans not only spent their incomes, they dipped into savings to borrow to pay for their purchases."[26] And of course we did, because the tax changes made in 2001 and 2003 had hardly any impact on the disposable incomes of most normal Americans.

The 2001 change in income tax rates gave the majority of taxpayers a rebate of just $300. The top 10 percent of American taxpayers, by contrast, saw their annual tax bill fall by more than $50,000. They—not the average American taxpayer—were the great beneficiaries of the Bush tax changes launched to lift America out of recession: the very people indeed whose saving and consumption patterns were already so well fixed—because of their excessive affluence—that they were almost entirely immune to the administration's determined attempt to trigger economic growth by making them more affluent still. If the administration had really wanted to kick-start economic growth in 2001 by boosting consumer demand, it would have directed its tax cuts *downward*—away from the rich, into the hands of middle America and the working poor—by cutting payroll taxes (which make up 60 percent of the taxes paid by the bottom 80 percent of income earners) rather than income tax (which makes up 60 percent of the taxes paid by the richest 20 percent).[27] But strangely enough, it chose not to do that—and we have to ask *why*? There couldn't be a slight matter of class bias here, could there? Surely not—what a wicked thought. Class bias from a Republican administration. Never!

If this is trickle-down economics, the money's going in the wrong direction

But you never know, because one thing at least is certain. For all the claims about rising tides raising all ships, we have yet to see any significant trickle-down effect on the distribution of wealth, and on the fate of general living standards, in the America presided over by George W. Bush. On the contrary, all the data suggest that inequalities in wealth in the United States are still rising and are now of an unprecedented scale (both comparatively and over time).[28] The data also suggest that the bulk of American workers have experienced at best only a limited increase in their living standards in the last quarter century, in spite of the remarkable growth and productivity performance of the U.S. economy, particularly in the 1990s.

The research data on the distribution of wealth are clear and disturbing. Reversing a long-term trend to greater wealth equality that began in 1929 and persisted through the 1970s, the last two decades have seen a sharp increase in inequality. "The share of the top 1 percent of wealth holders rose by 5 percent" between 1983 and 1998, Edward Wolff has reported, while "that of the bottom 40 percent showed an absolute decline. Almost all the absolute gains in real wealth accrued to the top 20 percent of wealth holders."[29] And that was at a time, between 1973 and 1995, when income inequality also surged and real wages effectively stagnated for at least the bottom 40 percent of U.S. wage earners.[30] There was modest wage growth between 1995 and 2000 but it was not sustained. Indeed, the weekly earnings of median workers—those in the middle of the income range—actually fell by 3.2 percent in real terms between October 2001 (when the recession ended) and late 2005.[31] Any increase in consumption that middle America has experienced of late has come not via any trickle down of wealth and income— except for that modest increase in real wages between 1995 and 2000—but from a steady increase in the *hours* worked and the personal *debt* levels carried by the average American household.

No one would deny that there was significant growth in the total stock of wealth and income inside the U.S. economy in the 1990s. What is remarkable, however, is how little of that growth actually trickled down into higher living standards for middle America. It should have done so, but it didn't. Instead, the fruits of the 1990s boom were largely monopolized by the top 10 percent of U.S. income earners, taken in the form of outrageously generous payments that chief executive officers (CEOs) made to themselves. Between 1997 and 2001, the top 1 percent of U.S. earners accounted for an amazing 24 percent of all the growth in aggregate wages and salaries. The top 10 percent took just a fraction under half of that growth. The bottom 50 percent held on to only 13 cents in every extra dollar.[32] The result was a change in the ratio of CEO salary packages to average earnings from 27 to 1 in 1973 to a staggering 300 to 1 by the end of the century.[33] If that was "trickle-down economics" at work, then Newton's laws of gravity are clearly wrong: under present arrangements in the United States, money trickles upward, it would appear, not downward, and in quite some volume.

If rising tides raise all ships, why is there still so much poverty in the United States?

The United States is not only the richest country on earth, but also it's the one that's most scarred by the persistence of poverty among affluence. Poverty is a notoriously difficult thing to measure and different countries do it in different ways. The United States, in fact, has one of the more restricted definitions of poverty—defining it in absolute terms, with different levels depending on family size—rather than as a percentage of average income, as is the norm elsewhere. Even so, it remains unique in the scale of its child poverty and second only to the United Kingdom among industrial nations in the severity of the poverty that its adult poor experience.[34] As we will see in more detail in chapter 4, 12.7 percent of all Americans lived in officially defined poverty in 2004—some 37 million Americans in total—down almost 10 percentage points from 1959 (the first year that an official measure was taken) but higher in percentage and absolute terms, year on year, for each 12-month period of the Bush administration. The real wealth of the U.S. economy (measured in terms of output and productivity) has risen since 1992 as never before—the tide has genuinely gone up—but not all the boats have risen with it. Certainly, prosperity has *not* risen for one African American in four, or for one Hispanic American in five, or for 21.9 percent of all American children. We all saw the images: when the waters rose in New Orleans, it was the poor who were left to sink.

Nor, within these tidal flows, have small boats found it easy to grow on their own. Within any one generation, individual mobility within the wage structure has proved extraordinarily difficult to achieve. Indeed, the rate of mobility has actually slowed slightly of late. As many as 77 percent of all low-wage earners in the late 1980s (those in the bottom 40 percent of the wage distribution) were still there a decade later—and that decade was, after all, one of unprecedented prosperity and growth.[35] And between generations, cycles of deprivation, like cycles of privilege, still conspire to lock the children of the poor into poverty as they age. Rundown housing, inadequate schooling, depressed neighborhoods, the predominance of low-paid work, and the absence of adequate skills and training programs all conspire to deny to large sections of the young American poor the full reality of the American Dream.[36] And that should come as no surprise. There's plenty of well-established research data to show—in relation both to whole economies and to groups and individuals within them—that unregulated markets *reproduce inequalities* rather than reduce them in scale.[37]

It's all very well for the well-heeled and privileged in this society to preach—to those who are not—the virtues of hard work, low taxation, and limited government, but let them try it for themselves. Shed the money and the car, lose the college degree and the network of well-connected friends, and resettle yourself in a dead-end street facing a local economy of low wages and high unemployment. Throw in a couple of children, too—the poor have the right to have little ones, have they not, just like the rich—and then see just how difficult it is, without help, to break out from the poverty that everywhere surrounds you. It's so easy to sing the praises of trickle-down economics and unregulated markets when you enter those markets with well-established skills and plentiful private funds. It's not so easy at all when what you inherit, and what you possess, is far more meager than that. A little bit of humility and compassion can go a long way. It's just a humility and a compassion that's not very plentiful these days, at least not among the Republican Right.

Let's try "trickle-up" economics for a change

Because all of this largesse by the Bush administration to the American rich doesn't appear to be helping the American poor—or indeed even middle America in the main—why not go at the thing from the other end? Over the course of the next few chapters, we'll see, many times over, a Republican propensity to go around the wood when they could go directly through the trees. If rich Republicans genuinely want the low paid to be better off, then there are more direct ways of achieving that desirable objective than giving themselves and their rich friends yet another tax cut. The fact that the Republican Party in the main doesn't go directly for the target must raise doubts about the genuineness of the party's commitment to helping the poor. But be that as it may, it remains the case that the most direct way to improve the lot of the low paid is to increase the national minimum wage: an increase that will, as its critics rightly claim, put a floor under low wages and ratchet up wage levels in total.[38]

There are think tanks within the Republican coalition that spend a vast amount of time preaching the dangers, to the American poor, of such interference in the "natural" workings of labor markets.[39] But if those dangers—of pricing people out of work by the creation of an "artificial" wage floor—are so obvious, why is such a vast effort of persuasion necessary? It's necessary, of course, because the dangers are overstated. It's necessary because raising the national minimum wage, as study after study has demonstrated, would have at most only the most marginal effect on levels of employment.[40] And that's not surprising, given that the vast majority of low-paid workers in contemporary America are employed in service sectors that are free of international competition. Raising their minimum wage doesn't affect the competitiveness of one service firm relative to another. It simply inflates prices across the service sector as a whole. People end up paying slightly more for their burgers—a modest cost, one would have thought, for a genuine erosion of poverty—particularly if at the same time raising the minimum wage helps to discourage subcontracting and boosts the purchasing power of the working poor. Even the CEO of Wal-Mart supports a higher minimum wage for that very reason.

If then there are sectors—and there are, not many, but some—in which wage increases can weaken the competitiveness of those U.S.-based companies that are obliged to compete with cheap labor-based producers abroad, then that is an issue to be addressed through trade and exchange rate policy (as we will see later). Industrious and low-paid American workers should not carry that cross alone. There is simply no justification for allowing unfair competition with underpaid workers abroad to add to the plight of the American working poor. We need a set of policies that will create a dynamic of rising wages here *and* abroad. Far from being a bad thing, a consistent raising of minimum wages in the United States—embedded in a new and more sophisticated trade policy—could be a key element in the generation of that dynamic, and we need to say so. The alternative—of a perpetual race to the bottom—will have social and political consequences too tragic to contemplate. Are Republicans really in favor of perennially low wages for one American family in five? Do they really think the minimum wage should remain frozen year after year, with a current real value lower now than in 1955? If they are, let them tell us, and let's see the electoral consequences of such honesty. And if they're not, then let them step aside, and allow the national minimum wage to rise incrementally as it should.[41]

This is the time for some old-fashioned honesty about the evils of greed

We need to remember who's going to benefit, and who's going to be hurt, if taxes are cut the Republican way. A successful campaign for a flat tax—a 17 percent sales tax is currently being canvassed by the Heritage Foundation[42]—would release, to quote Will Hutton, "little more than a feeding frenzy of the rich."[43] Even the International Monetary Fund has now published a report critical of the impact of flat tax experiments in countries abroad. By relocating taxes from income to goods, a flat tax would shift the burden of taxation *downward*—away from the rich on to middle America and on to the working poor. If that shift is not to be too excessive, government programs would also have to be cut on a very large scale and that would be a second hit on the poorest and the least privileged in the United States. Defense spending—and the flow of tax dollars to the firms wallowing in the corporate welfare of the arms industry—would not take the bulk of the reformer's knife. It would be the welfare programs of the poor that would feel the blade most.

For behind all the talk of cutting taxes in *everyone's* interest, the reality of the tax reform program pursued by the Republican Party after 2000 is that it was an exercise in looking after their own. It was the Republican-controlled House, after all, whose 2005 budget proposed to cut more than $50 million over five years off Medicare and Medicaid, food stamps, and subsidized heating bills. This, in the very session in which those same people voted to abolish the tax on estates of more than $4 million (roughly three estates in every thousand)—an abolition that would have cost four times more, in tax revenue lost, than the welfare cuts would save. Republican tax cuts in 2006 took just $20 off the tax bill of the typical middle-income household. They took $42,000 off the tax bill of households earning more than $1 million,[44] and every year it's the same. There's a class agenda at work in all these Republican tax reforms, one in which the rich and privileged in this society repeatedly demonstrate their determination to use less and less of their ever-rising wealth to help normal American families. In a classic piece of mislabeling, conservative Republicans habitually call their tax-reform program a "Contract with America." It's actually nothing of the kind. It's just a blatant exercise in selfishness, greed, and indifference, hidden behind a rhetoric of populism—and all the more shocking for the way in which it's packaged and spun. If the contract was really with America, the benefits of these tax reforms would be general—and they're not.

Not all government spending is bad, and Republicans know it

Finally, this more complicated issue might need to be tackled if the argument for tax cuts persists—the legitimacy of the claim, common in Republican circles, that by their very natures "big government" is bad and "unregulated private enterprise" is good. The polarity is a false one, and needs to be challenged at both of its ends.

On the "big government" end, we should point out that the Republicans in power after 1994 were not opposed to all forms of "bigness," no matter what they said. They were quietly happy with spending by the Pentagon and with the subsidization of American business and agriculture. They just drew the line at spending more and more on the poor. It's not public spending as such that seemed to be the problem here, even for those worried about the scale of the current deficit. It was what those tax dollars were spent on that was at issue. How else are we to explain that "in 2005 alone, when pretax farm profits were at a near-record level, the federal government handed out more than $25 billion in [farm] aid, almost 50 percent more than it pays to families receiving welfare;"[45] and yet it was welfare spending, not farm subsidies, that attracted Republican ire?

The conservative claim, as we saw, is that too much government spending crowds out the private investment vital to long-term economic growth. But this "crowding out thesis" is way too overplayed.[46] There's a case to be made for big government that fiscal conservatives regularly miss. Government spending actually stimulates private investment in economies operating at less than full employment, "crowding in" private investment rather than crowding it out. The public orchestration of private research and development (R&D) often can be a huge stimulus to growth. It certainly has been in the United States. The Pentagon has long been the U.S. equivalent of the much-vaunted Japanese industry ministry, MITI. It's not the case that the taxation that the Internal Revenue Service (IRS) gathers into Washington is somehow then "lost" to the private sector. It isn't. It's immediately recycled back into the economy through the government programs it sustains, in the process funding institutions (like schools) that are absolutely vital to the long-term health of both the private economy and the wider society. There are forms of public expenditure that progressives ought to question and contain—much of it "pork" added to spending bills to keep local interests placated and votes in place.[47] But it's quite wrong to imply that a private economy, low taxed and little governed, would easily sustain the vast range of public goods indicative of a civilized democracy. The test of spending by governments and private companies alike should be the outcome, not the actor—not who is doing the spending, but on what the resources are being spent. A private sector replete with industries of pornography and prostitution is not to be preferred to a public sector supporting art galleries and museums. Any society worth its salt needs a lot of public spending on lots of socially desirable things—and we need to say so.

Labor markets must be regulated, whether Republicans like it or not

Nor should we easily swallow the assumption that unregulated markets, particularly labor markets, generate patterns of reward that reflect genuine differences of skill and effort. How often do we hear, from the Republican Right, that the present tax code distorts the proper allocation of labor, by altering the prices and rewards of effort and initiative? But does it? Does a salary ratio of 300 to 1 between CEOs and the average worker mean that CEOs are three hundred times more skilled, industrious, and vital than the people they employ? No, it simply means that CEOs are in a better position—through their ownership and management of capital—to lay claim as their private salary to more and more of the collectively generated revenues of the companies they head. The strange thing about unregulated labor markets is that they often generate an *inverse* relationship between reward and effort, and between reward and competence. Think of all the incompetent CEOs who are still paid huge salaries or discretely ditched with generous severance packages. And think of all the really terrible jobs on which we depend: the collection of trash, the digging of ditches, the nursing of the infirm, the defense of the country at war. Are those the jobs to which an unregulated labor market gives the greatest rewards? No. An unregulated labor market gives most of what it has to give to those who monopolize a sellable skill, a piece of property, or a position of power. Of course, pay should reflect the years of study and sacrifice that people put into their training. There has to be some reward for skill, some differentiation of salary level. But how much? What is the right ratio of top salaries to bottom ones? Is it 50 to 1, 25 to 1, 6 to 1? There's genuine scope for disagreement here, but presumably most of us would agree that there has to be some limit to the kind of ratio that's acceptable. Henry Paulson reportedly earned $38 million in 2005 alone, as chairman and CEO of Goldman Sachs.[48] $38 million! If that's the kind of outcome that unregulated markets produce, then they're generating excess, not freedom, and they must be managed back into some proper proportion.

Sadly, it's not a form of management that we can expect from Republican tax cutters, is it? Just the reverse, really. Fat cats rarely slim voluntarily. Their diet usually has to be imposed. If, in these times of large budget deficits, someone or something has to be slimmed down, this is the key question to ask: Why start on programs for the poor, who are already thin, when in richer circles there is so much obesity waiting for the knife?

_____ 4 _____

Cutting "Welfare" to Help the Poor

Welfare states in the modern world aren't very old—60 or 70 years at most. Some parts are older—the German social insurance system started with Bismarck—but in general the provision of government help to the poor, the sick, the disabled, and the elderly is a recent phenomenon. Not all governments make that provision even now, but most do. Certainly in recent times, all governments in the advanced democracies have taken on a major welfare role, and that includes federal and state authorities here in the United States.

Yet in this, as in so much else, the United States has proved to be unique. Unique in coverage: No universal system of health care, free at the point of use, emerged here in the late 1940s as it did in much of Western Europe. Unique in delivery system: From the early 1950s, pensions and health care were tied directly to wage settlements here, in wage-and-benefit packages with few foreign parallels. Unique in timing: The United States set the pace in the 1930s with the New Deal, and again in the late 1960s with its own War on Poverty. Unique in vocabulary: The U.S. state pension system is known as *social security* and the term *welfare* is restricted to payments to the poor, giving it a stigma it lacks in much of Western Europe.[1] And unique in fragility: The United States is the only major industrial democracy formally committed to the "ending of welfare as we know it," through the 1996 Personal Responsibility and Work Opportunity Reconciliation Act.

The result has been the consolidation in the United States of a publicly financed welfare system, which, in comparative terms, is now both residual and modest. It's residual in that it leaves the bulk of provision for the sick and the old to the private sector. It's modest in that the public provision made available (pensions apart) is less generous than that now common-place in Western Europe and Japan.[2] For many American liberals, there's something profoundly embarrassing about the richest country on earth get-ting by with the most limited welfare system in the advanced industrial world. But that's not how the Conservative Right sees it. On the contrary, having a residual and modest welfare state is, for them, one of the key rea-sons why the United States *is* the richest country on earth. Protecting that economic success then requires U.S. welfare provision to be made ever more residual and modest over time. In a manner and scale without precedence elsewhere, *cutting welfare*—either to the bone, or away completely—is regu-larly and seriously canvassed by conservative forces in the United States as the best way to help the poor. Their argument goes like this.

There's not as much poverty in America as liberals like to claim

The liberal media are way too quick to exaggerate and at times misreport the data on poverty in the United States. We have to be very careful here. "For most Americans, the word 'poverty' suggests destitution," but in truth only a tiny portion of the 37 million people reported as living in poverty by the Cen-sus Bureau are poor in any meaningful sense of that term. "Overall, the living standards of most poor Americans are far higher than is generally appreciated." Most of them have a fridge, a stove, a television—normally two, both color—a microwave, air conditioning, and a car. The bulk of the American poor has ba-sic but decent housing and access to food and health care. In fact, "the average poor American has more living space than the average individual living in Paris ... and other cities throughout Europe."[3] This is not poverty by world stand-ards. It's in Asia and Africa that poverty stunts the growth of children. Not the United States. What poverty there is in the United States is often short lived. "More than half of all poverty 'spells' (time spent in poverty) last less than four months, and about 80 percent last less than a year."[4] There's a lot of upward *and* downward social mobility in the United States. One household in three escapes poverty within three years; and one rich family in three slips down into a lower income bracket during that same period. "In fact, very few people—only about 2 percent of the total population—are chronically poor in America, as defined by living in poverty for four years or more,"[5] and all societies have a stratum of folk like that. Poverty, after all, is natural. The poor are always with us, so it's ridiculous to criticize the United States for simply being like all the rest. We're not denying that there is real hardship for roughly one poor house-hold in three. We're simply saying that "even those households would be judged to have high living standards compared to most people in the world."[6] So we need to keep a sense of proportion when discussing poverty—a sense of proportion that, on this as on so much else, liberals normally lack.

What poverty there is in the United States is almost entirely self-induced

America is still a society in which, by hard work and personal effort, all things are possible. You don't have to be poor. Poverty is, in that sense, a question of choice. If you want to stay out of poverty, make sure that you stay first at school and then in work; make sure, too, that you don't have children until you've established a stable and well-funded relationship. School, work, and marriage are the great barriers to poverty here, and all three are readily available if you look for them.

So if you don't, that tells us something, not about the society in which you're poor, but about you as someone who remains poor when you don't need to. Why are you still there, trapped in your own poverty? Perhaps it's because you don't have the right skills or the willingness to acquire them. Or, perhaps it's because you blew off school and now are paying the price. There might even be an intelligence issue here.[7] Or, perhaps it is simply that you moved too quickly into casual and careless sex and are now looking for support from people less feckless than yourself. Not that everyone is guilty here, of course. There are innocents caught up in poverty, too—widows, the genetically infirm, and overwhelmingly the children you so casually bred—innocents who, if not helped, will find themselves trapped in a culture of poverty from which it is hard to escape. We know that "nearly two-thirds of poor children reside in single-parent families," but we also know that "if poor mothers married the fathers of their children, nearly 75 percent would immediately be lifted out of poverty."[8]

So there are things that can be done, and there is a role for public policy. But it has to be policy anchored in a clear recognition of at least three things. First, that, in the main, people put themselves into poverty, rather than being put there. Policy therefore has to be designed primarily to stop them doing that. Second, that it's not the rich who cause poverty, but the poor themselves. Tax the rich into oblivion—play class politics—and you'll end up with even more poverty. And, third, that public policy can only do so much and can easily overreach itself. "The government can force your parents to send you to school, but it can't force you to learn." There's a matter of personal responsibility here. "If you do not educate yourself or develop a marketable skill, the chances are you will be poor and powerless,"[9] and that will be nobody's fault but your own.

The big thing that's wrong with liberal welfare programs is that they create more poverty than they remove

The liberal welfare programs of the 1960s were designed on the premise that what the poor lacked, more than anything else, was money and skills. Liberal-minded politicians threw trillions of tax dollars into the urban ghettos, offering what they termed "a hand but not a handout." In the main, this largesse was well intentioned, although some of it, it should be said, did reflect a Democratic Party desire to build up a dependent client base. Even when welfare policy was well intentioned, it was entirely counterproductive. It got nowhere near the real causes of poverty, rooted as those are in illegitimacy and idleness. It simply transferred hard-earned resources from the working poor to the nonworking poor, in the process sending out entirely the wrong message about effort and personal responsibility, and squeezing the very people whose industry and personal morality were and remain the backbone of the American success story.

In designing their welfare programs, liberals ignored the warning, given long ago by Franklin D. Roosevelt himself, that "continued dependence on relief induces a spiritual and moral disintegration fundamentally destructive to the national fiber."[10] They choose instead to dole out ever larger quantities of that relief—to administer what he'd called in 1935 "a narcotic, a subtle destroyer of the human spirit"—tolerating as they did so the existence of far too many "welfare queens." The relief they doled out so indiscriminately to both the deserving and the undeserving poor then literally cost a fortune—$8.3 trillion since 1973 alone[11]—but failed entirely to remove the poverty it was designed to end. Even Jimmy Carter admitted as much: the liberal welfare system was "anti-work, anti-family, inequitable in its treatment of the poor and wasteful of the taxpayers' dollars."[12] But like all Democrats, he never tackled its inadequacies. He had far too many dependent constituencies to service to be able to match his understanding of the system's defects with policy adequate for its reform.

Many of today's social ills can and must be laid at the door of welfare itself

The War on Poverty was a disaster, and because it was, the liberal establishment in Washington stills bears a huge responsibility for the level and scale of deprivation in America's inner cities. As Ronald Reagan said in his last State of the Union Address, "Some years ago the federal government declared war on poverty, and poverty won." Like all welfare states, the War on Poverty, made it "profitable to be poor."[13] In doing so, it "degrade[d] the tradition of work, thrift and neighborliness that enabled a society to work at the outset," and then spawned "social and economic problems that it [was] powerless to solve."[14] What had started as a "safety net" quickly became nothing less than a "hammock."[15]

The incentive structures in its programs locked people into the very poverty on which the war was being waged. Welfare programs developed in the late 1960s and early 1970s made it far too easy for young men to shirk their parental responsibilities and for young women to have children without being able to afford them. "One out-of-wedlock birth every 35 seconds," Robert Rector told Congress in February 2005. Those same programs built in powerful disincentives to work, reducing the potential U.S. labor supply by nearly 5 percent and lowering the work effort of welfare recipients by as much as 30 percent.[16] They also helped to consolidate a culture of instant gratification and moral fecklessness among welfare recipients that ran counter to the work ethic that had lifted previous generations of the poor into their contemporary affluence. Far from raising living standards in America's urban heartlands, the War on Poverty created an *underclass* of people excluded by their welfare dependency from full participation in the values and practices of mainstream American life; and at the core of that underclass, this well-meaning but ill-informed expansion of welfare programs then marooned in poverty a whole generation of ghetto kids.

Suffer the little children. . .

It was, and still is, these children of the poor who are welfare's greatest casualties. These are the kids who lack the guidance of an ever-present and hardworking father. They're the ones who, in consequence, are disproportionately exposed to "emotional and behavioral problems, school failure, drug and alcohol abuse, crime and incarceration."[17] It's they who face the bleakest future, because "the longer a child remains on [welfare] in childhood the lower will be his earnings as an adult"[18] and the greater will be the likelihood of dropping out of school and ending up back on welfare when older. The driver here is *not* poverty. It's welfare itself. It's welfare, not poverty, that produces dependency, and it's dependency that lowers a child's IQ. Hold everything else constant—income, race, parental IQ, everything you want—and then test for cognitive capacity in kids on welfare and kids who are not. You'll find a 20 percent drop in cognitive capacity among kids who've spent at least a sixth of their life on welfare.[19] "The traditional welfare state's core dilemma," Robert Rector has written, "is that profligate spending intended to alleviate *material* poverty" actually "led to a dramatic increase in *behavioral* poverty . . . dependency and an eroded work ethic, lack of educational aspirations and achievement, inability or unwillingness to control one's children, increased single parenthood and illegitimacy, criminal activity, and drug and alcohol abuse."[20] The liberals' welfare programs did more than simply fail to solve poverty. They also damaged those for whom they were created.

Fortunately, there is a better way out of poverty than welfare

Once the true answers to poverty (school, work, and marriage) were recognized by the Republicans who swept to power in Congress in 1994, the solution was obvious. Instead of handouts and entitlements, the Gingrich Contract with America ushered in an era of personal responsibility, workfare, and the promotion of responsible parenthood. The 1996 Act took away entitlements to permanent welfare support, replacing the New Deal's Aid to Families with Dependent Children with a new Temporary Assistance to Needy Families program that linked welfare to a commitment to work or seek work. The Act set a firm time limit—five years—on the receipt of welfare and established targets for the percentage of recipients in work or job training schemes by 2001 and 2002, triggering a move from welfare to work. It also began systematically to reinforce the institution of marriage, by encouraging states to establish paternity and collect child support, and by obliging teenage mothers to remain in school and to live with an adult. According to its advocates, the 1996 Act worked. Contrary to the fears of increased poverty expressed by liberals at the time,[21] there were 2.3 million fewer children in poverty in 2001 than in 1996, the rates of poverty among African American children and among families headed by single mothers were at all-time lows, welfare caseloads were significantly down, the growth rate of illegitimate births had slowed, and employment among single mothers was up by anything between 50 and 100 percent.[22] With Earned Income Tax Credit and noncash benefits from the remaining 69 federal welfare programs added in, the number of people in poverty in the United States actually *fell* between 1996 and 2001 by more than 4 million—a rate of poverty down in just five years from 10.2 percent to 8.8.[23]

One section of the Republican coalition—anchored in the Heritage Foundation and in sections of the Christian Right—now wants a second round of welfare reform, focusing on a stricter and wider application of the work rules established in 1996[24] and on a more powerful advocacy of marriage. They want work rules added to the other main welfare programs—public housing and food stamps. They support the president's "healthy marriage initiative" and want to see it augmented by a wider advocacy of sexual abstinence before marriage. Their argument is that the 1996 Act was a step in the right direction. It began a welfare revolution that must now be carried forward—on the certain conviction that "by increasing work and marriage, our nation can virtually eliminate remaining child poverty"[25] within our lifetime.

The more Libertarian elements within the Republican coalition, however—those closer to the Cato Institute—are less comfortable with state orchestration of marriage vows than are those close to the Heritage Foundation. They remain convinced that even the 1996 reform failed to reduce out-of-wedlock births on any significant scale. Nor did it enable welfare recipients to become self-sustaining. They don't believe that even Republican-inspired welfare reforms can ever adequately do either of those things. So they favor a different tack: initially, the complete removal of welfare benefits from "young women who continue to make untenable life decisions,"[26] the return of all welfare funds from the federal government to the states, and eventually the replacement of *all* welfare payments with a negative income tax[27] and the complete privatization of welfare. Charities are so much better than governments, they insist, in dealing with poverty. They're more responsive to their donors and to their clients, more flexible, more efficient, and more effective. The federal government should therefore return "responsibility for the poor first to the states, then to the private sector."[28] Cato-based Libertarians see the 1996 Act as a mixed blessing—as a necessary first step, but one freezing the policy debate in the wrong place—by implying that, if properly designed, welfare can be made to work. No it can't, they say. Welfare will only work by being totally abolished. "When it comes to welfare," as Michael Tanner has written, "we should end it, not mend it."[29]

A LIBERAL RESPONSE

Oh, if it was only that simple. But, for the following reasons at least, it's not.

There's more poverty out there than you might think

It takes strong political nerves to get up in the morning, put on the expensive suit, and go tell Congress that being poor in the United States isn't really being poor at all. Perhaps those who feel this way should try it for themselves. After all, the United States possesses one of the more idiosyncratic and limited definitions of poverty in the advanced industrial world, one designed as late as 1963 by a minor civil servant in the Department of Agriculture.[30] What Mollie Orshansky came up with was not a relative measure of poverty but an absolute one—an income figure sensitive to family size and to rates of inflation—one that by 2004 defined the poverty threshold for a single individual as $9,827, and for a family of four as $19,157. Those are very low figures, especially if you live in an expensive urban area—just try living on welfare and even paying the rent in a place like Chicago[31]—and yet, even so, as we read in chapter 3, 12.7 percent of all Americans now live on incomes that fall at or below the official poverty lines. Even worse, of the 37 million people living in officially defined poverty in 2004, 13 million were children. That's equivalent to the entire populations of Sweden and Norway. The poverty rate for very young children in the United States in the first half-decade of the twenty-first century was slightly over 20 percent: that's one preschool child in every five. And around them are what the Economic Policy Institute (EPI) calls "the twice-poor," that is, Americans living on or below incomes that are only twice the officially defined level for their family size.[32] Amazingly, more than 89 million Americans fell into that broader category in 2003—all close to poverty and all accordingly obliged to watch every penny. Collectively, the poor and the twice-poor now constitute 31 percent of the population—that's 3 in every 10 Americans.[33] That's a lot of people in or near the poverty margin, no matter what Congress is or isn't being told by the people in suits.

What they experience is real poverty, in both the absolute and relative senses of the term. Currently, 39 million Americans are classified as "food insecure" and 40 percent of all those using food banks live in families in which at least one adult is working.[34] People in poverty here know, and know on a daily basis, that they don't have what most Americans have, and that they lack those things in a culture that repeatedly defines success in terms of consumption and income. The poor in America aren't only poor. They're continually reminded that they're poor by every billboard they pass. So it doesn't help them—or indeed us—to be told that most of them have cars. Of course they do. Given the absence of adequate systems of public transport in vast swathes of the United States, how else are they meant to get to shops or to the food bank? A car in the United States isn't a luxury. It's a necessity; an extra financial burden that can't be avoided if doing the ordinary things of life is not to become nearly impossible. The Western European poor don't need cars to anything like the same degree, because the scale of public provision—the size of the social wage that everyone enjoys regardless of income—is so much larger in those countries.

That's one reason why it's simply untrue to claim that the American poor are better off than most ordinary Europeans and better off than the entirety of the Western European poor. Sadly, they're not. On the contrary, the child poverty rate in the United States is currently *four* times that of northern Europe.[35] There are *only three* Western European countries whose poor children have a lower living standard than do poor children in the United States.[36] There are at least *nine* Organisation for Economic Co-operation and

Development (OECD) countries in which the cash and noncash benefits flowing to families in poverty exceed the flows reaching their American equivalents.[37] As early as 1990, there were at least *ten* OECD countries in which, after tax and transfers, the rate of poverty (measured in American terms) was lower than in the United States itself.[38] And at the start of the new millennium, life expectancy among African Americans was actually running *lower* than that of low-income Indians in the impoverished state of Kerela.[39]

If all this poverty is self-inflicted, then masochism in the United States is amazingly rife

If poverty is genuinely something that people choose, then it is remarkable how many people in America seem keen to make that choice. It's even more remarkable that the children of the poor consistently make that choice again and again as they get older; that women (especially single mothers) make that choice more than men; and that African Americans and Hispanic Americans consistently make that choice in greater numbers than do their white equivalents. There seem to be patterns here, patterns reproduced by lots of isolated individual decisions, but patterns that hold regardless of the individuals whose decisions call them into existence. And when patterns build up like that, it seems sensible to treat them like patterns. After all, if it looks like a duck and quacks like a duck, perhaps it is a duck.

This is why there's something particularly offensive about the speed and ease with which so many commentators on the American Right, instead of probing beneath the surface for the underlying causes of the "pathologies" of poverty they so dislike, move instead to demonize the poor, endlessly blaming them for making "bad choices" as though good ones were plentiful and immediately at hand. Telling young black women to marry the fathers of their children, for example, carries with it the premise that the men are there to be married. Yet "twelve percent of all black men between eighteen and thirty-four are [currently] in jail,"[40] a bigger proportion of "men away" than the United States as a whole experienced during the entirety of World War II. Unemployment rates among young black men are double those among their white contemporaries. "The problem is not that the nation's poorest women have systematically passed up good jobs and good marriage partners. The problem is that there are significant economic and cultural inadequacies in the choices available to them."[41] They, like the rest of America, value children; but unlike the rest of America, they cannot easily support them.

Conservative commentators roll into the ghetto, see individuals acting quite rationally within the parameters of what's possible there, and then condemn those individuals for not doing what they could have done had the parameters been wider. They see the last act in the drama, but never the prologue. Margaret Thatcher's great ally, Norman Tebbit, used to tell the U.K. poor to "get on their bikes and go find work," just as his father had before him. But when jobs are scarce, you have to peddle farther. If you're already trapped in urban poverty, the incline that you have to peddle up is steeper than in the suburban flatlands. If the world around you is racist, cycling alone can be dangerous if you're black. If it's sexist, women cyclists beware. The level playing field on which all of us are supposed to act with responsibility is just not there in a world scarred by inequalities of class, race, and gender that have built up over the generations. So advocate peddling by all means. Personal responsibility *is* the necessary last moment. We can all agree on that. But if the Republican audience genuinely wants the American social play to have the happy ending they desire, they will have to do something too about the inequalities and inadequacies that currently characterize the stage set on which it's being performed. If they don't work on the *positions* that create poverty, and instead focus only on the individuals currently occupying them, then all that can happen is that some of those individuals might escape to affluence. The positions of the poor will still be there, however, to be filled by the next generation of the underresourced. People will rotate in and out of poverty, but poverty itself will remain.

Given a chance, welfare works better than is claimed

The payment of welfare stands accused by many on the American Right of creating poverty and damaging those to whom it is given. With one important caveat—welfare traps—to which we will come later, the claim is literally ludicrous. Welfare did not create poverty in America. Poverty was here long before the New Deal and long before Johnson's "War." Neither set of welfare initiatives created their clienteles. They simply responded to their prior existence. The poverty of the 1930s was of a mass kind, the product of a general economic collapse that was rectified not by welfare programs but by the United States' mobilization for war. Within it, however, were categories of the poor that had existed before 1929 and that continued to exist after 1941—the temporarily unemployed, the genetically infirm, widows, and the elderly. By the 1960s, those categories of the poor had been joined by another, one explicitly excluded from the coverage of the original New Deal. To get any sort of legislative package through a Congress whose committees were dominated by southern Democrats, Roosevelt had excluded black workers in the south. Servants and agricultural workers gained no benefits from the core programs of the New Deal. They survived instead in the invisible southern poverty, poverty which—as prosperity returned with the war—then drew them out of the south into the cities and industries of the northeast and the midwest. In the first half of the postwar period, African Americans increasingly exchanged *invisible* southern rural poverty for its *visible* urban northern equivalent. It was an exchange to which the welfare programs of the 1960s were a belated response.

So it was a case of poverty first, and welfare second, and not the other way around. It was also a case of a welfare response that, when properly funded, took the rate of poverty *down*, not up: a response that over time definitely improved the lives of many categories of the American poor. The official poverty rate in 1959—the first year in the United States that it was taken—was 22.4 percent. By 1973, with the War on Poverty at its height, that rate had halved. Then, as programs were cut back in the 1970s and 1980s, the rate grew again. It was back to 14.5 percent by 1992, although it's slightly lower now, as we've seen. Behind the numbers there always was, and is, movement. More than 7 million Americans moved out of poverty in the 1990s, and 4 million moved back between 2001 and 2004. Behind the numbers, too, there was and is more than welfare. The growth rate of the economy also has to be factored in, but so too do the programs—three in particular. *Social Security* has had a huge impact on the plight of a key category of the American poor, providing an index-linked floor under the income of retirees. The poverty rate among the American old was 35.2 percent in 1959. By 1995, it was only 10.5 percent. *Food stamps* have played a vital role in maintaining at least a moderate flow of adequate food to families on low incomes—in 2000 helping some 17 million people.[42] In its last full year of operation (1995), *Aid to Families with Dependent Children* was providing money to about 14 million adults and children. None of these programs lifted any of their recipients into average-income lifestyles.[43] "None achieved spectacular results ... spectacular results are, of course, difficult to achieve."[44] But collectively they put a safety net under the American poor that, if absent, could only have intensified their poverty. There is thus an important if negative defense of welfare in the United States—that without it, the condition of the poor would have been significantly worse.

The charity illusion

Unless, of course, as the Cato people would have it, private charity would have stepped into the breach and done a better job. But there's just no evidence to sustain that claim. There's certainly no evidence that private charity could, or did, scratch more than the surface of the poverty experienced by the old, the infirm, and the widowed before the New Deal. And of the nature of things, no evidence can sustain the claim that if welfare was entirely removed (and tax levels cut accordingly), those benefiting from the tax cuts would then redirect all or most of their extra income into charitable endeavors. American altruism—although impressive by international standards—is not without limit, and because it isn't, the private sector can't be treated as a reliable and problem-free alternative to existing welfare programs. Charity-based welfare contains no mechanisms to guard against unevenness of provision, moralizing in the terms set for aid given, or the onset of "gift exhaustion" over time. The gathering of funds by private charities is in any case always time-consuming, intrusive, and administratively inefficient; and the distribution of funds as private handouts only serves to reinforce—for those who receive them—the very sense of dependency and impotence that conservatives are apparently so keen to avoid.

Members of the Libertarian Right talk the language of "rights" for the affluent and of "entitlements" for the poor, and they prefer charities to governments because only government programs are entitlement based. They imply that only the poor have an entitlement culture in contemporary America. They advocate dependency on wages but not dependency on welfare. They favor dependency on the stock market but not on the welfare check. They support the private dependency of married women on their husbands but not the public dependency of the poor on the state. That is, they rank different kinds of dependency without ever adequately explaining why just one of those kinds is inferior to the rest and without factoring in the entitlement culture of the corporate rich. But they're correct in this much at least. In a welfare regime based on charities, the poor do indeed lose all their entitlements. They get only what they're given. They literally have no *rights*. Is that what we really want—state-based or charity-based welfare systems that produce unevenness, particularism, and parsimony? Do we really want the poor in Alabama to be less protected than the poor in Massachusetts, or the Catholic poor less protected than Baptist poor in the south? I hope not. We need to remember that the best sort of charity starts at home, in a middle-class willingness to contribute through taxation to the provision of an adequate social wage that alone can guarantee basic quality-of-life rights to all Americans. It's not the sort of charity that the intellectuals at the Cato Institute favor, but it's the only kind of charity for which American liberals ought regularly to campaign.

The fallacy of the incompetent state

In any event, in making the pitch for the full privatization of welfare, the Charles Murrays and Michael Tanners of this world are not comparing like with like. They're also generalizing from an extraordinarily parochial base. They advocate the replacement of the American welfare system by an idealized and untested network of private charities, using as their evidence inadequacies in American public welfare policy since the 1970s. With few exceptions, they don't appear to have looked in any systematic way at Western Europe, where states have run welfare systems successfully for years. Nor have they engaged with—indeed have they even read—the fabulous and extensive scholarly literature on comparative welfare systems. If they had, they'd quickly have come to see that the great tragedy of Lyndon Johnson's War on Poverty was not that poverty won, but that the war itself was not pursued with sufficient consistency and zeal.

All governments—European and American alike—distribute income and dispense welfare. They're all, in James Galbraith's telling term, "transfer states," and inequality always shows what he called "the fingerprints of state policy."[45] The War on Poverty required those fingerprints to distribute income downward, and initially it did. General poverty levels fell. But command of the war then shifted. Under Reagan and the two Bush administrations, the fingerprints were deployed differently. Income was consciously moved upward. Welfare systems can always be made to fail, if inadequately financed and led. An agency such as Federal Emergency Management Agency (FEMA) will always fail if it's led by cronies and managed by fools. But by the same token, welfare systems can always be made to work well if supplied with sufficient funds and commitment. Indeed, take a welfare system up to about 40 percent of gross domestic product (GDP)—when it's servicing the entire community and not just the poor—and popular support for it will rise, not fall. That's been the universal Western European experience.[46]

Charles Murray is wrong: The limitations of welfare states are not structural and endemic. They're political and contingent. You get the welfare state you fight for. It's income inequality in the United States that makes welfare seem burdensome and unfair to those many middle-class Americans who are so financially hard-pressed by those above them that they're reluctant to fund those who stand below them on the social food chain. You can remove that pressure from middle America not by cutting welfare but by cutting inequality—by shortening the chain. Welfare provision works in Western Europe because income inequality there is less, and because European Conservative and Christian Democratic parties are genuinely compassionate in their conservatism. They have to be. To be elected, they have to say—as even Margaret Thatcher was obliged to do—that the "national health service is safe in our hands." But not here; here the Democratic Left is much weaker than in Western Europe, and the political and electoral center of gravity is accordingly much further to the right. Saving welfare doesn't require its privatization. It requires the Democratic Party to get its act together and to pull that center of gravity leftward in a more civilized direction again.

The limits of welfare-to-work programs in a world of low pay

The 1996 Act is the Republicans' ace card in their attempt to roll back the American welfare state, and they have one huge piece of evidence going in their favor: the dramatic fall in the number of people—especially young single mothers—in receipt of welfare since its passing. But the figures on caseload reduction, although real, are also deceptive, and we need to say so. They're deceptive in a *causal* sense: in that the full implementation of the Act coincided with a significant period of job growth in the American economy. When that growth stalled, so too did the rate of job take-up by single mothers.[47] The figures on caseload reduction are deceptive, too, in a *social* sense. People came off welfare, but then ran into a whole series of new problems that the figures don't catch. Women fleeing domestic violence lost a vital source of autonomy from the men who had violated them.[48] Young women with small children lost a significant percentage of their new wages on child care and transport costs; and the children themselves—whose enhanced well-being was, after all, a key aim of the new legislation—often found themselves in inadequate child care, looked after by undertrained and underpaid female staff. Women didn't stop providing child care. They simply stopped providing their own. And, overwhelmingly, the figures on caseload reduction are deceptive in an *economic* sense. Going off welfare, although it reduced the numbers, did not reduce the scale and rate of poverty among those who previously had been in receipt of aid. The Cato Institute's Michael Tanner has conceded as much, noting that "self-sufficiency appears to be eluding the grasp of many, if not most, former recipients."[49] And of course it is, because (quite predictably) the vast majority of the jobs into which former welfare recipients were moved turned out to be *low-paid* jobs. Welfare-to-work moved people from government-sponsored poverty to private sector–based poverty, adding to their transport and child care costs as it did so. Workfare changed the source of poverty, but not the poverty itself.

All of which underscores the key issue that the Right will *not* adequately address: how to restructure the American economy in ways that will reduce the number of low-paid jobs it sustains. Tanner wants welfare reduction to go hand in hand with the encouragement of enterprise and job creation. Fine, but where is the evidence that enterprise alone—without trade union pressure—will automatically create a high-wage growth strategy? There is none. If there were, China would currently have the highest wages on earth. Yet without that high-wage dynamic—put into play by government policy or by the strength of the labor movement—moving people from welfare to work won't bring down the rate of poverty. It will simply add to the pool of workers seeking low-paid jobs, reducing already low levels of pay as it does so and forcing even more Americans into that most intolerable of situations: full-time work that fails to provide an adequate living wage. Oh, if only the Republican coalition in the United States would put half the effort it does into welfare reform into the design of a labor market policy protective of adequate wages. That would be an effective antipoverty policy indeed, but don't hold your breathe. That kind of sanity is definitely not coming, not from this generation of Republicans anyway.

The "welfare poor" and the "working poor" are on the same side

Republicans likes to present themselves as champions of the working poor against the welfare poor, implying that the interests of the two groups are in tension and painting the Democratic Party into a "tax-and-spend" corner as they do so.[50] But the argument is false in both of its premises: The interests of the two are not in tension and the Republicans are not the defenders of the real interests of the working poor.

The existence of a large group of full-time workers—paid so little that they themselves are on the margin of poverty—actually traps the welfare poor a second time. If you're on welfare, you're poor. If you get out of welfare and into work, you'll still be poor, because the move will only take you into the bottom tier of the poorly paid. If the people in that low-pay group are then financially pressed—and they definitely are—it's not because of the weight of any welfare taxation that they carry. It's because their wages are low. It's not taxes that make them poor, but the lack of income growth. What really hurts the low paid is not the poverty of the people below them but the greed of the people above.[51] As we read in chapter 3, the truly unique feature of the recent American income story is the proportion of total income growth taken by the ultrarich. You remember, 24 percent of all income growth in the U.S. economy between 1997 and 2001 was taken by just 1 percent of the population, and it was taken at the end of a quarter-century in which wages remained flat for the majority of working Americans. What the working poor need is not welfare retrenchment but higher wages. They *and* the welfare poor need the creation of a high-wage, high-growth economy to ease the burden of poverty on them both. They both need full employment and rising wages in an economy in which there is a fair distribution of rewards. That's the kind of economy that the Republicans always promise in the run-up to elections, but it's also the kind of economy that after the elections, for 80 million Americans at least, the party regularly fails to deliver.

The promise, however, does indicate one thing: Even Republicans agree that public policy can make a difference. The existence of the working poor is not an act of God that's as "natural" as poverty itself. It's the direct product of an unregulated market system in which the rights of workers are regularly eroded and taxation policy is repeatedly redesigned to favor the already privileged. Relative wages are always "much more a matter of politics, and much less a matter of markets, than is generally believed."[52] Even before the 1996 Act and the later Bush tax cuts, the United States came in last—and by a huge margin—in the number of low-income families raised to half-median income by government programs: only 38 percent of families in the United States, as against 87 percent in Sweden and 78 percent in Germany.[53] The problems of the working poor are "directly traceable to actions of the government, the most prominent [being] the redistribution of tax burdens, government hostility to trade unions, and an indifference to preserving the real value of the minimum wage."[54] It's not the welfare poor who live off the hard work of ordinary Americans. It's the super-rich. It's time to straighten out the twisted logic of an argument that blames the poverty of the nearly poor on the existence of those even poorer than themselves, while the rich get away blame free. If poverty, and the fear of poverty, is genuinely to be lifted off the shoulders of those at the bottom of this society, those in its upper layers will need to do the lifting, not by cutting welfare to the poor but by cutting welfare to themselves.[55]

Welfare doesn't trap the poor in an underclass—we do

Welfare critics are right on at least this: There is a "welfare trap, work disincentive" issue in any welfare system. As people come off welfare and lose benefits, the effective tax rate on their own earnings can be extraordinarily high. Depending on the rules, in the move from welfare to work you might lose 60 cents of welfare provision for every dollar you earn, and effectively be only 40 cents better off—a rate of taxation against which the rich regularly howl when experiencing it themselves. So there is a problem of "disincentives to work" associated with welfare, one on which the Right regularly latch. But it's not the only, or indeed the main, problem currently facing young mothers in search of good jobs in America's inner cities. Good jobs are scarce because the middle-class workers have left those cities, taking the jobs with them. Available child care is poor because the programs have been cut. Young men are scarce because incarceration rates have been systematically ratcheted up. Suburban flight, welfare retrenchment, drugs, and the rise of a prison economy are the real villains here. As Barack Obama said, "the people of New Orleans just weren't abandoned during the Hurricane. They were abandoned long ago—to murder and mayhem in the streets, to sub-standard schools, to dilapidated housing, to inadequate health care, to a pervasive sense of hopelessness."[56] Underclasses don't create themselves. They're created. You can't be trapped unless somebody does the trapping.

The great thing about traps, however, is that they can be sprung. The solution to the disincentive effect of welfare payments is to phase in benefit reductions slowly—allowing people to earn and receive benefits in parallel until their incomes reach a tolerable level. Middle-class college kids paying back student loans experience a similar kind of phasing. They're allowed to link the repayment of their loans to the growth of their salaries and to pay lower than market rates of interest as they do so. So if it works for one class, it should for another. It costs money, of course, and it goes to the poor, so it's not a solution that appeals to many Republicans. Their preference is the more penal one: cutting off the flow of aid, to force people to make "right choices" and get themselves out of the ghetto. But that's easier said than done. Cut the money from teenage mothers, and you leave their babies even more disadvantaged than before.[57] Deny those mothers adequate training programs and child support and to what then can they turn? It's as likely to be vice as virtue,[58] particularly if, at the same time, three-strike incarceration policies are taking away the men who might support them—and taking them away in ever greater numbers for ever longer periods of time. There is a problem of illegitimacy rates among young African American women, rooted in a longer-standing crisis of the African American family that stretches back to the Civil War and beyond.[59] Welfare didn't cause that problem. At most, it amplifies it at the margin, and thus cutting welfare alone won't solve it. Cycles of deprivation aren't broken by denying help to those locked within them. Breaking entrenched patterns of social exclusion requires the deployment of *more*, not fewer, resources, and it requires the careful orchestration of policies from the full range of government agencies seeking to deal with them. Faced with entrenched social exclusion, you don't pull welfare out. You put it in. Liberal solutions aren't easy. They aren't cheap and they aren't quick. But at least they are solutions. Cutting welfare is not. Cutting welfare can only make the social exclusion of the poor worse.

Poverty is a matter of choice—it's just not a choice made by the poor

The ultimate irony here is that poverty, as the Republican Right regularly claims, is indeed a matter of choice. It's just not a choice that the poor themselves are called on to make. It's a choice made by the rest of us. In the main, for most of us, by how we vote, and for those who govern us, by how they legislate. They and us, not the poor, have the power to choose. We can choose, as an economy and a society, to meet the arrival of intensified global competition by outsourcing production, lowering American wages, and increasing income inequality. Or we can choose to reset the way we organize the economy and regulate trade to pull jobs back to the United States and to improve the quality of work and levels of remuneration attached to them. There is a choice to be made. If we take the first route, we'll create new sources of poverty for those low-skilled American workers currently in employment and extra barriers for those trying to move into work from welfare dependency. If we take the second, we'll have to dismantle much of the hidden welfare state now going to the rich, and perhaps not just to them. A proper system of rent subsidy for people on low incomes, for example, may have to be financed by phasing out the enormous tax subsidy currently provided to those of us fortunate enough to be buying rather than renting our houses. But at least the more affluent among us have a choice. The poor do not. Or perhaps more accurately, the affluent have the choice of making a big difference by making a small sacrifice. The poor, by contrast, have to labor mightily just to change their individual circumstances by merely an inch.

"Poor people and investment bankers have one thing in common. They both spend considerable energy thinking about money."[60] Which is why, on this topic at least, the Republicans are both right and wrong. They're right: when discussing poverty, policy is ultimately a matter of making right choices. But they're also wrong. Over and over again, the choices they make are the wrong ones—and we need to say so.

——— 5 ———

Reforming Social Security

President Bush made "reform" of the Social Security[1] system the center-piece of his 2005 State of the Union Address. He warned us then—as on many other occasions later—that for young workers, in particular, the system had "serious problems that will grow worse with time." So serious, in fact, that by 2042 "the entire system would be exhausted and bankrupt." He presented an image of a system based on payroll taxes that was running out of payroll, and he argued for its replacement, little by little, by a system based on voluntary personal retirement accounts. He was very careful that night to reassure older workers that none of these changes would touch them. He also hedged his proposals about a series of limitations on how and where young workers would be allowed to invest, in order to reduce the risks involved in the new responsibilities he was planning to lay on them. But he was clear. The Social Security system needed to be reset—made "permanently sound," as he put it—and that resetting had to involve at least its partial privatization.

Both his specification of the problem, and his preferred and widely canvassed solution, were (and remain) fully in the mainstream of Republican thinking. Five major themes run through conservative analyses and prescriptions for Social Security reform, each visible in what the president chose to say. Their general argument goes something like this.

The demographic base for a viable system of Social Security has changed qualitatively since the system was first created

In the 1930s, there were 16 people available for work for every retiree eligible for the new system of Social Security; and with an average life expectancy of only 61, few of those 16 could legitimately anticipate any kind of pension at all. But that's no longer the case. Now the ratio of workers to retirees is about 3:1, and falling. It'll be 2:1 soon, when the baby boomers start retiring. Government actuaries project that the ratio will be lower still by century's end. As a population, we're aging: as recently as 1960, only 1 American in 10 was over 65; by 2025, that figure will be 1 in 4. We're not breeding or dying in the same proportions or at the same rate as earlier generations did. We're having fewer babies and we're living longer; and because we are, a Social Security system designed to meet the needs of the 1930s will have to be changed. Some 5 million Americans received Social Security in 1945; 47 million do today. Young workers in particular have lost faith in the system. There was even a poll showing that twice as many of them "believe in flying saucers as believe they will receive a Social Security check when they retire."[2] Something has to change.

Those demographic changes mean that the financing of Social Security—1930s style—will not work in the long term

Right now, there's no immediate financial crunch. The payroll taxes levied on the salaries of the baby boomers are still much larger than the monies being handed out to current retirees from the Trust Fund: not least because the relevant tax levels have been raised at least 30 times since Social Security was first legislated. But this excess of revenues over expenditures won't last. Sometime around 2015, the Fund will begin to pay out more than it takes in. Even then, for two or three decades at least, it'll be able to survive by drawing on the surpluses built up in the years when workers did outnumber pensioners. But eventually—around the year 2040—the money will all be gone. Then, to balance the books, pension benefits will have to be cut, or the age of retirement raised, or levels of taxation significantly increased. Accordingly, the country faces "a looming fiscal crisis as the baby boom generation moves into retirement."[3] It is a crisis that, according to the Trust Fund's critics, will be ever more expensive to resolve, the longer it's allowed to fester. "We have a huge fiscal gap, a huge generational imbalance, and we can't let one generation's social insurance be paid for by bankrupting" the next.[4] "Estimates suggest," the Cato Institute's Michael Tanner has said, "that each year we wait to reform Social Security costs between $150 billion and $600 billion more. That sure looks like a crisis to me."[5]

The existing system has deeply disturbing consequences for the wider economy, which will only intensify if allowed to continue unreformed

Even now, Social Security has some pretty unpleasant *indirect* consequences that we would do well to avoid. True, it provides some security for 95 percent of all Americans in their old age. But that very security discourages private savings, and America's uniquely low savings rate is one of the key things undermining the economy's long-term competitiveness. "Social Security," Cato's Ferrera and Tanner have argued, "likely reduces U.S. GDP by 10 percent or more each year."[6] Americans are not saving and investing enough. Instead, they're getting big government on the cheap, because politicians are able to raid the Trust Fund surplus to finance programs they would otherwise have to cover with new taxation. In that way, Social Security is currently making a double contribution to the creation of an undesirable culture of welfare dependency: entrenching dependency on state handouts in old age, and dependency when younger on other welfare programs its payroll tax indirectly helps finance. Right now, there is no Trust Fund. It's been raided to oblivion by welfare-minded politicians, replaced by a set of worthless government IOUs that a later generation will have to pick up and pay. Even the liberals' claim that Social Security is mildly redistributive of income from rich to poor isn't right. Social Security isn't redistributive downward but upward—disadvantaging African American men worst of all because most of them (and the low paid in general) don't live long enough after retirement to recoup the money they've paid into the system. Those monies end up by default in the pockets of the more affluent longer-living old. Which is why it's so much better, the conservative argument runs, to let the low-paid workers build up their own investment accounts while they're working, enabling them by their own savings to break out of cycles of poverty that otherwise debilitate them.

A more market-based funding system would give future generations of pensioners a better and a more secure pension

Ultimately, Social Security is just a big pyramid scheme, and a very poor one at that. The pension it generates is appallingly low. If the private sector had designed it, people would have been jailed for fraud. If Social Security is all you've got to live on in old age, you'll be very poor indeed. So rather than compound its defects by ignoring them, leaving future generations to cope with the huge tax increases or substantial benefit cuts, the system should be progressively privatized as quickly as possible. The rights of existing workers must be protected, of course, but the financing of pensions by younger workers needs to change. If workers entering the labor force now are encouraged or obliged to build up their own Individual Savings Accounts (ISAs), four benefits will follow over time. First, young workers will avoid overpaying into the Social Security Fund, in effect no longer transferring so much of their earnings into the pensions of the baby boomer generation. Second, the rate of return that they'll earn on their private savings will be much greater than that guaranteed now by federally provided Social Security (their pensions, when they eventually arrive, will be *bigger*). Third, those pensions will be entirely theirs. No set of politicians will be able to take them away from the workers who've saved for them. A market-based solution, that is, will make pensions not only larger but also more secure. Fourth, it will set workers free from the existing curbs, imposed by the Social Security system, on their liberty to buy what insurance they want from whoever they want. "The larger crisis," Michael Tanner has written, "is not about the system's finances. . . . It is about a system where workers have no real ownership of their benefits, and where low- and middle-income workers cannot accumulate wealth that they can use in retirement and pass along to their heirs."[7]

The route to a secure and prosperous retirement for all lies in the creation of a system of personal investment accounts

These accounts are now being canvassed by the Cato Institute and others as *the* way forward, and as the one most widely adopted outside the United States—most famously in Chile—to overcome the lack of viability, unfairness, and low rates of return that are endemic to government-run, pay-as-you-go pension schemes of the Social Security type. Advocates of such a transition argue that the introduction of such personal savings accounts, if properly organized, can avoid the central criticism often made against such a radical move—namely, that the first generation building them will be double-burdened by the simultaneous need to pay existing pensions and to save for their own. Those transition costs will be cushioned, advocates of privatization claim, by the enhanced economic growth triggered by the savings and investments of young workers, by the temporary continuation of a reduced payroll tax, by the taxation of the returns on these rapidly expanding ISA nest eggs, and by much-needed cutbacks in other government programs. The great strength of ISAs, Cato President Edward Crane has written, lies in their capacity "to take advantage of the higher returns available from private investment, what Einstein called 'the most powerful force in the universe'—compound interest."[8] ISAs, not Social Security, are the way forward, because by "investing through the private system and earning modest returns, the average two-earner couple would retire with a trust fund of about $1 million in today's dollars,"[9] enough to pay them more than Social Security off the interest alone.

A LIBERAL RESPONSE

So if Peter Ferrara and Michael Tanner are right, and average couples could end up controlling their own million-dollar trust funds if Social Security was privatized, why should liberals object? The following reasons spring to mind.

Don't take the jewel from the crown

The first reason is this: We need to say to right-wing doom merchants in the debate on Social Security that the scheme they're critiquing is actually one of the New Deal's finest legacies. The Social Security system initiated under Roosevelt's leadership in 1935 has developed into one of the strongest state-provided pension systems in the industrial world. So before we knock it, we should praise it. It is, as George McGovern said, "a true success story."[10] Under the New Deal, the United States equipped itself with a near-universal publicly provided pension system, and it did so well before most other industrial democracies.[11] Then, with genuine bipartisan support, later administrations transformed that near-universal system from its original character as a limited safety net for the aged poor into a pension scheme giving the vast majority of U.S. citizens a unique and unprecedented peace of mind—a guarantee that for the first time in American history, their living standards would not cataclysmically fall with retirement, and that if disabled at work, they would not be left to starve. There is still poverty in old age for many Americans, of course, because many Americans are poor; however, with the Social Security system fully developed, even the poorest Americans are now guaranteed that retirement will not make that poverty worse. The key development here occurred under Republican rather than Democratic leadership—under Richard Nixon in 1971—when the level of Social Security payment was not simply raised but also index linked. This move was part of a steady expansion of Social Security's coverage and benefits from the 15 percent of the U.S. workforce originally covered to the 95 percent now within its umbrella—currently, more than 130 million workers and their dependants. In December 2003, Social Security provided monthly payments to 47 million beneficiaries—and that was one American in six.[12]

The critics are right in this—the "expense" of Social Security has in consequence grown. Grown, indeed, to the point at which the United States, when compared with other industrial democracies, now has one of the more generous of state-provided pension schemes. That is presumably one reason why conservatives—keen, as Grover Norquist once so famously said, to reduce government "to the size where I can drag it into the bathroom and drown it in the bathtub"[13]—have set their sights on Social Security privatization with such determination. The Cato Institute has had privatization as a major policy goal since 1980. The Heritage Foundation has been equally active, as has Norquist's Americans for Tax Reform organization. No wonder, because in the sphere of pension provision, with all its actuarial uncertainties, state provision really works.

If it ain't broke, don't fix it

We should say, too, that much of the scaremongering about the viability of the Social Security Trust Fund is just that—scaremongering. The dire scenarios that are regularly painted, by those who see the Fund drained of all monies by 2040, rest on a set of problematic premises that are rarely aired, let alone contested. The main one is the yield from the payroll tax, but that undershoots its required level only if two other things undershoot as well: the growth rate of the U.S. economy and the total wage fund that it sustains. The conservative's worst-case scenarios are normally built on the trustees' growth rate projection for the economy of only 1.5 percent per annum over a 75-year period (and a productivity growth rate of only 1.3 percent): growth and productivity rates that the U.S. economy has regularly exceeded, and by some margin. In fact, there's an important and serious paradox here: that those who would have us believe the Trust Fund to be doomed (because of low growth rates in the economy as a whole) would also have us believe that individual savings (withdrawn from the Fund and invested on Wall Street) would simultaneously soar in value. But it's not obvious how this would be achieved, unless we are to project a bubble economy in which the real economy stagnates but paper assets inflate—hardly a basis for long-term pension stability—or unless we buy into the argument that payroll taxes alone depress economic growth. A much more realistic projection would have the economy expanding on average at 3 percent per year between now and 2040, and productivity at 2.5 percent, with wages rising at least in line with growth.[14] If that happens—and all that's being projected is that the U.S. economy will function as well in the next half-century as it has in the last—then there will be more than enough money in the Trust Fund, secured by U.S. Treasury bonds, to continue paying full benefits well past 2040.

If you're genuinely worried, try tinkering instead

That may be to bend the stick too far the other way.[15] It may be that a payment shortfall will eventually open up—although it's hard to see why it should come as early as 2040—but if it does, all the policy makers would then have to do, to put matters right, would be one or more of three very modest things. They would have to (1) make small adjustments in the payroll tax rate;[16] (2) alter slightly the investment strategy adopted by the Fund;[17] and (3) raise, or indeed entirely remove, the $90,000 cap on payroll taxation currently in place.[18] The image we're being given by the Trust Fund's critics is of an America burdened by the old. Yet, in truth, the rate of aging of the population is far lower—and will continue to be far lower—than the rate of growth of the economy as a whole. Compound interest works on economic growth, productivity improvements, and wage levels as well as on ISAs, which is why running the economy at full employment, and triggering labor-saving capital investment and associated productivity and wage growth, would be a much more effective guarantee of Trust Fund solvency in 2040 than any privatization proposal currently on the table. In fact, the creation of ISAs, by redirecting part of the payroll tax, can only intensify the problems of balancing the Trust Fund's books. We need to say—loud and long—that if the Conservative Right really is concerned about the Fund's long-run viability, a modest set of tax and benefit changes is easily available to it. The fact that such a set is not being canvassed by them must at least put on the table the question of the real motives involved in their call for rapid privatization: Is it pensioner security or social privilege?

If you want to mend something, focus your efforts on the bits that are really broken

One of the great paradoxes of this whole debate about Social Security insolvency is that a part of the U.S. pension system *is* genuinely in crisis—it just doesn't happen to be the government-provided section of it. The other great leg of retirement support in the postwar United States has been a system of company-financed pensions negotiated into existence by trade unions in bargaining processes with major corporations. In 1994, these pensions were in place for at least 45 percent of all Americans between the ages of 21 and 65. But that employer-based pension system is now in an internal free fall. Major U.S. corporations claim that they can no longer afford its continued provision, citing intensified competition in domestic and global markets as the cause. Accordingly, three things at least are now under way. Many companies are resetting their pension schemes for their younger workers from "defined benefit" to "defined contribution" plans—no longer guaranteeing a pension of a certain value, but only a flow of funds into some 401(k) or its equivalent. Verizon, Lockheed Martin, Motorola, and even IBM have all gone down this route, shifting pension investment risks from the company to the worker. A number of major corporations have reneged on the pensions they promised—General Motors for one, United Airlines for another. And firms going bankrupt, like Enron, have often raided their pension funds as a first line of defense, taking away pension rights to pay off debtors, ease the burden on shareholders, or provide golden parachutes for a chosen few.

Time and again, we are told in this debate that taking pension provision away from the government, and placing it in the private sector, increases pension security. But nothing could be further from the truth. "Social Security is now the only secure source of retirement income that retirees can count on."[19] No serious politician is willing—if present practice is any guide—to risk the wrath of the gray vote by reducing current pension rights by so much as a dollar. In the private sector, however, chief executive officers in trouble regularly completely restructure or do away with the pensions that, in easier times, had been traded for moderate wage settlements. And the irony is that, when they do, it's the much-derided government funding system that then rides to the rescue, in the form of the Pension Benefit Guaranty Corporation.[20] It's the big corporations, not the government, that have the worse record for robbing pensioners: robbing them as workers by holding their wages back in return for pension funding, and robbing them as pensioners by defaulting on some or all of the pension provision they had previously promised. We need to remember that every time we are told something different.

Remember that privatization can damage your health

As the advocates of privatization do occasionally concede, playing the market produces losers as well as winners. It takes skill, capacity, and time to play the market well, and markets, particularly money markets, have a way of going down as well as going up. What Social Security provides is just what it says—security. People know exactly what flow of funds they can rely on as pensioners, and they know that those funds will be continually indexed to inflation. The critics say that that flow is too small, but even they recognize that (political intervention apart) it is secure. Indeed, the more they recognize the risks involved, the more they follow the president's example and hedge ISAs around with politically imposed constraints. In his 2005 State of the Union Address, the president promised "careful guidelines for personal accounts ... a conservative mix of bonds and stock funds" plus protection from "hidden Wall Street fees" and "sudden market swings on the eve of your retirement."[21] But if such a scale of constraints is necessary by pensioners taking money out of Social Security, why do it in the first place? Why go to a casino to gamble, when staying away from one ensures that your pension will remain secure? And why make that move now, when the other leg of the pension system—company-based private pension provision—is looking less and less secure? Why trade one secure leg and one insecure leg for two insecure ones? It makes no sense.

Except, perhaps, for this one reason: The only people who make money long term in casinos are the people who run them, which is presumably why the privatization of Social Security is so attractive to sections of Wall Street. The 130 million new ISAs would be literally, for them, a license to print money. The administrative costs of private brokerage will act as an extra tax (albeit a private one) on the money held back from the payroll taxes going into the Social Security Trust Fund. It is almost certain that those private fees would take out of any privatized system far more monies than are currently absorbed by administrative overheads in the Social Security system. Estimates vary, but normally the gap between the two is projected to be at least several percentage points.[22] And because the Social Security system is one that provides benefits to the disabled and the widowed, as well as to the old, where are we to find private insurers prepared to pick up their cover, at rates that are in any way comparable to the rate of payroll tax? Presumably the gap in charges between the two systems will be higher again for anyone unfortunate enough to lose a limb, a spouse, or a parent before their pension kicks in.

The dangers of speculation

Those extra charges might be worth absorbing, of course, if ISAs were indeed a guaranteed route to the accumulation of million-dollar trust funds by the average American earner. But are they? The answer is almost certainly that they're not. The numbers put together to sustain this part of the privatization argument are, to put it mildly, extremely optimistic. The 7 percent annual rate of return available to well-managed ISAs often cited by the advocates of privatization would indeed double an investor's money every decade; but that rate was achieved in the United States in the postwar period only by widening the gap between stock prices and the earnings of their underlying assets to a dangerously large 33:1. You have to factor in the 1990s stock market bubble before projecting future rates. Projecting the same 7 percent forward for another half-century would give us a gap between stock prices and underlying earnings of something in excess of 200:1 by 2055. A speculative bubble of that scale would be unsustainable. Because of that, and if we take the economic growth assumptions used by the Social Security trustees as our guide, a rate of stock price growth of 3.5 percent seems far more likely.[23]

So there won't be quite so many millionaires as promised, particularly because of that other piece of evidence on which the advocates of privatization tend not to dwell: the one documenting the way in which significant numbers of American workers, no doubt for very pressing and immediate financial reasons, raid or empty their savings accounts long before those savings mature.[24] Some 47 percent of American workers currently work for companies that don't even offer 401(k) plans, and less than half of all private-sector workers currently take advantage of them even when they are offered. Social Security's coverage is near universal. Privatization's coverage will not be. We therefore need to ask: Where is the security in all of this? And, where is the gain to the society at large, in the reproduction, within the pension system, and of the unevenness of coverage that so bedevils American health care?

Take the direct route to income equality, if equality is actually what you want

The capacity of savers to enjoy Edward Crane's compound interest bonanza will critically turn on how much they are able to put into their personal savings accounts. Any privatization of Social Security will only compound income and wealth inequality in the United States, not level it as the Conservative Right now claims. True, a rising tide raises all ships, but as we read in chapter 3, compound interest makes big ships bigger on a grander scale than small ones. Whatever else the privatization of Social Security will or will not deliver, an egalitarian society is certainly not going to be one of its outcomes. In data collected since 2001, "the Social Security Administration found that Social Security provided more than half of the total income for almost two-thirds of households comprised exclusively of those aged 65 and over, and provided at least 90 percent of income for a third of this group."[25] We also know that Social Security accounts for 55 percent of the income of older women, and that for many elderly unmarried women, it is often their *only* source of income.[26] It is hard to see any kind of private savings account that can give similar proportions of the working poor, and particularly the elderly female poor, the indexing protection of the current system or the cushioning of their pension rights against low earning years as is the case now.

Indeed, something is particularly unseemly in the Libertarian insistence that Social Security should be privatized because it is failing the poor, when Social Security currently provides so great a proportion of the income of those who need that income the most. As Henry Aaron has rightly said, Social Security is by "far and away the most important U.S. antipoverty program."[27] And it's the Cato people who want to do away with it. If they really want to improve the lot of America's working and elderly poor, they can take at least two far more direct routes. Instead of campaigning to rundown government-provided pensions, the Cato Institute could campaign for, say, a doubling by the government of the pensions provided to the lowest paid, with means-testing of Social Security benefits for the rest. And it could support a significant increase in the minimum wage, attacking poverty directly at its source. After all, poverty in work is due to low wages, not to payroll taxes, and African Americans die, on average, earlier than white Americans, not because they lack ISAs but because they're disproportionately poor. Alas, as far as I'm aware, no such Cato campaigns have been forthcoming.

It pays to place this issue in a wider, more comparative context

As its critics often point out, the U.S. Social Security system is built on a confidence trick. Young workers are told that they're paying into a fund that will be waiting for them when they retire. But, in reality, they are paying into a fund that then pays the pensions of the existing old; so that when it comes time for them to retire, they will need a new generation of workers committed to the same illusion. Like pension schemes in many other industrial societies, Social Security is a pay-as-you-go scheme, and it has all the strengths and weaknesses that schemes of that kind necessarily have.

The strengths come early. When the scheme is young and the ratio of workers to retirees is high, the money that flows into the Fund is far in excess of the money being paid out. That is particularly true if—as was indeed the case for most of the postwar period—the productivity and wages of those workers were rising rapidly. Then generous schemes could be, and were, consolidated, thus delaying until now any day of reckoning when the growth rates of productivity and wages slowed and the demographics changed. At that moment, altering the system becomes particularly difficult, because any attempt to replace it with a actuarially sound one—one in which workers genuinely save for their own retirement—then creates, for the generation caught up in the transition, the "cost" of simultaneously saving for their pension and funding the pensions of others. The change is also difficult because the regular repetition of the illusion helps to build up in the minds of those paying the payroll tax a quasi-property attitude to the pensions promised: a belief that they have in some meaningful sense already "bought" their pension, which the government is therefore obliged to give them. Many governments in other countries have lately faced these endemic elements of pay-as-you-go pension schemes and have quite properly ducked them.[28] Once in such a system, reform at the margin, not a fundamental resetting, seems the appropriate order of the day. The system works as long as the illusion holds, and breaking it brings transition costs of too great a scale to make the resetting worthwhile.

The big canvassed exception has been Chile, but the Chilean experiment is now widely recognized—outside ideologically blinkered circles at least—to have been a disturbing failure.[29] Many of the Chileans who opted for the private accounts, particularly those on low incomes, found the yield too low to sustain their retirement, and lower in many cases than the pensions provided to their equivalents by the state system. Heavy administrative fees also eroded their benefits—in a private system that is still heavily underwritten by the Chilean taxpayer—to the point, indeed, that pension reform was a key issue in the election campaign that brought the center-left's Michelle Bachelet to power in 2006. Even the parties of the center-right campaigned during the 2006 election for public subsidization of contributions to private accounts—hardly what President Bush could have had in mind when suggesting in 2004 that the United States could learn some "lessons from Chile, especially when it comes to how to run our pension plans."[30] If there were lessons to be learned, President Bush didn't seem to realize that they were entirely negative ones.

Don't let the flows of money fool you

Those who would privatize Social Security treat it as a dead weight on the economy in at least two different senses: as a barrier to saving (and hence investment and economic growth) by this generation of workers and as a debt burden (and hence a barrier to consumption and economic growth) on generations of workers to come. But neither is true. The payroll tax is itself a major form of saving—taking money from the consumption of workers now and depositing it in the Trust Fund. That money is not then lost to the economy. It finances public expenditures on other programs and it finances the spending of the old. It only slows economic growth if you subscribe to the theory that savings trigger investment, rather than—as Keynesian economics would have it—the other way round, and if you believe that the balance of bondholding and equities in the contemporary U.S. economy is too bond-heavy. If it is, that balance can be altered in many ways, without touching Social Security at all. And debts do not flow between generations, but *within* them. If, at some point in the future, governments have to borrow money to finance pensions, they will borrow that money from institutions actually functioning and people actually alive at that time.[31] Each generation has to decide on the appropriate balance between the consumption of the young and that of the old, and between the holders of government debt and the recipients of government spending. Decisions in

one generation do not predetermine those choices for the next, because
beneath the circuits of money that lubricate consumption and welfare in any
one generation, real resources move. A generation can only consume what it
makes. Social Security doesn't increase or decrease that total stock of goods
and services. It just gives the old a secure claim on a small part of that total
stock. What, we must ask, is in any way wrong with it doing that?

Ultimately, it's a question of values

In the end, as always, this discussion comes down—as all important ones
do—to a question of values. How important is it to you to give your parents,
as they age, a secure and prosperous retirement? If it is important, then two
things should follow.

First, if the prosperity of the old matters to you, then far from curtailing
Social Security, you should be pushing to raise its minimum levels. Current
levels of provision are—as its critics say—still too low to lift out of poverty
the elderly Americans who depend on Social Security alone. Not privatization, but expansion, should be the order of the day. Not less Social Security
but more.

Second, if the security of that prosperity also matters to you, then so too
should the defense of the existing system, because Social Security provides
benefits that

> .... no government Thrift Savings Plan or 401(k) can match: an inflation-
> indexed annuity, life insurance and disability insurance. Social Security's guar-
> anteed benefit does not depend upon the outcome of the stock market and is
> not tied to the decisions of individual investors. Rather, Social Security auto-
> matically adjusts the benefit to reflect a worker's earning history, which insures
> a worker against underestimating her earning ability. Social Security also fol-
> lows workers from job to job, and, unlike a private fund, is not affected by
> breaks in payment in times when workers are unemployed. Private accounts
> lack the important social insurance properties of Social Security. Social Secu-
> rity adjusts for inflation; is guaranteed to last an entire lifetime, no matter how
> long; is shielded from stock market losses; and, when young workers become
> disabled or die, provides substantial income replacement to multiple beneficia-
> ries across generations (e.g., to surviving family members for their lifetime).
> Private accounts and 401(k)s have none of these protections.... In essence
> private accounts would fundamentally shift the risk from the government to
> the individual, changing the Social Security program into an "Individual Inse-
> curity" program.[32]

This is not to say that the present rules and trustee policies should not be
reviewed. Undoubtedly, they should. Change *within* the system is visibly
needed, both to generate a better rate of return for the Fund as a whole and
to strengthen the benefits flowing to groups currently disadvantaged under
existing regulations—most notably, African Americans and elderly women

among the poor.[33] The roots of inequality in this society do not lie in its pension scheme, but that inequality is definitely reproduced there. So any serious attempt to eradicate poverty in this (the richest society on earth) must have, as one of its dimensions, pension reform.

Markets, however, are the great creators of inequality, so they are the least suitable device for its elimination. Those who advocate market-based pension systems in preference to government-funded universal provision would be much more convincing if they were also advocating programs of income equalization—so that everyone within the market could operate on a level playing field. But no such advocacy is forthcoming from the members of what Jacob Hacker has so aptly labeled as "the personal responsibility crusade,"[34] which is why the ostensible concern of the Social Security privatizers for the poor and underprivileged ultimately sounds so bogus. We need to say back to them, over and over again, that *they are simply wrong*. We may indeed need to make many incremental changes to the Social Security system, now and in the future, in order to maintain its capacity to meet its important social function. But we can be absolutely certain of one thing. The privatization of the system, either in part or in whole, is not going to be one of those necessary changes. Any privatization that is done will simply be right-wing Republican ideology run amok.

_____ 6 _____

Bringing Health to the Health Care System

L ike people abroad, people here tend to believe that we possess "the finest health care system in the world."[1] That claim is the common currency of the health debate in many countries these days. But what is
less common elsewhere is the scale of anxiety evident across the entirety of
the United States about the cost and availability of the health care of which
we're so proud. And that's not surprising because, for all its huge strengths,
American medicine also has huge problems, problems that are understood
in a broadly similar fashion on both sides of the aisle.

- The American medical system has a problem of *size*. In 2003, U.S. spending on
  health care, at $1.7 trillion, took up 15 percent of gross domestic product
  (GDP), nearly twice the percentage common in other industrial democracies.[2]
- It has a problem of *costs*. Since 2000, premiums for health insurance have been
  increasing at an annual rate of around 10 percent, far quicker than general
  rates of inflation and wage growth.
- It has a problem of *access*. In August 2005, 46.6 million Americans lacked any
  health insurance, and maybe twice that number spent some months in 2003
  and 2004 without health coverage of some kind.
- It has a problem of *public fundability*. The two great federally funded systems of
  health coverage (Medicare for the elderly and Medicaid for the poor) take up
  between one-quarter and one-fifth of the entire federal budget, and without
  major tax hikes, they face insolvency within our lifetime.

- It has a problem of *private fundability*. Increasingly, employer-sponsored insurance coverage is being reset, with higher copayments and deductibles levied on employees, and with more limited access to medical services per dollar of coverage provided.
- It has a problem of *quality control*. As many as 195,000 people may well be dying in American hospitals each year because of avoidable medical errors, and as many as 1.5 million may well be misdiagnosed.
- It has a problem of *public confidence*. Opinion polls regularly show most Americans placing the reform of health care high on their domestic political agenda, with significant minorities prepared to put on record their dissatisfaction with the status quo. And not just ordinary Americans—presidents, too, and of both parties. As George W. Bush put it in his 2005 State of the Union Address, he and the entire American population clearly understand that Congress needs to "move forward on a comprehensive health care agenda," and to move forward immediately and with some speed.

The problem, however, is that speed is unlikely here. The consensus on the *need* for reform does not extend to any agreement on the *nature* of the reforms needed. On the contrary, on the reform agenda the parties are deeply, even negatively, divided. They are divided in that they disagree with each other on what should be done. And the division is a deep and negative one in that each side sees in the other's proposals the genuine risk of making a bad situation worse. On health care—arguably the most important political issue touching the daily lives of each of us—deep ideological differences scar the political landscape. Politicians and policy advisors feel passionately about what to do, precisely because the problem with which they struggle is so important to each and every one of us. The conservative case, broadly speaking, goes something like this.

> **There are serious problems in the U.S. health care system—just not the ones talked about by liberals**
>
> There are things wrong with the way in which U.S. health care is currently provided and managed, but we won't correct any of them if we continue to incorrectly specify what they are. Liberals continually talk the system down. They endlessly make use of meaningless international comparisons, and they go on and on about the more than 40 million Americans who lack health insurance, when the true figure is only half that.[3] They forget to take out all the uninsured children covered by Medicaid, the adults who're only temporarily without cover, and the many young and healthy Americans who *choose* to be uninsured. And they tend not to mention that, anyway, the uninsured get emergency care at hospitals whenever they need it, care that the rest of us pay for in higher insurance premiums. Instead, liberals advocate ever more government intervention into every aspect of health care, when it's that very intervention that inflates demand and prices across the system, putting health care coverage out of the reach of so many hard-pressed Americans. If people were free to

choose health insurance packages appropriate to their circumstances, many more would do so, but they can't. Government regulations get in the way. The problem here is not the *under*regulation of the entire health care industry but its *over*regulation. The U.S. health care system is already far too close to socialized medicine for its own good, "with all the increased costs and rationing of care that follow,"[4] and it needs to back away.

The present situation is untenable and must be changed

The government already directly finances health care for more than a quarter of the American population and that "translates into nearly half (44 percent) of all medical care in the United States."[5] In 2005, Medicare and Medicaid cost the federal government more than the cost of national defense. Add spending on Medicaid by state governments, and the bill exceeded that of Social Security. It's a bill that, unless brought under control, is likely to *double* by 2015. It's currently growing at twice the rate of GDP and heading for a revenue deficit *six* times larger than that projected for Social Security. Spending here has its own internal motor of expansion. The federal government has an open-ended commitment to match state Medicaid spending, so states have an incentive to spend on Medicaid to draw down matching funds. The beneficiaries of that spending are then sealed from the cost of their own care, which only leads to "increased demand, overconsumption, higher prices, and enormous waste."[6]

- It leads to *waste*, because the unscrupulous are free to scam the system, and even more honest folk are free to consume medicines that don't actually bring measurable health benefits. (Researchers at Dartmouth College estimated that 20 percent of Medicare spending is so wasted.)
- It leads to *higher prices*, particularly to non-Medicare and non-Medicaid recipients, because the government systems underpay, and medical suppliers cross-compensate by inflating prices elsewhere. (Cato estimates that price inflation on non-Medicaid prescriptions to be at around 13 percent.[7])
- And it leads to *increased demand and overconsumption*, because removing price sensitivity "induces patients to consume more medical care"[8] (43 percent more in the widely cited RAND experiment designed to test this out).

The problem here is government intervention

Everyone knows that markets work best when prices are left free to reflect individual preferences and needs. This currently is not happening in the U.S. health market because of *three* different but linked distortions introduced by public policy.

- By making care free at the point of use, Medicare and Medicaid remove any incentives on the elderly and the poor to ration their use of health care in an appropriate manner. Free coverage also builds up in those groups patterns of welfare dependency of the kind associated with Social

Security. The elderly and the poor lose independence. Their capacity to own and to choose their own health care is diminished, as is their propensity to join private insurance schemes that finance better-quality care. In fact, free government coverage crowds out private coverage. Put a free program in, and you build in incentives for people buying private coverage to abandon that election. The taxpayer then picks up the tab for people who previously picked up their own. By reducing the pool of risk-spreading customers in private heath insurance, you drive up the costs of those insurances for honest customers who choose not to free-load on the state. Drawing people into Medicaid who might otherwise provide their own coverage actually reduces the public program's capacity to adequately fund those who genuinely need its help.

- By giving tax breaks to employer-sponsored insurance programs, public policy favors that form of saving for health care over others, significantly distorting the market for health insurance in the United States. Currently, this tax break is the largest in the entire tax code—$126 billion annually. The tax break encourages people to hold more health insurance than they would otherwise. It favors spending on health care over other forms of spending and saving, and it gives employer-provided insurance the edge over other forms of health insurance—so disadvantaging workers in firms too small to participate and people excluded from employment altogether.[9] It also inflates demand and prices. No less a figure than Milton Friedman reckoned that third-party payment systems (private and federal together) inflated per capita spending through the 1990s by a factor of two.[10]

- By regulating medical standards in a centralized and bureaucratic manner—through institutions like the Food and Drug Administration (FDA)—governments add significantly to drug costs and slow down the rate of technological innovation vital to improvements in the long-term quality and efficiency of health care in the United States. By "requiring insurers to cover certain types of care and restricting their ability to set premiums,"[11] state regulations inflate costs and price people out of health insurance altogether. The latest Cato analysis "found that the costs of health care regulation outweigh the benefits by two-to-one and make health care insurance unaffordable for roughly 7.5 million Americans."[12] Cato estimates that 4,000 more Americans die each year from costs associated with health care regulation than do from lack of health insurance and that the annual cost of health regulation for each American household averages more than $1,500.

Liberals will take us toward socialized medicine

Liberal solutions will only make a difficult situation worse.

- Further regulation on drug companies will damage the U.S. health system and the competitiveness of a key sector of the U.S. economy. The toleration of uncapped medical liability suits will line the pockets of trial lawyers, inflate medical costs, and drive doctors (and patients) out of the system altogether. Expansion of "free" government coverage will force taxpayers to bear costs hitherto borne voluntarily by the private sector and will encourage employers to cut back on private health care provision. "It's a shell game," Michael Savage said. "They 'give' you 'free' health care, then enslave you with a tax burden so heavy you go into cardiac arrest from the load."[13]

- Moving toward any form of a "single-payer system" will significantly reduce the freedom of Americans to own and choose their own health care. It will take control away from doctors and patients and will give it to politicians and bureaucrats. The result can only be longer waiting lists for patient care, diminished quality of care, and greater amounts of patient suffering and death. "Socialized medicine requires a culture of submission."[14] Socialized medicine "free rides" off the dynamism of market-based health care provision, and it must be avoided like the plague. Apply it to California, the Pacific Research Institute has recently estimated, and the number of physicians would drop by 23,000, access to medical technology would diminish, waiting times would lengthen, and about $9 billion of "free" health care would be wasted on people who didn't really need it.[15]

- Even Republican administrations and Congresses can get this wrong. The new Medicare prescription drug coverage is a move in entirely the wrong direction. We can't afford it. It's poorly targeted. It invites price control. It was slipped through Congress on some pretty dodgy statistics, and it's a form of corporate welfare. Once again, legislators are making the hard-pressed young finance the consumption of the privileged old, having taxpayers pick up the tab, and cutting "corporations a check just for providing the drug coverage they are already providing."[16] In the end, everyone will suffer because the new program will also reduce savings, drive up drug prices, and even (via its likely impact on payroll taxes down the line) hit jobs and slow economic growth.

The way forward must be a market-based approach

It's time to put control back into the hands of consumers by strengthening competitive forces within the health care system and by giving individuals direct control of what they save and what they spend on the protection of their own health. "To control health costs, we must give consumers an incentive to spend money wisely."[17] Markets have to be allowed to work in health care; and so we must ...

- Change Medicare from a system in which politicians define benefits to one in which seniors choose the benefits they want. We should give them a *voucher* with which to purchase health coverage from a variety of competing private insurers or with which to make a deposit in a health savings account (HSA). We should make the voucher bigger if the seniors have expensive medical needs. We should allow retirees to supplement the voucher with their own money if they choose to and to spend any unused health savings funds on nonmedical items. We should even go so far as to allow current workers to place their Medicare payroll tax in their own personal retirement HSA.

- *Introduce 1996-type reforms into Medicaid.* We should pass control over spending down to the states by freezing federal funds and distributing them as a block grant. We should allow the states full flexibility on eligibility and benefits in Medicaid programs. We should encourage them to target only the truly needy, by "eliminating eligibility for those most likely to land on their own feet,"[18] and we should have them replace open-ended entitlements with vouchers or tax credits, which the poor can then use to buy health coverage or to create their own HSAs.

- Develop *savings accounts* as the main way of financing health coverage for adults of working age. We should let people become the "stewards of their own health care dollars rather than force [them] to rely on their employer to spend those dollars wisely."[19] A proper system of HSAs, combining personal savings accounts with low-cost, high-deductible health insurance for catastrophic expenses, would be "the opposite of federal control.... patient control."[20] Because individuals, not bureaucrats, make the best decisions about their own health needs, empowering them is the best way to bring demand and costs down, and access up.

- Make out-of-pocket medical expenses tax deductible (removing the bias in favor of third-party payers), *deregulate* the health insurance and pharmaceutical industries, and relax the regulation of medical professionals. We should allow individual patients and medical providers to strike their own agreements on malpractice protection. We should "improve access to health care through incentives to purchase less comprehensive insurance, expand high-risk pool coverage, finance charitable safety net care, and deregulate state insurance regulation."[21] We should create a system in which people take responsibility for their own health costs, a "genuine free market in health care, from cradle to grave."[22]

A LIBERAL RESPONSE

That all sounds sensible and reasonable, doesn't it? So what could possible be wrong with it? This much, at least.

The key weakness here is "access," not "costs"

Pick up the Cato Institute's latest "solution" to the crisis of the U.S. health care system—Cannon and Tanner's *Healthy Competition*—and check out what they say are the "real problems" bringing that crisis into being. They turn out to be "costs ... quality ... [and] bureaucracy,"[23] but not *access*. Not access, in a health care system, in the richest country on earth, in which one American in seven can't get any regular health care coverage at all. At 15.7 percent of the population uninsured in 2004, that proportion of the excluded puts the United States alongside Mexico and Turkey in the Organisation of Economic Co-operation and Development's (OECD's) list of worst health providers. Virtually every OECD country manages to provide health coverage to the vast majority of its citizens, but Mexico, Turkey, and the United States do not.[24] And because we don't, the Institute of Medicine estimated in 2002 that as many as 18,000 unnecessary deaths occur here each and every year.[25] Lack of access to adequate health care is literally killing us. That's *the* problem with which this discussion must begin: the problem of why the most expensive health care system on earth fails to provide even minimum levels of adequate coverage for such a significant portion of its population.

There's a framing issue here. Problems of cost, quality, and bureaucracy have to get in line. They're not important to the 46.6 million Americans who in August 2005 weren't in the system,[26] or at least they're only important to those 46.6 million if they're the prime cause of their lack of access. But they're not. At most, they're a second line of causation, not the first. Americans have problems getting health care primarily because, uniquely here in the United States, we treat health care as something to be bought—bought like any other thing we buy. And we treat it as something to be insured against, because when we're really sick, we'll need to buy lots of it all at once. Buying health care, and buying health insurance, costs money—lots and lots of money. The critics are correct on that at least. But money isn't evenly divided in the United States. If you're poor, you can't afford health care.[27] If you don't have a job, or if you work for a small employer who's also strapped for cash, you and your employer can't afford the insurance. And even if you can, if you're young and healthy, there'll be a thousand more pressing calls on the money on which you're just getting by. When the OECD ranked countries by equity of access to physician care in 2000, U.S. access turned out to be more sensitive to income *even* than in Mexico.[28] When the scale of *un*met medical needs was mapped in 2001, 15 percent of the uninsured reported such a need against 4 percent of those with medical insurance.[29] Inequality, poverty, and inadequate health insurance go together here. They form an iron triangle. To tackle one, you have to tackle the rest. Those who would fully privatize American medicine seem to know that. They simply won't take on the wider inequality issue—at most, insisting that "redistribution issues should be debated separately"[30]—and so they can neither privilege nor solve the problem of unequal access.[31] We, by contrast, must.

Separating work and health

As so many commentators have said, in comparative terms "the most striking feature of the American health care system is the absence of a statutory universal health care program and [the presence of] an employment-based fringe benefit in its stead."[32] Unequal access to health care is endemic to such a system—one in which people who are paid so differently have to rely on employer-provided insurance for the bulk of their health coverage.

Voluntary safety nets and federally sanctioned access to hospital emergency rooms for the uninsured can at best only ameliorate that inequality, because inequality itself is structured into the system. There's a huge amount of research material out there making two things as clear as it is possible to be. One is that the length, intensity, and stress of work in many American factories and offices actually make people sick. The way we organize work here puts work and sickness together, and as we'll read in chapter 10, if we want to separate them, we'll need to deal with the terms of employment as well as the terms of health. The second is that tying health coverage to work doesn't work well—at least it doesn't work well for everybody—because employees in small businesses are much less likely to be offered coverage than employees in large companies, because layoffs and job switching often lead to irregular coverage even for those who are offered it, and because certain categories of workers are prone not to be offered coverage at all (particularly, part-time and temporary workers, low-paid and women workers, young workers and those from minority communities).[33]

This access problem is a deep one in the current health system. It's not just that so many Americans lack secure health coverage and so miss or delay seeking medication until their illnesses intensify—although that certainly happens.[34] It's also that those with health coverage live perpetually with the fear of its loss: its absolute loss, with unemployment or job change, and its incremental loss, as benefits are eroded in annual reviews or as coverage is denied as illnesses become catastrophic.[35] How often do we hear of Americans working full-time jobs for low pay, juggling *which* pills to take of the many they need, and struggling to balance spending on medicine, food, and fuel when their incomes will not cover all three? And how often do we hear of even better-paid Americans working on, long past retirement age, for fear of losing their ability to buy the medication that they require? The *stress* and *deprivation* associated with a health system based on the purchasing of health care has to be set against the claim that only through private purchasing do health consumers get genuine *control* and *choice*. Perhaps the Cato people should try it. Put themselves in rural Tennessee, live on a low wage for a couple of years with a chronic illness, see the state government cut back on its health care plan for the poor and uninsured, and then find out exactly how much "personal control of health care decisions" they really enjoy.[36] Not much—not much at all. It's easy to type this kind of self-delusory nonsense, but it's much harder to live it.

Focus on supply-side issues, not demand-side ones

The impression so often created by conservative critics of Medicare and Medicaid—and of the tax break given to employer-provided private health insurance—is that the great driver of health costs is the excessive and unnecessary *demand* for medical services and products created by health consumers who don't directly pay for what they get. But, in reality, no such overindulgent inflationary dynamic is currently at work in American medicine. There's simply no evidence of systematic overconsumption of routine medicines by the majority of U.S. health "consumers." On the contrary, at least 80 percent of all the demand flowing into the contemporary American health system comes—entirely legitimately—from the 20 percent of Americans with genuine and serious illnesses. In 2002, "a mere 5 percent of Americans incurred almost half of U.S. medical costs."[37] Americans actually "visit a physician or go to a hospital *less* often than people in other developed countries,"[38] although you wouldn't think so, if all you read are conservative critiques of pill-popping seniors bleeding the rest of us dry through their excessive zeal for unnecessary medicine.[39]

Nor are federal- or state-provided funds the great triggers to rising costs. Costs are rising in American medicine. That we know; but they're rising primarily for reasons of technology and demography, not politics. Doctors can now do things that they couldn't do a generation ago, and cutting-edge medicine is increasingly sophisticated and expensive.[40] Both independently and as a consequence of that, we're now living longer than ever before and gathering ever-higher expectations of the doctors who keep us alive and well. What's striking about this much-cited dimension of the U.S. health crisis, however, is that it isn't uniquely American at all. Every health system in the industrial world is dealing with a similar cost explosion—there's a cost-containment problem everywhere. Between 1990 and 2004, expenditure on health provisions rose faster than GPD in all 30 OECD member countries except Finland, not just in the United States.[41] What's actually unique about our experience of that general inflationary phenomenon is that we spend more, and get less back for each dollar we spend, than do the best of our equivalents abroad. It's the *expense of what's supplied* in the U.S. health system, rather than the *excess of what's demanded* there, that constitutes—alongside the access issue—the real problem facing us today, and we need to say so.

If you doubt that, just look at the figures. The United States tops the list in the technology and sophistication of the medicine being practiced in its health system. It also tops the list in spending on medicine. Overall, indeed, although Americans make up less than 5 percent of the world's population, we "account for roughly half the money that goes for doctors, drugs and other health expenses on [the] planet." But "line up the nations in order of longevity or infant mortality ... and the United States does not even make the top twenty," and "the places we trail, in addition to the usual suspects—Sweden, Norway, Switzerland and Canada—include Greece, Hong Kong and Martinique."[42] The United States currently ranks dead last (13 out of 13) on 3, and second to last (12th place) on 16 of the main indicators of health status in the advanced capitalist world.[43] The latest World Health Organization (WHO) rankings of high-performing health systems lists the

United States as 33rd, below Costa Rica and just above Cuba. Even the British occasionally do better, although they spend way less than the European average on health care provision. When researchers from the United States and United Kingdom recently compared the health of large samples of men between the ages of 55 and 64—men with similar lifestyles and ethnic backgrounds—they found the British to be significantly healthier, even though their American counterparts consumed health care that cost nearly twice as much.[44] It wasn't a finding that the researchers could explain, but it did point to the capacity of health systems less generously funded than the American to produce outcomes that are measurably better. What you pay for—in health care provision in the United States at least—is not always what you get. There's a "value-for-money" issue here that we need to confront, and soon.

"Fragmentation," not "overregulation," is the deepest weakness of all

Conservatives and Libertarians like to portray government involvement as *the* problem in American medicine: inflating costs—on the demand side by giving free care and on the supply side by overregulating health providers and insurance companies. This, as we saw, was largely the way advocates of privatization currently explain America's unique lack of access to medical cover by the poor: not that people are disproportionately poor here, but that regulations disproportionately inflate costs. But the converse is actually true. Costs inflate in the U.S. health system faster than in equivalent health systems elsewhere because our system is *less* regulated than others are. Not overregulation, but the fragmentation of the system into a myriad of ostensibly competing units, is the extra bit that the United States brings to the cost-inflation table. Although the U.S. government "pays directly or indirectly for more than half of the nation's health care ... the actual delivery ... is undertaken by a crazy quilt of private insurers, for-profit hospitals, and other players who add cost without adding value."[45] Within that "quilt," prices escalate because nobody controls the system as a whole. Doctors don't. Consumers don't. The government certainly doesn't. Insurance companies try, but they fail. Indeed, in a real sense, there's no one system for anyone to control. There are just "ten thousand little health care systems," and as such, a veritable "plague of administrative and clinical fragmentation."[46]

That very plague then adds a powerful inflationary dynamic of its own. The well-insured are left free to seek expensive care that guarantees benefits, however small. Hospitals are left free to exploit their local monopoly positions, able to set prices at will, and no one purchaser of any one drug is large enough to constrain the capacity of those supplying it to set whatever price they deem appropriate. The inflationary dynamic at work here is partly one of *defensive medicine*—doctors overmedicating for fear of later litigation if they don't. It's also one of *cost-shifting*. Maybe two to three million people

are now employed to pass the costs of particular treatments from one insurance company to the next, in a paper chase that absorbs maybe 20 percent
of the entire health bill. And it's also one of *fee-setting*. Most physicians set
their own prices, and until the era of "managed care," the insurers largely
paid what the doctors billed without questioning the clinical judgments
involved. The 1990s experiment with "managed care" ended that at least—
shifting control from doctors to insurers—but only at the cost of an administrative arbitrariness that alienated all of us from the system, and yet still
failed to stem the rise in costs. The average U.S. family now spends $11,500
a year for insurance policies whose average price has risen by a staggering
73 percent since 2000, policies that show no sign of significantly lowering
their rate of price inflation over time. The cost of medicine is no longer just
a problem for the American poor. Paying for health insurance is becoming a
general middle-class problem in states as geographically and socially separate
as Texas and New York. Little wonder then that, in a recent poll taken by
the Center for American Progress, 89 percent of those questioned agreed
with the proposition that "the health care system in our country is broken,
and we need to make fundamental changes."[47] The question is no longer
about the need for change, but only about its direction.

A solution focused on demand and regulation will not solve weaknesses rooted in supply and fragmentation

There's much that can't be known about the future of U.S. medicine, but
this much at least is clear. The direction of change favored by both moderate
and radical elements within the Republican coalition will simply make that
future worse.

Take the moderates first: President Bush clearly favors the strengthening
of portable HSAs, medical liability reform, and (if his budgets are any guide)
financial limits on Medicaid. True, it was his administration that pushed
through the Medicare Drug Prescription Bill in the face of opposition from
fiscal conservatives and Libertarians within his own base—but even that bill
was constructed in such a way as to reinforce the incremental drift to privatization. Historically, Medicare offered retirees a choice: let the government
pay your medical bills directly, or finance a private plan that will do it for
you. Most retirees chose direct payment. This time, however, they weren't
given that choice. To receive the drug benefit, they *had* to sign up with a private insurer, and remarkably, under the terms of the Republican legislation,
Medicare was specifically prohibited from using its bulk-purchasing power
to help those private plans get lower drug prices.[48] Instead of choosing
between Medicare and private insurers, retirees now have to choose between
a myriad of private insurance providers—more fragmentation and more subsidization of private insurers and drug companies. By privatizing the new
drug benefit, the Bush administration created an extra and unnecessary layer

of complexity and cost, which then had the usual and entirely predictable consequence—namely, a low rate of take-up of the new benefit by the most vulnerable and poverty-stricken groups among the seniors at which it was aimed. More stress for health consumers and more profits for the usual suspects—hardly an adequate way forward.

The Cato Institute's proposal for vouchers to replace Medicare and the phasing out of federal health care support in favor of individual savings accounts are just bigger steps in this same wrong direction. Their proposals only make sense if excess demand, caused by the irresponsible use of free medicine, was the prime driver of costs in the American health system—but as we've seen, it's not. The Cato people are not proposing to leave the seriously ill without access to proper medical care unless they can afford it. On the contrary, they're advocating vouchers calibrated by risk: with bigger vouchers for the genuinely ill. But the delivery of that would be a bureaucratic nightmare open to huge abuse—who, after all, would make the final judgment in each case here—and if it's not the patients themselves, then where's the enhanced consumer empowerment that supposedly justifies the proposal in the first place? And because spending on the seriously ill makes up 80 percent of all the spending in the system, where's the gain in reduced demand and lower costs? There's gain to hard-pressed employers: shifting risk, as with pensions, off their shoulders and on to those of their employees. But where's the gain to the employees themselves, faced with a plethora of complex plans covering a multitude of medical conditions they currently lack but may one day face? That's much harder to discern.

No, there are simpler and more direct ways of containing health costs than this. As with Social Security, the Cato people are going around the woods rather than moving directly through the trees. A voucher system and individual HSAs run the risk of splitting "consumers" in the American health market into the rich and the poor, the young and the old, the healthy and the sick, adding to the premiums and out-of-pocket expenses of the second of the two in each category as they do so. You don't get guaranteed universal health coverage by disaggregating those who need it. You get guaranteed universal coverage by guaranteeing equal access to all, regardless of their status. You get guaranteed universal coverage by *managing* health markets rather than by surrendering to them.

The special features of health markets require special kinds of market regulation

Not all markets are the same. We'll see that later in relation to labor markets, and we need to see it now in relation in health care markets. Labor markets and markets for baked beans are different because you can leave baked beans unsold on the shelf for months without adverse social consequences, but you can't leave labor unemployed even for a day without those consequences immediately coming into view. You can go to a number of car companies and compare prices, or move between gas stations looking for the cheapest fuel, and exercise real (if limited) consumer power in the process. But no two medical operations are the same; unlike your car, if one doesn't work, you can't just trade it in for another. As Charles Morris has said,

> ... buying health care, at the end of the day, is not like buying television sets. It is not the affluent, healthy, probing consumer.... that accounts for the spending. Mostly, it's people who are sick, frightened and not likely to be thinking clearly. You are in hospital, festooned with stitches and tubes, and your doctor comes in to tell you about chemotherapy—do you reach for your laptop?[49]

No, of course you don't.

In economic terms, this all comes down to a disagreement about the way prices work as signals in markets. You have a choice. You can go with the right-wing health economists and argue that, by lowering the price of health care at the moment of consumption, insurance (public or private) causes rational economic actors to overconsume. But if you do, you need to realize that your perfect solution—rational consumers making carefully calibrated health choices—will only come into existence if everyone in the market has equal purchasing power as well as equal knowledge, and if you can find some way to enable people to buy "big" operations (expensive ones) when they need them, even if their income is—in the moment—too small. Income equality, well-informed consumers, and risk-pooling are essential prerequisites of your market-based solution; so if you're serious about your health reform, you'll need to be serious about them, too.

But why go that way at all? What's the sense of even formulating the issue in those terms, when in reality people are often being asked to make life and death decisions (should I have a heart bypass operation, or will medication be enough?), when they can't know what each outcome would actually be, and when even the professionals can only talk in probabilities? The pill may be purple, but is it any good? How can the general consumer know? And why hang on to systems based on private insurance, when by its very nature a private insurance system must shake out high-risk candidates in favor of low-risk ones and charge heavier premiums to the ill? Health insurance, after all, suffers from a particularly acute version of the well-known problem of "adverse selection,"[50] and the famous RAND Corporation study in the 1970s showed that higher cost-sharing reduced both necessary and unnecessary medical spending in broadly the same proportions. So why not go the other way and recognize that given the inevitability of imperfections in consumer knowledge about medical conditions and options—and the heavy presence of drug advertising by pharmaceutical companies dedicated to private profit growth—a free market of consumers and suppliers is as likely to generate poor decisions as optimal ones?

Unregulated health markets bring together reluctant profit-seeking insurers and underinformed and unpredictable consumers. That's hardly a recipe for well-financed and well-prioritized health care, no matter how ideologically committed you might be to free-market solutions over managed-market ones. In a very real sense, the genuinely sick are invariably too ill to shop around systematically, and we'd do well to design a health system that has the recognition of that inability at its core.

The time for reform is now

We certainly won't get to such a design by overglorifying the system we've inherited or by misunderstanding its history. There's nothing quintessentially American about the present arrangements, no matter what right-wing politicians and shock jocks periodically claim. The creation of the contemporary health system has been far too haphazard for that. Employer-provided insurance coverage was the accidental product of a class compact struck in the 1940s between strong companies and industrially militant labor unions. Medicare and Medicaid were later add-ons—products of urban unrest *and* conservative political maneuvering in the 1960s: the first the result of Johnson's War on Poverty, the second the unintended consequence of a conservative move to block it. Progressive social forces extended health coverage down the American social ladder in the 1940s and 1960s, but they failed to push that coverage all the way. They failed under Truman in the 1940s, and they failed under Clinton in the 1990s—in both cases because of opposition from the medical community, who feared loss of professional control, and from employers who preferred their own benefit-based system. Throughout the postwar period, that is, "the triple trench" of "weakly organized workers, constrained citizenship rights and the disproportionate power of business and institutional interest groups"[51] combined to block any attempt to create the kind of universally accessible health care systems emerging in the rest of the advanced industrial world.

But that triple trench is no longer the force it once was. The political space for reform is opening again as the current arrangements begin systematically to unravel. That space is reemerging in part because of professional dissatisfaction with managed health care. The private rule of the insurance companies satisfies no one, and certainly not the doctors whose autonomy it erodes. It's emerging because the nation's emergency rooms can no longer easily meet their legal obligation to treat the flood of patients—insured and uninsured—now crowding their corridors.[52] It's also emerging because, in this age of intense international competition, both large and small U.S. companies, and foreign ones like Toyota, are no longer prepared or able to carry the expense of large health benefit packages.[53] Indeed Toyota recently redeployed a car plant to Canada—to single-payer Canada!—because of the burden of health costs in the United States. And it's emerging because the fallout from that corporate retreat—the general shifting of costs and risks to ordinary working Americans through greater copays, higher deductibles, and the withdrawal of all coverage by more and more small U.S. companies—is educating all of us in the need for substantial health care reform.[54] The unreformed American health system is well on its way to the very worst kind of rationing system—rationing health care by excluding the poor while allowing those with insurance to get whatever health care they demand, regardless of its value. The very visibility of that move is making the present arrangements progressively more difficult to defend. We need a better rationing system. The only question is which one.

Choosing the best way forward

The choice we face is not, as Michael Savage and others would have it, between the free enterprisers and the Marxists and socialists. Nothing stymies clear thinking on this key topic faster than the far too rapid deployment of either *pejorative labels*—"Russian-style" medicine against "American free enterprise"—or *false polarities*—"single-payer systems with long waiting lists" against "market-based systems with none." Those pejorative polarities distort because they obscure. They obscure the fact that all medical systems are regulated. There's always a role for government somewhere. They obscure the fact that all medical systems have greater demands placed on them that they can immediately meet. There's always rationing. Sometimes rationing in time (someone has to wait). Sometimes rationing by price (someone can't afford). And they obscure the fact that all medical systems are complex. There are always patients, professionals, suppliers, and regulators. The trick is not to play clever labeling games. The trick is to find a set of arrangements that can minimize the rationing and the complexity, and create clear lines of control and accountability that can be democratically accessed. The trick is to find a set of arrangements capable of maximizing the quantity and quality of medical outcomes without placing excessive cost burdens on the surrounding economy and society. High-quality, high-efficiency, low-cost, and publicly accountable medicine should be our target, and the question is how best to reach it.

The real choice we face is between options canvassed by those "who start with a private insurance (individual responsibility) model and try to fix the problems that a competitive market poses for equity and access" and those who "begin with a public insurance (social justice) model, like Medicare, and try to adapt it to deal with issues such as overall cost or misuse of health care."[55] If the argument here is right, and a more privatized and market-based system can only intensify existing levels of inequality in health care, then we clearly need to move toward the social justice model because "on balance," as Leif Wellington Haase has so persuasively argued, they "make much more sense."[56] The task we face is therefore twofold: to stem the drift toward the incremental marketization of an employer-based insurance system in decline, and to develop a public insurance-based model that is electorally credible. Indeed, we won't manage the first of those two tasks if we don't also manage the second, and doing the second will be (and indeed is) extraordinarily difficult in our present political circumstances, given the increasing weight of market orthodoxies in the entirety of American public life over the last two decades, and given what Mark Schlesinger has quite properly called "the corrosive power of market thinking."[57] But just because a thing is difficult doesn't mean that it shouldn't be tried.

Progressive alternatives

The most radical reconstruction of the U.S. health system from a social justice point of view would be what Paul Krugman calls a "VA system for everyone," that is, a reconstruction in which federal and state authorities ran the hospitals as well as financed them. A less radical move in a similar direction would be a "Medicare for everyone," some kind of Canadian-style *single-payer* system of universal health coverage financed through general taxation. In a single-payer system, private insurance would be replaced by public insurance, with medical services provided by the existing set of private practitioners, including primary care providers, specialists, hospitals, and clinics. That would bring at least three huge advantages into play. Everyone would have access to medical services, regardless of their income and employment status. Employers would be free of the cost burden of the insurance they now provide. And because the government alone would administer and purchase services, running costs would be reduced and the capacity to slow the rate of growth of medical and drug costs would be enhanced. Indeed, according to its advocates, the scale of the savings involved by the introduction of a single-payer system could be so great as actually to reduce overall health spending while extending coverage to all Americans.

The big problem with such a move, however, is the range and number of interests that would mobilize against it. The private insurance companies would be the great losers, and they are unlikely to go quietly from the scene. The other potential losers—small businesses providing no coverage, workers with established medical benefits, and physicians with affluent lifestyles—might be more inclined this time than last to tolerate reform, given the fragility of their current privileged position. But the insurance companies would certainly fight any single-payer proposal, and they would play on fears of big government among employers and workers alike. Which is why some *hybrid* scheme—strengthening the role of public insurance alongside existing private insurance coverage—seems to many people on the left to be a more realistic alternative.[58] There are lots of schemes out there of that kind, all now seeking political support. Consider the following:

- In 1993, the Clintons had a "play-or-pay" proposal—that employers pay health insurance for their employees or pay into a general fund that provides health insurance to those who lack it—and that scheme remains available for use.
- There are elements of play or pay in the current and much-discussed Massachusetts initiative, under which all residents will have to have health insurance coverage, with the coverage of the poor financed by a mixture of federal money, payments by employers providing no coverage, and taxes on individuals who are able to buy coverage but don't.
- There's a lot of support in progressive circles for the generalization of the Federal Employee Health Benefits Program—one in which federal employees and their dependents choose coverage from one of a number of federally regulated private insurers and in which the membership pool is big enough to keep premiums down. The Center for American Progress is currently canvassing such a generalization.[59]
- The Century Foundation's Charles Morris has recently suggested a similar scheme: a universally available, federally regulated basic health plan, with subsidized premiums for the elderly and the poor.[60]
- The Foundation has also published a more complex proposal from Leif Wellington Haase, in which the federal government would establish and sponsor three different insurance packages and make purchase of at least the basic package mandatory, with subsidies again for the old, poor, and disabled.[61]
- And there are others. The Democratic Leadership Council, for example, issued a blueprint in July 2006, "Saving the American Dream," which contained a commitment to affordable health care for every American family.[62]

There's quite a choice out there, and the best of them all widen access, lower costs, and strengthen quality controls by reinforcing the role of public institutions in the management of what is still a privately provided system. That is certainly the minimum direction in which public policy on health care now needs to go.

It's time to "go to the mattresses"[63]

We need a move in that direction as a matter of urgency, and we should say so. We should say loud and clear that it is entirely *unacceptable,* in the most affluent society on earth, for 46 million Americans to have no regular health coverage at all and for perhaps an additional 100 million Americans to be continually worrying about their capacity to sustain adequate coverage. We should also say that it is quite *ridiculous* that access to proper health care should depend on the company people work for, on whether they work at all, and on what kind of benefits package they manage to negotiate. And we should say that it's *bad medicine* for those who lack insurance to use hospital emergency rooms as their first and last port of call. We should insist on the *unfairness* of a system denying basic coverage to so many while providing super-profits for insurers and drug companies alike, and we should label as *obscene* any system of health finance under which the sicker you are the more expensive coverage becomes and the more difficult it is to acquire.

"Health care must be affordable and accessible to all, irrespective of health, age, income or work status."[64] Adequate health coverage is not something you should have to buy. It's something you should have by right. It is, after all, one of the major rights guaranteed by the UN Universal Declaration of Human Rights. In the area of health perhaps more than any other, "no man is an island." The health of each of us is the responsibility of us all. Of course, we also have a responsibility to each other to live a healthy life— there are issues of self-inflicted illness with which any affluent society has to deal—but that is only one of the health responsibilities we carry. We also carry the responsibility to help others obtain the health care they need and to create a reasonably level playing field of economic and social rewards on which healthy lives can be easily lived. There's a relationship between poverty and illness at play here, as well as one between affluence and excess, that we need to remember. Inequality actually makes people ill. Inequality also denies to many who are ill the capacity to "buy" back their health. We need therefore to design a health care system free at the point of use, and a society in which that freedom, because shared, is not abused.

Market-based health reform will not give us that system or that society. Conservatives regularly praise markets as instruments of freedom and denigrate democratic politics (and politicians) as corrupt and self-seeking. But markets are not instruments of popular control in societies in which income is as unequally divided as it is right now in the United States. Market actors don't respond to the totality of human need. They respond only to needs that are linked to purchasing power. So to be affluent in a privately funded health market is indeed genuinely to have "consumer power," but it's a power to exclude as well as to consume—a power to lay claim to more than your fair share of limited health resources by pricing those resources out of the hands of those who are less affluent. To be only moderately well-off in a privately funded health market, by contrast, is to have the appearance of consumer power but invariably not its reality—certainly not the full reality. Instead, the bureaucrats in the insurance scheme have that power and the insured don't. And, of course, to be poor in such a system is to have no power at all—just the freedom to know bad health and early death.

Democratic politics, by contrast, do have the potential to be genuinely responsive to the full set of American health needs, if those who care about universal health care can mobilize enough numbers to overcome the defensive leverage of the special interests. The rich and the poor, after all, each only have one vote. American politics is not always democratic, because money gives political leverage and because special interests are so entrenched—especially around issues of health reform. But the potential for democratic change is always there. Change is possible, if it can be *made* to happen. It's up to progressive forces in contemporary America to realize that potential, by uniting around a health platform based on universal access and by campaigning for it with vigor and determination. Progressive health reform is there for the taking, but it will have to be taken. There will be a fight, probably a truly enormous fight—which is why, on this issue perhaps more than on any other issue in contemporary domestic politics, it is genuinely time for us to follow the man's advice: time to say, "enough already— away with all this right-wing nonsense," time, on this issue at least, to go to the mattresses.

Immigration Control in a
Land of Immigrants

E mma Lazarus's injunction on the base of the Statue of Liberty could not
be clearer. "Give me your tired, your poor, your huddled masses yearning
to breathe free." It was never so simple, of course. "The wretched refuse
of your teaming shore" always had to negotiate their way past Ellis Island.
Even in the late-nineteenth-century heyday of open borders, one would-be
immigrant in every 150 never made it out of there, and as many as one in
three of those who did eventually chose to return home. And after 1882, the
border was never entirely open—not open first to the Chinese, then from 1917,
not open to people from India, Indochina, Arabia, and Afghanistan (the so-
called Asia-Pacific Triangle), and from 1924 not open to people from countries
other than those from which the majority of Americans had already come.
Immigration in the United States, that is, has long been regulated, and regulated
in ways that traditionally benefited immigration from the western hemisphere.

Being regulated, immigration into the United States has also periodically
been "reformed"—sometimes to reinforce that European privileging, as in
1952, or to lessen it, as in 1965 and 1990. Over time, immigration acts have
set (and then varied) limits on the totals of immigrants annually allowed
into the country. They've regulated the places from which those immigrants
have come, by setting national quotas, and the skills required to come with
them, by issuing work visas. They've opened American borders to refugees

from political repression and natural disasters, and to family members of people already here. Between 1943 and 1964, Congress even created a guest-worker system for Mexican agricultural laborers, and in 1986 attempted to stem the flood of illegal immigrants, again mainly Mexican, by proposing penalties on those employing undocumented workers. And legislation has periodically altered the terms under which people can visit the United States, study here, or work in American factories and offices on a temporary basis. There has been a lot of immigration legislation.

The big moments in that legislative flood have come in, broadly, 20-year phases, each one triggered by the leftover business of its predecessor. We're into another of those phases now, picking up the pieces left in place from 1965 and 1986. Two pieces in particular come to mind: (1) the dramatic change in the scale and regional origins of recent immigration (the unexpected legacy of the 1965 Act), and (2) the number of undocumented immigrants now working in the United States (a number whose growth the 1965 Act inadvertently triggered, and the 1986 Act failed to stem).

- In December 2005, the House of Representatives voted to erect a 700-mile fence along the southern border of the United States, to increase the number of patrol agents by 10,000 over five years, to make illegal immigration a felony, and to require employers to identify illegal workers by checking their status against a national database.
- Throughout 2006, this House legislation existed alongside—and in significant tension with—a Senate bill passed with bipartisan support in May 2006. The Senate bill, proposed by Republican Senators Martinez and Hagel, divided illegal immigrants by length of stay. It allowed those here for more than five years to pursue citizenship after paying a fine and back taxes, and passing an English language test and a background check. It sent home illegal immigrants here for less than two years, while allowing those here for more than two years but less than five privileged access to green cards distributed from specially created "ports of entry" in their home country. The Senate bill also proposed fence building—370 miles of it along the Mexican border—and a guest-worker program admitting 400,000 guest-workers a year.
- Between the two, 2006 saw a proposal, from President Bush, to give temporary guest-worker status to 325,000 foreign nationals a year. It saw another, from Senator Arlen Specter, to create a three-year guest-worker program, with workers free to stay for three additional years if they so wished, and yet another—a so-called "no amnesty guest-worker program"—from Representative Mike Pence, requiring even long-standing "illegals" to briefly leave the country, register as temporary workers, and return (a kind of "self deportation"), with the prospect of U.S. citizenship still available, but way down the line. Eventually, it was the House bill, amended in committee but still with its 700 miles of fence, that was sent to the president for his signature in the dying moments of the 109th Congress.

At stake in these various legislative proposals was neither the volume nor the internal composition of *legal* immigration, although the scale and character of those issues did loom large in the background of this dispute for some of its participants. The hot-button issues this time were *illegal immigration* and *border security*—primarily border security to our south. And unlike other debates discussed in this book, this was not a fight that primarily pitted Republicans against Democrats. Here, the major line of cleavage lay, and still lies, inside the Republican Party itself. On this issue, more than on any other in recent times, right-wing elements within the broad conservative coalition have mobilized *against* their own liberal wing and against their own national leadership. In consequence, this is also a debate in which you find real bitterness—angry accusations of "betrayal," "cowardice," and "selling out," as well as of "error"—from anti-immigration forces whose general argument takes the following shape.

The U.S. border is porous, allowing in a flood of immigrants

By common consent, the number of people currently in the United States without proper papers and documentation totals at least 12 million,[1] with more arriving daily. Perhaps as many as 3 million in 2004 alone, if Michael Savage is right—enough, as he put it, to fill "22,000 Boeing 737-700 airliners, or 60 flights every day for a year."[2] This, in the context of what some are calling "the second great migration": one similar in scale to the wave of immigration around 1900 that created the modern American population profile. The two great migrations are said to be both similar and different. They're said to be similar in that both waves altered the number of foreign-born people living here. The current migration has taken that figure from 1 in 20 in 1970 to 1 in 8 today. The two are different in that the first great migration was regulated in ways that the current one is not. Unlike last time, at least one-third of America's current foreign-born population is here illegally. The flow of illegal immigrants may not be as large as Michael Savage suggests—the average annual figure often cited is nearer 500,000—but it does have the geographic focus he mentions (namely, Mexico). One-third of all foreign-born people in the United States are currently Mexican; "over half of all Mexicans in the United States are illegal immigrants; and in the last decade 80 to 85 percent of the inflow of Mexicans into the United States has been illegal."[3]

These people are entering illegally because legal immigration is controlled by tight quotas—quotas of skill and quotas of global region—that fail to match the number of people from Mexico wanting to move north. Existing legislation allows for 19 million extra legal immigrants over the next two decades. Critics of the Martinez-Hagel Senate bill say that, if passed, that number would rise by a factor of five: not 19 million by 2026, but probably 103 million.[4] Even bleaker scenarios put the figure higher still—200 million is sometimes mentioned—but even when more conservative projections prevail, the point is clear. The United States is said to be facing demographic change of an unprecedented scale, one that will permanently alter the ethnic and cultural makeup of the entire population. It is also said to be facing a mass challenge to the legality and effectiveness of its immigration codes. In trying to block that change and

challenge, critics vary in what they emphasize. All are troubled by the scale of
illegal immigration and want it stopped. But many on the Right are concerned
about the scale of immigration, period, and they want some kind of morato-
rium on entry to the United States, illegal or otherwise.

It's not just a matter of numbers; we're actually letting in the wrong kind of immigrant

Critics concerned with the scale of immigration as well as its legality also
worry about the proportion of unskilled workers, relative to skilled ones, in
existing immigration flows. They point to the tight limits set on the number of
skilled workers allowed into the United States, in a policy mix that allows family members of existing immigrants to enter, regardless of the skills they bring
or lack. Where is the economic sense, these critics ask, in inflating the pool of
the unskilled and the poor, in a world in which economic competitiveness
turns on the quality of human capital and social inequality only fuels urban
tensions? After all, "If low-skill workers were the key to economic growth,
Mexico would be an economic powerhouse, and impoverished Americans
would be slipping south over the Rio Grande."[5] Opening doors to what
Michael Savage called "a deluge of human flotsam and jetsam"[6] may well have
made sense in the past, when manual labor and semiskilled industrial workers
were the bedrock of American economic growth. But we now live in a world of
intense competition between knowledge-based industries—a world in which
the average skill level of a labor force can make the critical difference between
global success and failure. Of course, not all the conservative critics of current
immigration policy favor privileging even skilled immigrants. Some think the
skilled should be excluded too, to give homegrown American scientists a
chance,[7] but there is widespread agreement among critics of current immigration policy that leaving the door open to the global poor no longer makes any
kind of sense at all.

Such immigration threatens American national unity

Some of those critics—but critically not all of them—then go the extra inch
and raise objections to the places of origin of so many contemporary immigrants, as well as to their lack of skills.

They argue that more than economics has changed in America, that the
political context of immigration has changed as well, and that because it has,
the rules of immigration now need to be reset. We live, they say, in a new age
of political correctness, an age of multiculturalism, an era in which minorities
within the United States have come to expect recognition and rights linked to
their minority status rather than to their individual standing as citizens. Older
immigrants came mainly from Europe. They left the old country behind and
arrived determined to assimilate, knowing that they had to and that they would
have to wait in line for the benefits of the new society to which they'd come.
They might not feel those benefits, but their children would. Things are different now. The new immigrants don't arrive from the same places. Nor do they
arrive with the same expectations and flexibilities. They come from Asia, bringing completely different cultures and languages with them. They come from

Mexico—so many from Mexico—not leaving their country so much as just slipping across its northern border. And these Mexican migrants do not come to assimilate. Many come to work, but many do not. They come to live off our welfare services or even to recolonize land that was once Mexican—to pull the southern United States back into a Hispanic linguistic and social orbit from which it was wrenched by military force in the 1840s.[8] They come in search of the good life, and they expect it now.

In the worst fears of such critics, what we face in the contemporary United States is not the traditional melting pot of cultures subsumed into a common Americanism, but the emergence of an increasingly balkanized society riddled with ethnic tension—"the United States as a Bosnia of continental proportions"[9]—one in which illegal immigrants "get bumped ahead of every-body"[10] and in which Americans no longer even speak the same language. They fear that Mexican immigration without assimilation threatens to end the Anglo-Protestant cultural dominance on which, they claim, American greatness has been built.[11] California is already heavily bilingual. It will soon, Pat Buchanan says, be the Quebec of the United States. In such a bleak scenario, "differences between legal and illegal immigrants fade into a generalized belief that a brown-skinned, Spanish-speaking tidal wave is about to swamp the white-skinned population of the United States."[12] This is not immigration, we're told. It's invasion: the creation of a nation within a nation, a gradual transformation of the American southwest, California, and Texas into a veritable "Republica del Norte." What Mexican soldiers could not hold by force in the nineteenth century, Mexican immigrants will take by stealth in the twenty-first. We need to recognize this, and resist it accordingly.

Illegal immigrants bring crime, disease, and terrorism with them

When the criticism of existing immigration policy switches from issues of scale to issues of legality, the case being made switches with it. Then what we hear is that all illegal immigrants break the law by coming here, and all of them continue to break the law by staying. They are all, in that sense, genuinely criminals. And although the majority of them are not engaged in an active life of crime (most, indeed, come illegally simply to do honest work), among their number are active criminals and, post-9/11, active terrorists as well. Tom Tancredo has written of "the corruption that is spreading through the United States that is linked to Mexican-based drug cartels and the Mexican mafia. . . . Some of the most violent criminals running loose in the United States," he tells us, "are illegal immigrants."[13] Apparently, "we are in the middle of a mounting epidemic of preventable crime by illegal immigrants . . . Americans murdered, raped and assaulted by criminal illegal aliens."[14] This "violence by illegal immigrants [then serves] as one of the largest causes of financial loss to emergency departments around the country." It is also a violence that is triggered by illegal immigrants who harbor (and so reintroduce) "fatal illnesses that American medicine fought and vanquished long ago, such as drug-resistant tuberculosis, malaria, leprosy, plague, polio, dengue and Chagas disease."[15]

We're told that terrorist groups keen to enter the United States face lax security systems to our north and to our south—Mexico and Canada both—and that the United States has a uniquely long and open border to police. According to Michael Savage, 190,000 illegal immigrants from countries other than Mexico "melted into the U.S. population ... during the first nine months of 2004" alone, including "people from El Salvador, Nicaragua, Russia, China and Egypt, not to mention Iran and Iraq."[16] So "if Al Qaeda wanted to smuggle in a nuclear weapon, America's southern border is a very inviting place to start."[17] Add to that the proposal in Section 240d of the Senate bill to prevent local law enforcement agents from arresting aliens for civil violations, as distinct from criminal offenses, and the United States is poised to create what the Heritage Foundation's Kris Kobach has called a new "terrorist loophole."[18] Four of the 9/11 hijackers had been stopped for speeding before the attack, and they could have been arrested by better-briefed police officers. Why take that law enforcement power away?

Illegal immigration costs the rest of us jobs and wages, taxes and space

Don't let anyone tell you that illegal immigrants make the rest of us prosperous by doing the grunt work that other Americans won't do, for wages that other Americans won't accept. The truth is entirely otherwise. Illegal immigrants take the jobs that native-born Americans would gladly do if they were offered to them, at wages that would be higher if immigration was lower. Unemployment among adult Americans rose by 2.3 million between 2000 and 2004. The number of employed adult immigrants rose in the same period by exactly the same amount.[19] Even the Clinton Labor Department admitted that half of the wage losses experienced by low-income Americans in the 1990s was caused by immigration. Mexican wage rates act as a weight, pulling down the wages of the rest of the labor force. Big agribusiness gets the benefit of cheap labor in its fields but honest businesses suffer from unfair competition and other workers suffer, too. Their living standards are squeezed by the downward pressure released by illegal immigration on jobs and earnings economy-wide. Over the longer term, those same living standards are held back by slower rates of technological improvement in the industries whose costs low-immigrant wages subsidize. All American workers suffer, and the poor suffer the most. Illegal immigration has undermined the capacity of African Americans to realize the promise of the 1960s[20] and legal immigrants from Mexico have suffered most of all, with their pace of assimilation and acceptance slowed by the illegal presence of huge numbers of their fellow countrymen and women, from whom they find it so hard to differentiate themselves.

Illegal immigration creates poverty, not prosperity. It overburdens social services and the American welfare state, and it fills up an already crowded American landscape. Illegal aliens and their children cost U.S. taxpayers probably $10 billion a year in Medicaid, uninsured medical costs, aid to schools, food stamps, free school lunches, and jail time—and "the cost of providing free health care for illegal immigrants is one of the primary reasons the price of U.S. health care continues to rise."[21] "Right now, 34 percent of all LEGAL Mexican immigrants are on welfare, and 25 percent of illegals are getting government assistance."[22] The pressure placed on the school systems and hospitals in areas of high illegal immigration is accordingly daunting. "Every year 65,000 illegal aliens graduate from our nation's schools.... Who pays for that?" Michael Savage has asked. "The Mexican government? Sorry Señor, You do and I do.... It's all part of the *No Illegal Alien Left Behind* program"[23] that's bleeding America dry. The folks in Washington might get their grass cut cheaply and their laundry done but the rest of us "are owed tens of billions of dollars in reparations from Mexico for feeding, clothing and providing health care for millions of illegal aliens over the last several decades."[24] It's time to stop the rot and get the money back.

This is a problem made in Washington, one that can be solved there

We've lost control of our borders, so the argument runs, because of politics in Washington. Outside the Beltway, significant majorities of ordinary Americans want action taken on illegal immigration and restrictions placed on the flow of migrants given green cards to work here legally. But not inside the Beltway: there, an unholy alliance of corporate interests, labor unions, and politicians seeking immigrant votes regularly combine to pass inadequate laws and to conspire against their full implementation. Border patrolling is regularly underfunded. Companies employing illegal immigrants are systematically ignored. Periodic amnesties for illegal immigrants are either proposed or passed. One passed—under Ronald Reagan himself—in 1986. It was presented as a solution to illegal immigration, but it was actually a trigger to even more. Too often in Washington, leftists consumed with guilt about their own affluence turn a blind eye to the illicit arrival of the Mexican poor, and passionate free-traders argue for the dismantling of border controls, not just on goods and capital but on people, too.

The Democratic Party has been the great sinner here. It relies heavily on the votes of recent legal migrants, and it is unwilling to criminalize their family members by cracking down on those here without proper authorization or papers. Rush Limbaugh for one regularly reminds his listeners of what's afoot here. According to him, they're "trying to recruit these people and legalize them on the spot just to make them voters."[25] They're trying to build a new constituency for big government.[26] But elements in the current Republican leadership are proving equally spineless on this matter—"running scared," as Rush Limbaugh has it, "pure cowardice in action."[27] They are the "gutless ... country-club, blue-blood Rockefeller-type"[28] Republicans who also want that migrant vote and are prepared to surrender principle to get it. Not all of them, of course—certainly many House Representatives are currently taking a principled stand on border and repatriation issues, and they deserve the support of all right-thinking Americans. But of late, Senate Republicans have been a different matter. They contain maverick and liberal elements with their own presidential ambitions and are definitely part of the problem here, not part of the solution.

Any kind of amnesty is the wrong kind of solution

So what is the solution? Definitely not any kind of amnesty, nothing as soft and spineless as a $2,000 fine and a compulsory English class. To allow illegal immigrants to stay—either unpunished or only moderately penalized—would

send out completely the wrong kind of signal. Far from ending illegal immigration, it would encourage it. It did in 1986, and it would again. What we
have to do is close the border, stopping illegal immigration altogether. In the
short term, that means deploying the national guard and reinforcing border
patrols. In the longer term, it means building an actual fence, all along the
southern edge of the United States. (Some bloggers have even suggested that
the Mexicans be invited to build the wall themselves, as a boost to their own
economy—thus increasing the capacity of the Mexican government "to offer
their people an incentive to stay home. A living wage springs to mind."[29]) In
addition, illegal immigrants already in the country must be denied any access
to schooling and health care, and the companies that employ them must be
heavily fined. If the demand for illegal labor is cut off in this way, then the
supply will dry up. And, it will definitely dry up quicker if people illegally in
the United States are rounded up and sent home. All of them rounded up.
All of them sent home. Not just those in the border states, but every single
one. Not everyone thinks that's practical—Rush Limbaugh for one does not,
and attrition, not mass deportation, is Pat Buchanan's policy of choice[30]—but
Tom Tancredo certainly does, and he is by no means alone in that belief.
"Those who don't go home," he told the House in December 2005, "you
deport."[31]

A LIBERAL RESPONSE

So what could possibly by wrong with that? This much, at least.

You don't have to be a Democrat to disagree with Tom Tancredo

All you have to be is George W. Bush and recognize that "it is neither
wise nor realistic to round up millions of people, many with deep roots in
the United States, and send them across the border."[32] Not only is it
not wise, it's not practical or politically expedient either. You can't build a
2,000-mile-long fence; even if you did root out every illegal immigrant, all
you'd end up with would be 12 million versions of what Congressman Pence
referred to as "the horrific images in the world press the night Elian Gonzalez
was taken into custody." Which is why Pence, and many Republicans more
liberal than he, believe that "this idea of putting everybody on buses and
conducting a mass deportation is a nonstarter."[33]

Even if it were not—even if somehow all illegal immigrants could be
expelled—the resulting economic fallout would be catastrophic. "The economics are simple," New York City's Republican mayor has argued. "We
need more workers than we have,"[34] and we rely on immigration to provide
them. According to liberal and Libertarian Republicans, powerful forces of
supply and demand are at work here, forces that make border security counterproductive, if used alone. "Coercive efforts to keep willing workers out"
have not only "spawned an underground culture of fraud and smuggling,"

the Cato Institute told the 108th Congress, and "caused hundreds of unnecessary deaths in the desert." They've also "disrupted the traditional circular flow of Mexican migration, perversely *increasing* the stock of illegal Mexican workers and family members in the United States."[35] Michael Bloomberg made the same point even more graphically when appearing before members of the 109th Congress:

> It's as if we expect border control agents to do what a century of communism could not: defeat the natural market forces of supply and demand and defeat the natural human desire for freedom and opportunity. You might as well sit on your beach chair and tell the tide not to come in.[36]

Patrolling the border of Pat Buchanan's mind?

None of that satisfies Pat Buchanan, of course, because he sees amnesty lurking in the detail of any guest-worker program and "loss of country," as he puts it, in the weakness of the border security being proposed by liberal Republicans. But then Pat Buchanan has a very particular view of what is actually going on here, a view that can and should be challenged in at least the following ways.

The present immigration situation is neither as threatening nor as novel as he would have it. Certainly in terms of scale the proportion of foreign-born people in the United States—at 12 percent in 2004—is still lower than in 1890, when that number included several of Pat Buchanan's German, Scottish, and Irish ancestors.[37] The United States has survived this scale of immigration before—it survived the arrival of the Buchanans, after all—and it will do so again. Moreover, there's nothing unusual in people coming to work in the United States and then going home. That was a common feature of Mexican immigration, in particular, from the end of the Mexican-American War right through to the passage of the 1965 Act. It was that Act's creation, for the first time, of a quota for Mexican migrants that inadvertently triggered this new phenomenon of the illegal Mexican immigrant. Pat Buchanan would have us understand this flow of predominantly Latin American migration as something intensely alien to an American culture rooted in western values; yet, in reality, the bulk of those migrants come from former Spanish colonies. They come, like him, with Roman Catholicism as their religion. They come with strong family values and a powerful work ethic. Pat Buchanan is also highly critical of the decline of U.S. morality and popular culture and yet criticizes immigrants for not assimilating into it. He would surely do better, from a conservative perspective, to welcome this addition to the bloc of social forces uneasy with abortion on demand, gay rights, and explicit sexuality. What Mexican immigration brings isn't "alien behavior. It's admirable behavior, the antidote to the excessive individualism that social conservatives decry."[38]

Getting the history right

To those who would contrast an old-style melting pot America with a future of Balkanized ethnic tension, we should ask for the restraint of historical accuracy. Ethnic—and indeed racial—tension has been, and remains, central to the American story. Try asking Native Americans whether the old-style melting pot was one in which the newly arrived Europeans assimilated into existing native Indian culture. Try asking the descendants of African slaves if those who arrived first set the cultural tone for those who arrived later. After all, black America was here long before Irish America, Italian America, or Polish America. The very choice of those three major ethnic groups in the United States should remind us that, to the degree that Samuel Huntington and others describe American culture as Anglo-Saxon and Protestant, they write out of the American story, among other things, Catholicism, the Romance languages, and European Jewry.[39] It's Mexicans and organized crime today. It was Italians and organized crime in the 1930s—and Hollywood makes a fortune these days glamorizing things like *The Godfather*. There's nothing new in this nativist fear of cultural change linked to immigration or in the politics of "last man in, shut the door." Benjamin Franklin expressed that same fear in 1751 about the arrival of Germans in Philadelphia. But they assimilated. They didn't initially speak English, but within three generations they were bilingual. In fact, German settlers in the midwest reportedly maintained bilingual public school systems until World War I made it impolitic to do so. By that measure, current immigrants and their children are actually learning English "faster than their predecessors [did] a hundred years ago."[40]

Mexican immigrants aren't qualitatively different in this regard, just newer in the immigration cycle. The data we have do suggest higher rates of bilingualism among current second-generation Hispanic immigrants than among European immigrants of the first great wave, but it also shows that by the third generation, speaking English predominates in all Hispanic households.[41] People at the bottom of English-speaking social structures *have* to learn English to make progress up them. The German immigrants certainly did. The Mexicans will no doubt follow suit. The only thing that will block the rapid assimilation of Mexican immigrants into mainstream American life—if that is the outcome we want—is the very hostility to their presence in the United States that the politics of the right encourage. The only thing that will keep more of them here than actually wish to remain is the difficulty of going back and forth across the very wall being built to keep the rest out, and the only thing that will keep them poor—and a burden on the welfare state—is discrimination against them in American labor markets. If we want the new wave of immigrants to assimilate, all we have to do is let them. And, as we do so, we too will change. Streets run in two directions, after all, and they always work best when their lanes are open to traffic moving both ways. What would America be today if an earlier generation of Pat Buchanan's had frozen U.S. culture in the mind-set of the 1840s? At the very least, it would be racist, homophobic, anti-Catholic, and anti-Semitic. Immigration is one of the things America does best, and cultural change is one of the *positive* benefits of the American immigration story. We need to recognize that and celebrate it.

Framing the issue the Columbus way!

Mexican immigrants—at least in the hands of the more strident defenders of the American border—stand condemned for bringing disease, crime, and terror to the American heartland, as though *Guns, Germs, and Steel*[42] are not central to the entire American story. Christopher Columbus was not a legal immigrant, as far as I'm aware, and although he went back to Spain twice after "discovering" America—a pattern of return of which many "no amnesty" advocates would doubtless approve—he didn't leave these shores because he couldn't get a green card. He went home to restock, the better to seize more American land in the name of imperial Spain when next he returned. Indeed, there is something particularly ridiculous about the current claim of an impending Mexican "Reconqista" when you think back to what has actually happened in North America since Columbus arrived. Over that intervening period, the United States was expanded by conquest and held united by war. From the very beginning, "the building of America" was a national project with a fair degree of ethnic cleansing at its core, not to mention a good bit of slavery on the side. Anyway, there's just no credible evidence of any Mexican plan to retake the American southwest—historically, the urban and rural poor have never been an independent imperial force, and Mexican workers are unlikely to break that pattern—but the rhetoric that sometimes surfaces among Mexican radicals is understandable nonetheless. The American southwest is itself a product of conquest, and we would do well to at least acknowledge that, before raising the fear of an impending invasion by forces that actually exist only in the imagination of the paranoid few.

As for disease and terror, how more American could the story be? When the *Mayflower* arrived off Cape Cod in November 1620, its capacity to successfully land its tiny band of exhausted pilgrims was entirely the product of the prior arrival of European diseases that had all but decimated the local Indian forces that might otherwise have repelled them.[43] And as we now know—but tend not to mention in polite conversation—in the century and a half after 1492, a staggering 95 percent of the pre-Columbian Native American population fell victim to deadly European diseases—either by direct contact or indirectly via contact with infected tribes[44]—so that European settlement largely expanded into areas left empty by American versions of the Black Death.[45] True, European settlers brought superior weaponry, and that was important; but the most vital thing they brought were killer

illnesses. They traded smallpox, measles, influenza, typhus, and even bubonic plague for syphilis. Not a pleasant trade, it must be said, but a trade
on such a scale as to render current claims about Mexican immigrants over-
using local hospitals trivial by contrast.

Let's not be so quick to discount the benefits of immigration

Michael Savage would have us believe that the Mexican government owes
ordinary Americans a big reparation check, because of all the expenses
imposed on the rest of us by the presence of so many immigrants, legal or
otherwise. But this really is to count with one eye open and one eye shut.
Ledgers always have two columns, and before we can judge the debit side,
we need a list of assets, too.

There's a clear scholarly consensus—even among economists troubled by
the impact of immigration on wage levels—that, in overall terms, immigration brings positive benefits to the society in total. Quite how much is hard
to quantify: the National Academy of Sciences in 1997 thought it might be
around $10 billion a year.[46] No serious argument is currently circulating
that immigration by professionals and skilled workers is anything other than
entirely desirable. Roy Beck apart, the general consensus seems to be that
the presence of such immigrants in the United States directly enhances the
competitiveness of U.S. industry, and it contributes to technological growth,
labor productivity, and rising general standards of living. Illegal immigration
is more problematic, of course; at the very least, it visibly provides labor to
a number of important American industries, including construction, hotels
and restaurants, retailing, and agriculture—industries that otherwise would
experience crippling labor shortages and industries whose costs are significantly reduced by the immigrant presence.[47] The American consumer clearly
benefits from these lower costs: cheaper housing costs, food costs, and costs
of domestic service. The bigger question is whether those benefits come with
a price: the price of higher unemployment and lower wages for that section
of the native-born labor force whose skills and employment prospects are
similar to the immigrants' own.

In periods of rapid growth—such as those enjoyed by the U.S. economy
in the 1990s—that question tends to be buried, as immigration, rising real
wages, and falling unemployment all go easily together. But in periods of
recession and jobless growth, like now, it tends to reappear, and the argument is heard again that immigrants take American jobs. (As we saw earlier,
there's widespread concern about this in African American quarters, in particular, that black workers are especially vulnerable to Mexican competition.) But the best research data we have would suggest that the concern,
although understandable, is misplaced: because the kinds of jobs on which
competition is fiercest are likely to remain plentiful over time, and because
the skill sets of immigrants and native-born workers are likely to continue
to be different. The Labor Department's own employment projections

anticipate the creation of an additional 7.7 million unskilled jobs in the U.S. economy in the first decade of the new century, with more to come in the decades to follow.[48] And those will be decades in which the indigenous population will continue to age and become more educated and, for both those reasons, will become less willing and less suitable to fill jobs at the bottom of the employment food chain. That unwillingness and lack of suitability is already in place. Currently, there is a significant mismatch between the skills of unemployed Americans and the skill requirements of the jobs taken by undocumented Mexican workers.[49] That mismatch is likely to continue because, in general, the shape of the skill distribution among immigrants is hourglassed: Immigrants arrive with either very high skills or very low ones. The skills of most native-born Americans are, and are likely to remain, more in the middle range. Immigration doesn't threaten that indigenous skill pattern. It actually complements it.

The thorny question of wages

The issue of immigration and wages is more difficult to resolve. Here, there is a genuine academic dispute. It's not a dispute about the impact of highly skilled immigrants on professional wages. Immigrants with professional skills tend to be among America's highest earners. No, the argument is focused elsewhere: on the impact of the presence of so many unskilled workers on the earning capacity of indigenous labor, similarly unskilled.

The most quoted study here—by George Borjas and colleagues at Harvard—suggests a 3 percent reduction in average wages between 1980 and 2000 because of immigration, and a cut in wages for high-school dropouts of around 8 percent.[50] But that attribution has not been without challenge from across the entire academic-political spectrum. Using an alternative methodology, academics at Berkeley found no significant correlation between proportions of immigrants in city labor forces and average wages for unskilled labor. Academics using Borjas's data but different assumptions have reported overall wages unaffected by immigration and an impact on the wages of workers without school diplomas of 5 percent rather than 8 percent. Factor in the extra demand created by the wages of illegal workers. Factor in additions to the capital stock. Factor in the high concentration of illegal labor in just a limited number of industries. Suddenly, the general impact of immigration on indigenous wages begins to look more benign.[51] The most we can safely say here is that if the flow of illegal immigrants does indeed hit the earning capacity of the indigenous unskilled, it does so only at the margin and only in specific industries. And if we are concerned about that margin—and we ought to be, because we're talking about the poorest of all American workers—then excluding immigrants is definitely not the quickest way to fix it. The quickest way to fix poverty, among both indigenous and immigrant American labor alike, is to raise significantly the minimum wage and to improve by legislation the working conditions of the lowest paid.

Ultimately, there's only one certain way to determine whether illegal immigrants are, or are not, doing jobs that native-born Americans would want for themselves if those jobs were properly rewarded, and that's to ensure that those jobs *are* indeed properly paid. Raise the minimum wage. Send in the factory inspectors. Block off the super-exploitation of both illegal immigrants and the indigenous poor simultaneously, and do it, not by criminalizing immigrants, but by criminalizing those who so cruelly exploit both groups of vulnerable workers. Epiphanies are always wonderful things to watch, so seeing the Republican Right suddenly concerned with the wages of the lowest paid is genuinely touching. But let's see just how deep and genuine that concern actually is. Let's see Republicans bringing in, and enforcing, legislation that really will stop illegal immigrants undercutting local wages—legislation, that is, that fines or jails the employers who pay less than a much-improved minimum wage, rather than attacking those who are struggling to keep body and soul together as they work long hours in appalling conditions for a mere pittance.[52]

Illegal immigration and the welfare burden

Conservative critics of the current influx of a Spanish-speaking immigrant labor force regularly bewail the impact of that influx on America's social infrastructure—specifically on its hospitals, its schools, and its jails. You remember Michael Savage's question about who pays for all this "welfare." His answer, of course, was that we do—that the tab is picked up by honest American taxpayers. And he's correct: Right now the children of immigrants from Mexico get more help with school meals and medical coverage than the American average, and there's more going out from the public coffers to support their families than the immigrants are putting in. But that imbalance is not primarily the result of them being here illegally or being Mexican. It exists because they're newly arrived, badly paid, and poor. And there's nothing particularly new or shocking in that.

The newly arrived have always been poor in the U.S. immigration story. When the Irish, the Italians, the Germans, and the Poles arrived, they too arrived poor. Their children didn't fail to burden the U.S. welfare state because there was something particularly superior about late-nineteenth-century European immigrants or something particularly feckless about contemporary Mexican ones. The earlier generations of the immigrant poor didn't burden the U.S. welfare state because there was *no* welfare state to burden. They and their children lived initially in levels of squalor that none of us ought now to wish on anyone. They depended on charities and political parties for help with employment, housing, and health because no public institutions existed to provide those vital early supports to them. No doubt there was an imbalance of payment then, too—the charities gave more to the newly arrived poor than the poor gave back to them. But over time—through education and individual effort—those immigrants and their children did raise their skill levels and their earning capacity. Over time, they did get to a point at which they could begin to contribute more to the welfare support of others than they took in welfare support for themselves. That is already happening again now, among the second generation of this most recent influx of poor immigrants, and it will continue to happen. If Mexican Americans currently draw slightly more heavily on the U.S. welfare system than do Americans in general, that is a temporary condition. Assimilation and spreading affluence among the newcomers will solve it. The denial of basic services and mass deportations most definitely will not.

In any case, those same conservative critics of excessive immigration also regularly bewail the absence of sufficient workers to sustain the baby boomers in their retirement. Yet immigration—both legal and illegal—is by far the most effective source of that extra necessary labor. Tom Tancredo blames illegal immigrants for rising health costs. The claim is, at best, shortsighted. The immediate burden illegal immigrants place on local welfare services, although undeniably heavy in certain localized areas, is both temporary and solvable with federal help. The long-term assistance those same immigrants can provide to those same welfare services will be permanent and more general. The median age of American workers is currently 34 years old. By 2025, it will be 43 years old; as Commerce Secretary Gutierrez recently put it, "every 60 seconds, a baby boomer turns 60." We're running out of workers, and in this we're not alone. All developed industrial societies currently need more labor and more babies. All of them—the European Union and Japan alike—are recalibrating their immigration laws to meet that need. As Gutierrez said, relative to them, "we have an incredible advantage here. We can stand out from the pack by using our well-honed skills from 230 years of assimilating immigrants."[53] Between 2000 and 2004, the U.S. population grew by 12 million. More than 5 million of those were immigrants. The age and fertility profile of those immigrants was significantly younger and more active than that of America as a whole, and the skill levels and education performance of their children is already on the rise.[54] Their presence here offers the promise of an enhanced stock of able-bodied workers in the decades to come. Thus, if conservatives try to shut them out as they deplore the welfare crisis, it's hard to avoid the conclusion that—although the critics of Mexican immigration presumably want, like the rest of us, more workers and babies to sustain them in their old age—they want that sustenance to be provided by workers with a particular color of skin.

Shades of Ross Perot

The Michael Savages of this world are quite mistaken to propose, as a solution to the flow of Mexican labor, that the Mexican government give their people a living wage. They're also wrong to imply that only corruption in Mexican politics is preventing that from happening. Leaving aside the inconsistency of argument here—with Michael Savage advocating more government management of the Mexican economy while decrying govern-ment interference with the economy at home—the whole proposal ignores the legacy of two centuries of economic underdevelopment. Contemporary Mexican politicians and workers, like their equivalents everywhere, are con-strained by the past. Living standards in Mexico and the United States were not that different in 1776, but they are now because the nineteenth-century Mexican economy failed to grow as fast as the American one. No one alive today is to blame for that nineteenth-century failure. They just have to oper-ate within the limited amount of industrialization and infrastructure that it left in place, an amount that all through the twentieth century triggered a regular and steady flow of Mexican labor north to work in the agricultural businesses of the American southwest. That flow of labor was genuinely migratory, mainly coming north and going south with the seasons.[55] It was also a flow that paid the real price of underdevelopment: destitution at home and appalling working conditions on the road. Those leading the charge against contemporary Mexican migration often present the U.S. worker or tax-payer as the real loser in the immigration story. They should try being a Latino migrant working long hours for low wages in an American chicken factory, or a Mexican child left behind by parents going north in search of a better life.[56] Losing a tax dollar is one thing, losing a parent is quite another.

Mexican workers don't hold the prime responsibility for the changed pat-tern and volume of their migration into North America. That responsibility lies with the North American Free Trade Agreement (NAFTA). The Mexican economy had been a success story in the 1950s and 1960s—growing *faster* even than the Japanese economy for most of that period—behind policies of import substitution and oil exploration. But by the late 1980s, Mexico had gone through a major oil-based debt crisis and a policy shift to free trade—one that culminated in the launching of NAFTA in 1994. That agreement (among other things) progressively and incrementally exposed modestly subsidized Mexican agriculture to competition from heavily subsidized U.S. agribusiness.[57] In 2002, Oxfam estimated the average rural subsidy per farmer in Mexico to be just $720 a year, whereas in the United States it was $20,800.[58] As the two subsidy systems interacted, the Mexican elite may have benefited, but in general, Mexican farm incomes began to fall. They fell at a rate of 4.3 percent per year throughout the 1990s.[59] A new iron triangle then opened up. Tax dollars flowed out from Washington to the American West—$180 billion dollars worth in the 2002 Agriculture Bill alone, mainly going to big companies.[60] Ever-greater volumes of their subsidized agrarian produce then flowed south across the border, threatening the living stand-ards of the more than 20 percent of the Mexican population still working in agriculture; in consequence, Mexican workers left the countryside in ever-greater numbers—maybe 2 million in total since 1994—with some then finding work in U.S. factories at the border, but others moving even further north, unable to sustain themselves at home.

We need to remember that the great flows of permanent immigration from Mexico that so concern Pat Buchanan are of very recent origin. In the 1980s, before the signing of NAFTA, illegal migration from Mexico averaged about 140,000 people a year, and the total undocumented population was fairly stable, at around 2.7 million. People came and people went home. After the signing, by contrast, illegal immigration averaged more than 500,000 people a year—the vast majority of whom did not go home. On the contrary, they stayed, to take the total number of illegal immigrants now in the United States up to its present level (of probably 11 to 12 million). *Two-thirds* of all undocumented workers now in the United States actually arrived after 1994.[61] If the American Right want those inflows to slow, and the Mexican economy to sustain (and retain) its own people, then the policy weapon to achieve it is in their hands. Instead of building a wall to keep Mexicans out, they should turn off the tap: Stop the subsidies to U.S. farming that bring so many Mexicans here in the first place. Conservatives don't like giveaways. So stop giving it away. Turn off the largesse given by Republican politicians to the agribusiness interests that sustain them. Live up to the Right's traditional antigovernment stance and stop the public funding of *all* American industries, including the agrarian one. Then see what happens, over time, to migration flows. Successful farmers don't migrate—American farmers certainly don't; so why should Mexican ones?

Try not to make a bad situation worse

The golden rule of politics is normally this: If you're in a hole, the first thing you should do is stop digging. That rule needs to be applied here because we are genuinely in a hole. The critics of illegal immigration are entirely correct on that point. Illegal immigration does present us with a cluster of genuine problems that public policy must at the very least *not* make worse. It's clearly undesirable to have 12 million people in the United States without authorization and proper documentation. Their presence does, indeed, call into question the effectiveness and legitimacy of the entire legal system. But it's also clearly undesirable to see those same people then exposed, as a result of their illegal status, to terrible wages and working conditions, open to super-exploitation by unscrupulous employers, and forced to live a subterranean life without adequate access to legal protection for themselves and their families. Nor should we be happy with a situation in which heavy pressure is placed on schools and hospitals in border states, and on the honest taxpayers who reside there, or with people waiting abroad for green cards being passed in line by those who slipped across the border undetected. And because those illegal immigrants are generally paid so badly, we shouldn't be happy either with a situation in which they're forced to live in poverty, and in which their willingness to work for so little then makes whatever contribution it does—big or small—to poverty wages for others. As Michael Dukakis has recently noted, currently "millions of illegal immigrants work for minimum and even sub-minimum wages in workplaces that don't come close to meeting health and safety standards."[62] That is clearly something that we need to end.

Illegality, exploitation, differential welfare use, wage pressure, and queue-jumping are all real problems. They're just not problems that will be solved by criminalizing the people caught up in them. Putting up a wall will not stop the flow. People can always get around walls. It certainly won't keep out terrorists. None of the 9/11 terrorists slipped into the United States across the Rio Grande, and there's no reason to suppose that the next lot will either. Anyway, only half of all illegal immigrants entering the United States do so across the Mexican border, so how many walls are we proposing to build?[63] All a wall, or a set of walls, would do is cost a very large amount of money[64] and break the circularity of migration by stopping those already here from easily returning home. Criminalizing illegal immigration, and deporting illegal immigrants whenever they're found, would simply add to those costs[65] while driving those immigrants further underground. It would add hugely to the fear and stresses they already carry, and it would leave them even more vulnerable to exploitation by their employers. Any mass deportation would also inevitably backfire, and at some speed, certainly in public relations terms, but probably in economic ones as well. In a place like Arizona, for example, the spending power of illegal immigrants is already a significant component in the local structure of demand for goods and services—outstripping that of even highly paid physicians by a factor of 2.5:1—and across the country as a whole, large-scale deportations would inevitably create acute labor shortages (and associated price hikes) in industries as disparate as leisure and entertainment, construction and agriculture, cleaning and food preparation.

To then compound the mass deportation of illegal immigrants by also denying basic welfare services to their children and dependents would be simply inhumane and profoundly un-American. Is anyone actually proposing that hospitals literally dump people without papers on the streets? Any guest-worker system put in place in the wake of that dumping would run counter to the American tradition of granting eventual citizenship to those who enter legally and work. Indeed, if that new guest-worker system ties workers to specific jobs, and makes eventual citizenship dependent on employer support, it will only increase guest-worker vulnerability to exploitation. And if it's applied to Mexican immigrants alone—if it becomes a kind of second *Bracero* program—its creation will only institutionalize and exacerbate the racism that is currently slowing the assimilation of existing Latino immigrants. You can't split the Mexican American population in two, and force one half to go back to Mexico, without turning the other half into second-class citizens in the country from which you've just expelled their important family members—so it would entirely counterproductive to try.

So what should we do?

The only way out of this impasse is to separate its immediate participants from the processes generating their contemporary plight, and then to deal with each half of the problem in different ways.

We should start by celebrating the contributions made by even illegal immigrants to contemporary American prosperity. We should celebrate their capacity for hard work that sustains basic services, their willingness to live in (and revive) depressed urban areas, their propensity to spread out beyond the normal "big six" immigrant states into every corner of the United States,[66] and their commitment to the building of strong families, powerful churches, and stable communities of a traditional American kind. We should accordingly support programs of registration that allow immigrants already here to build up entitlements to citizenship—that is, we should support a general amnesty—paralleling that with a quickening and expansion of the flow of legal immigration from Latin America during the period through which the amnesty holds. And we should protect the integrity of the amnesty by limiting the flow of family members allowed in after citizenship to immediate relatives and by setting a clear endpoint: a moment after which anyone still unregistered would be deported, and any employer giving work to the unregistered would be heavily penalized. In other words, we should bring the existing flow of illegal migrants into the orbit of law, and use the legal system to turn off *demand* for such illegal workers in the future. Walls will not keep people out, but a properly funded and adequately computerized system of identification numbers certainly can. Its creation should be a common rallying point for all the nonracist players in the contemporary immigration drama—because it's visibly in the common interests of honest employers, native-born workers, and legalized immigrants alike.

But that's not all we should do. To get rid of an underclass—Mexican or otherwise—we have to do more than influence the social background and national origins of the people occupying its lowly positions in any particular generation. We have to get rid of the lowly positions themselves. To stop people competing for poverty wages, we need to do more than simply half the number of competitors, by sending those here illegally home. We also need to remove the poverty wages for which they compete in the United States and the super-poverty wages from which those coming illegally are trying to escape. The first of those issues is easier to tackle than the second, but we need integrated programs that are capable of addressing them both. Poverty wages in the United States have to be legislated away by raising (and then enforcing) the national minimum wage and by requiring that even workers on temporary work visas are paid no less than the prevailing wage paid to their native-born equivalents. And over time, poverty wages in Mexico have to be eased by removing any U.S.-induced pressure to keep them down. As we'll argue more fully in chapter 10, fair trade, not free trade, is a key part of any solution to the U.S. immigration controversy. At the very least, we need a significant reduction in public subsidies to large U.S. agricultural companies, a reduction that will free public funds for much-needed antipoverty programs at home. Higher wages in the United States will, of course, be a spur to further illegal immigration. That's why penalizing employers who use illegal immigrants will be so vital. But higher wages will also remove the need for a migrant labor force that survives by trading its low skills for low pay and will create instead an entirely different dynamic at the base of the U.S. labor market. Putting a solid floor under the wages of low-skilled, native-born, *and* immigrant workers will enable the living standards of both groups to grow together, with all the positive social consequences of generalized affluence over time. The only way to protect the American Dream is to share it, and the best way to share it is to design public policy that allows everyone to dream together.

8

Is God Necessarily Conservative?

Y ou would definitely think God was conservative, if all you listened to were the radio programs of the Christian Right. And there are lots of such radio programs around these days—so many, indeed, that you have to work rather hard to avoid them—radio programs that all push a particular and a similar message. It's a message that links public policy to a set of religious values. It's one that sees those values as everywhere under challenge and in retreat. It's one that treats the major social ills of contemporary America as the consequence of that challenge, and it's one that urges people of faith to fight back. It tells them to bring their own conservative social agenda to the political table and to hold the Republican Party responsible for its implementation.

This was not always the case. In the past, as now, the attitudes of the American electorate were heavily shaped by religious convictions, but historically those convictions were as often liberal as conservative. Indeed, from the very moment they arrived in the United States, most Irish, Italian, and Polish Catholics voted Democrat rather than Republican, and the candidates they supported were invariably progressive on economic issues if not always on social ones. White southern Baptists voted Democratic, too—they did so pretty consistently from Reconstruction to Civil Rights—although their Democrats were invariably on the conservative, even racist, wing of the party, and the bulk of the Jewish vote—certainly in the Northeast—was solidly in the New Deal camp after 1932. So there's nothing new about the connection between religion and politics in the United States. What is new is the way in which, of late, the political face of American religion has been monopolized by the right. What's new is the conservative impact on national politics of a rising tide of evangelical Protestantism.

Although the history of evangelical Protestantism is as old as that of the United States itself, it's normal to link its recent political history to the organizational initiatives of two men—Jerry Falwell and Pat Robertson—the first setting up the predominantly Baptist Moral Majority in 1978, the second hosting the more ecumenical *700 Club* television program before creating the Christian Coalition of America in 1989. What they began, others then copied, putting into place organizations of a bewildering number and complexity. Not all the Christian organizations now politically active on the American Right are evangelical, Protestant, and white. There are Catholic players here, too, and a number of conservative organizations and individuals rooted in the African American community. But white evangelical Protestantism is the main force behind many of the leading organizations now seeking to speak on social issues for Christian America: among the more influential of which are Focus on the Family, Concerned Women for America, The American Family Association, The Family Research Council, The Traditional Values Coalition, The Campaign for Working Families, The Free Congress Foundation, The Center for Moral Clarity, The Ethics and Public Policy Center, and The Discovery Institute. For the purposes of this chapter, it is these organizations to which we will refer collectively as "the Christian Right."

Between them, they and their supporters now command a vast array of radio stations, their own television networks and news agency, a host of think tanks, and several universities. Their reach and impact is correspondingly remarkable. Reportedly, "the radio commentaries of Focus on the Family's James C. Dobson alone are heard by more than two hundred million people every day in ninety-nine countries on more than five thousand radio outlets."[1] So not surprisingly, perhaps, a Gallup poll taken in 2005 found that 41 percent of Americans classified themselves as "born again" or evangelical Christians, and 59 percent of Americans said that "religion can solve all or most of today's problems."[2] More significant still for our purposes here, four out of every five white evangelicals voted for George W. Bush in 2004 and made up more than one-third of his entire electorate.[3] What Christian conservatives think is therefore important to Republicans, and what their leaders say they think is broadly of the following kind.

America as "a city upon a hill"

The uniqueness of America lies in its Christian character. America was created by men and women of faith, refugees from religious persecution. They came to these shores "to do justly, to love mercy, to walk humbly with our

God," believing that if they dealt falsely with that God, they would ultimately by "consumed out of the good land" on which they had landed.[4] There was a subordinate Catholic strand in that early American story, but nonetheless the values to which all decent Americans now adhere are understood as predominantly Protestant in origin: values such as individualism, freedom of thought and conscience, equality, and self-improvement. America prospered, so the argument goes, because it was a society built on these Christian values. The separation of church and state established in the Revolutionary Era guaranteed the right of every American to worship as he or she thought fit, but that separation was not designed to divorce religion from politics. On the contrary, religious values were from the beginning of the American story—as they must now remain—a vital source of guidance for the design of public policy, with the Bible itself as the main repository of those values. Indeed, according to Beverly LaHaye of Concerned Women for America, "politicians who do not use the Bible to guide their public and private lives do not belong in office."[5]

Conservative Christians differ on whether the New Testament should be treated as simply the main or as actually the only source of guidance on political issues. The more fundamentalist and evangelical such Christians are, the more the Bible is taken as the literal Word of God, and as such entirely true, complete and definitive in its own terms. The Bible is everywhere in the promotional literature of the Christian Right. The self-proclaimed mission of Concerned Women for America, for example, is to "protect and promote Biblical values among all citizens—first through prayer, then education, and finally by influencing our society."[6] The Traditional Values Coalition is similarly committed to "living, as far as is possible, by the moral precepts taught by Jesus Christ and by the whole counsel of God as revealed in the Bible."[7] So whether or not they're actually committed to the view that the Bible contains the full and authoritative word of God—when polled in 2004, 53 percent of all Americans and 83 percent of all evangelicals believed that the Bible was literally true[8]—all the major Christian think tanks and campaign organizations agree that Christian religious teaching has an importance, a legitimacy, and a priority that no other source of values can command. For daily guidance, they say, go to the Bible; if in crisis, turn once more to Jesus. Indeed, being "born again" is, for evangelical Christians at least, an essential stage in the personal journey back to a better and (for many) a more conservative politics.

The social ills of secularism

Many leading conservative Christians are convinced that most modern social ills are the direct consequence of the inability or refusal of many people to be born again in that fashion. They treat themselves and their churches as a persecuted and misunderstood minority. They insist that their religious convictions are regularly dismissed and derided by liberal policy makers and media pundits. They see their influence blocked by policies that deny the presence of Scripture in public buildings or prayer in public schools—to America's great and continuing cost. This "de-Christianizing of America" is, for Pat Buchanan at least, a key element in a more general "death of the West" that he uses to explain our current moral malaise,[9] and he's not alone in that view. The taking of prayer out of schools in 1962 was condemned as recently as 2002 by the evangelist Joyce Meyer as nothing less than "a violent assault against the future of the kingdom of God." "Satan knew," she told the delegates to the Christian Coalition convention, "that if he could take spirituality away from children ... the next generation would not be able to do the kingdom of darkness any damage."[10] Indeed, taking prayers out of public schools in this way is seen by many on the Christian Right as simply one example of that "constant attempt to strip our Judeo-Christian roots out of every nook and cranny of American life"[11] that has so eroded American values over the last half-century.

Such socially conservative Christians often assert a direct causal link between a multiplicity of modern general and specific ills and the secularization of American public life since 1960, a secularization they blame entirely on liberals. They explain the rise in crime in this fashion. They understand the upward trend in teenage pregnancies in a similar way. They lay much of the blame for declining moral standards on pornography and the entertainment industry, and they see both as driven by liberal Hollywood elites. Some conservative Christians—at the more extreme fringe of their coalition—even link things like Hurricane Katrina,[12] the scandal at Abu Ghraib,[13] and the attacks on 9/11[14] to this retreat from core religious convictions in American social life. Many leading Christian conservatives regularly describe modern America as a country without a proper moral compass and insist that the reestablishment of that compass—by the reintroduction of religious values into U.S. public life—is *the* political task of the age. It's a task, moreover, that the vast majority of them seem to believe can only be achieved by the election of Republican-dominated Congresses and born again Republican presidents. No Democrats here, only Republicans, because on their conservative reading of the Bible, Jesus Christ's political color was clearly red, not blue.

Marriage as "the union of a man and a woman"

Christian conservatives are aware that the transmission of solid religious values is no automatic process. It requires institutional support, particularly in times of moral crisis as they believe these to be. Many focus on the importance of schooling in that institutional support system, and seek to influence the content and delivery of the education curriculum. Others see the mass media as a huge negative influence, and seek ways to offset its impact—particularly on the young—by developing media outlets of their own. Most see a vital role for the courts in the protection of traditional practices and attach overwhelming importance to the selection of conservative judges. But the key institution to which the vast majority of conservative Christians look for the transmission of values is the family—understood as a permanent union between a man and a woman, sanctified by and before God—and the intensity of Christian Right politics now is, in large measure, a reflection of the extent to which they see the traditional family as everywhere in melt-down.

Many leading Christian conservatives feel that the American family is being challenged on two fronts. They see it threatened by the prevalence and toleration of sexual relations outside marriage—both premarital sex and marital infidelity—so that many of them actively campaign for sexual abstinence, abhor divorce, set their face against the distribution of family planning advice or contraceptives to the young, and oppose foreign-aid packages that fight AIDS by distributing condoms. They also see the institution of the traditional family as threatened by the prevalence and toleration of homosexuality in the wider community. Indeed the wedge issue here for the Christian Right in the first decades of the twenty-first century is less sexual promiscuity of a heterosexual kind than nonpromiscuous sexual activity of the homosexual variety. Members of the Christian Right treat homosexual acts as a sin and their defense as a left-wing practice. They see homosexuality as a socially learned form of deviant behavior proscribed by God, and they campaign vigorously against its receipt of any form of social recognition or acceptance. In particular and of late, they have set their face firmly against any extension to gay couples of the legal rights and privileges associated with marriage. They've argued that recent judicial decisions extending equal rights to gay and heterosexual couples actively undermine the sanctity of marriage as an institution, put at risk the stability of the wider society, and endanger the moral conduct of future generations of young Americans.[15] Many of them have now joined President Bush in demanding a constitutional amendment defining marriage as a union between a man and a woman.

The horrors of abortion and feminism

The other wedge issue on which many Christian conservatives have actively campaigned since the 1970s is that of abortion. Organizations speaking for the Christian Right are unambiguously "pro-life" and entirely opposed to the rights granted to pregnant women by *Roe v. Wade* (not for them, a woman's right to choose). They plant their flag firmly on the side of the embryo, insisting that life begins at conception and that abortion is literally murder. They vary in the degree to which they're prepared to take direct, even illegal, action to stop this murder. Fringe groups within their number are prepared to physically attack abortion clinics and the staff who work there. The majority of the organizations of the Christian Right, however, are not. Their focus is elsewhere—on the election of legislators willing to restrict or eliminate the right to abortions, and on the selection of judges prepared to give any pro-abortion legislation the narrowest of interpretations. This narrowness is vital, so Christian conservatives contend, because only unwarranted judicial activism since the 1970s has allowed the scale of abortions to grow to its present holocaust-like proportions—to such a scale, indeed, at 30–40 million aborted fetuses, as to make this *the* time for Christians "unashamedly [to take] up the cause of pre-born children in the name of Jesus Christ."[16]

The antiabortion campaign, so central to the contemporary politics of the Christian Right, then sits alongside other campaigns of a related kind. The Traditional Values Coalition, for example, has recently been busy opposing the "murder of the elderly through active euthanasia,"[17] and many socially conservative Christians have been equally active opponents of embryonic stem cell research, on the grounds that it too constitutes the slaughter of "innocent life at its earliest stages."[18] But, oddly, antipathy to murder does not always translate into opposition by organizations of the Christian Right to the taking of life by the state. On the contrary, The Traditional Values Coalition, for one, makes a specific exception to its general pro-life argument in the case of the death penalty. The Coalition supports the death penalty—indeed it strongly advocates it—on the grounds that the Bible is clear on the responsibility of government "to provide peace and security for its people," a responsibility the Coalition interprets as giving "the government the power to take the lives of those who murder others and to wage war against our enemies."[19]

What the pro-life position does often translate into is a generalized anti-feminism and a desire for the restoration of more traditional gender roles. James Dobson of Focus on the Family, for example, and Beverly LaHaye of Concerned Women for America have both long been strong advocates of the patriarchal family and the stay-at-home mom—consistently arguing that women have a divine obligation to submit themselves to their husband's authority and that whenever women leave the home for paid work, their children suffer. "Careerism may satisfy for a while," Janice Shaw Crouse has argued, but "nature will not forever be denied; women are beginning to see the costs of imbibing the unnatural cocktail of self-centeredness served up by radical feminism."[20] Pat Robertson, of the Christian Coalition, has been more explicit still. Strident antifeminism is God's Work, he has reportedly said, because "the feminist agenda is not about equal rights for women. It is about a socialist, antifamily political movement that encourages women to leave their husbands, kill their children, practice witchcraft, destroy capitalism and become lesbians."[21]

The need for a new crusade

The great claim of the Christian Right is that the United States needs to rediscover its traditional values and to live by them. To do that, so the argument runs, political loyalties must be determined by the positions that potential legislators take on social and moral issues rather than on economic and material ones. There's a culture war going on—"a battle over values, beliefs and the cultural basis of western civilization"[22]—one in which people must vote their conscience, not their pocketbook.

Domestically, that means supporting candidates who oppose gay marriage and a woman's right to choose. It also means supporting candidates who are economic conservatives. Leading figures on the Christian Right tend to interpret traditional American values as meaning low taxes and limited government rather than any modern version of the New Deal. God, apparently "never authorized government to tax in order to provide matters such as housing, food, child-care [and] health-care." He required governments, no less than individuals, to obey the eighth commandment—"thou shalt not steal"—and that holy injunction stretches out to taxes. Domestically, the key requirement therefore is for America to "return to its moorings, once again embracing the biblical concept of limited government,"[23] which is presumably why, in 2004, "the Christian Coalition of America listed making the Bush tax cuts for the rich permanent its number one legislative priority."[24]

In foreign policy, taking the proper side in the global culture war means supporting Israel and the invasion of Iraq. The obligation on the Christian

Right to support the state of Israel and its current hard-line stance against the Palestinians is rooted in the force of Old Testament arguments about Jewish rights in the Holy Land. "I have many Palestinian friends," the Reverend Franklin Graham has said, "and my heart breaks for them. ... But I have to look at the Scriptures. Whose land is it? God created this earth." Palestine "was God's and He gave it to the Jews."[25] Likewise the vast majority of the Christian Right are committed supporters of the war in Iraq, because—to varying degrees—they see the United States as engaged in some kind of Holy War. Moderate elements within the Christian Coalition do recognize the right of Muslims to worship as they choose, but even moderates believe in the superiority of Christian teaching to that of Islam, and they see the only route to salvation as that through Jesus Christ. More radical evangelical Christians go the extra inch—and condemn Islam as not only misguided but as evil.[26] And if it's evil, it has to be fought.

A LIBERAL RESPONSE

So what should a liberal answer be to arguments of that kind? Maybe something like this.

The hijacking of evangelical Protestantism

The Christian Right likes to present itself as the voice of an older, safer, more traditional America, and it uses a literal reading of the Bible to sustain its positions. The impression given is of continuity and conservatism that stretches back through time—certainly down the decades and even the millennia. But the impression is a false one, and the reading of the Bible made to support it is highly selective. The conservative politicization of contemporary evangelical Christianity is actually modern, dating back only to the 1970s. And in spite of how conservative evangelicals now choose to understand their own history, the issue that initially galvanized the modern Christian Right was actually not abortion, or even homosexuality. *Roe v. Wade* was initially welcomed by some leading evangelical ministers, and met with silence by most.[27] The fight back on this issue came initially from Catholics, not evangelicals. It was the 1975 decision of the Internal Revenue Service (IRS) to take away tax exemption from the Bob Jones University that apparently spurred the Christian Right into life,[28] and certainly there was as much racism and anticommunism as homophobia in the early politics of the modern movement.[29] If Randall Balmer is right, the stand against abortion was something added in the early 1980s, and added consciously, to reinforce a segregationist message, and it was initially added almost as an afterthought.[30] So there's no tradition here. What's now presented as the necessarily conservative politics of evangelicalism is a modern and recent construct, and we should say so.

We should say, too, as so many liberal evangelicals now do, that what was constructed in the 1970s and 1980s by the leaders of the Christian Right constituted a sharp break from the main lines of social teaching normally associated with evangelical Protestantism. It is worth remembering that "the last two Democratic liberals to be presidents of the United States were Southern Baptists—and by their lights devout ones!"[31] It is also worth remembering that early generations of evangelicals were as likely to campaign for progressive causes as for conservative ones. Many evangelical Protestants opposed slavery. They fought for civil rights. They wanted better labor conditions, even votes for women. They certainly wanted a strong wall between church and state, the very wall that modern conservative evangelicals are so keen to take down. And they were generally ecumenical in their attitude to other Christian nominations and to people of other faiths. The extreme wing of the contemporary conservative evangelical movement can say, along with Randall Terry, that "we are called on by God to conquer this country. We don't want equal time. We don't want pluralism."[32] That intolerance, however, is not what evangelical Protestants traditionally preached. For them, the church was like a bird. It had a left wing and a right wing, and it flew best when combining the strength of both.[33] So before we deal in detail with the politics of the Christian Right, it is worth saying to its modern rank and file that the general right-wing stance of the contemporary evangelical movement is an *add-on*. So add it on if you want to, but don't for a minute imagine that right-wing politics has always gone hand in hand with the religious beliefs you hold so dear. It hasn't, and it needn't again.

The dangers of religious fundamentalism

With President Carter, it's also worth pointing out that religious fundamentalism always sits uneasily with the civil liberties of a democratic system, even if that fundamentalism is Christian.[34] The Religious Right has no difficulty spotting the authoritarianism of Islamic fundamentalism. It does it all the time. But many conservative Christians appear to be less sensitive to the authoritarianism implicit in their own certainty of faith. At the very least, being convinced that you alone have a direct line to God means that you must see the religious beliefs of others as in some way inferior to your own. At the worst, being convinced of the certainty of your religious position must predispose you to treat people of other religious faiths as essentially wrong—certainly misguided and possibly evil.[35] Either way, a commitment to religious certainty sits ill with the central democratic value of freedom of conscience. It puts an inescapable tension into the politics of the Religious Right. They want both to be free to worship as they wish *and* simultaneously to have their religious icons placed at the center of the public school and court systems. But where's the freedom in that, for those of other faiths or of no faith at all? There is none. There's only what President whether Jim Crow worked for them. No, of course it didn't, and it won't for the gay community either. If people are genuinely equal, then they're equally entitled to marry. And if the entitlement is equal, why then do we need another word?[42] We don't.

Respecting a woman's right to choose

When the Religious Right turns its fire onto the issue of abortion, it moves onto firmer ground. Abortion is not an easy issue for any of us, liberal or conservative, and the United States is not alone among modern industrial democracies in struggling with the moral agendas involved. Catholic democracies in particular—France, Ireland, and Spain—have legal codes that are more restrictive of abortion than those created by *Roe v. Wade*. Even industrial democracies whose legal codes set the limits wider than we do, nonetheless do set limits. "So forget the fiery rhetoric of the far Right. Nobody is pro-abortion."[43] Few of us can be comfortable with time limits that allow abortion after the fetus is viable. Few of us can be comfortable with barriers that give women rights in one state but not in another. But nor should we be supportive of a total ban on abortions under all circumstances, because that entirely takes away a woman's right to choose. It would deny women the right to abort in the wake of rape and incest, and it would simply drive the practice back underground—where it would endanger the lives and health of the women involved, with all the inconsistencies associated with income and racial inequalities among the women themselves. Working-class women, women of color, and girls of a particularly young age would all suffer disproportionate amounts of personal danger if abortions were banned entirely. We should say that. We should cite the many religious organizations that support abortion and planned parenthood.[44] We should point out that the number of abortions fell throughout the 1990s, even with a Democrat in the White House.[45] We should say that the U.S. legal code has now narrowed the right to abortion to an already dangerous level, and we should fight for a woman's right to choose, within the limits of the law. And, overwhelmingly, we should put the weight of our case on the prevention of conception, as part of a pro-choice position that wants abortion to be "safe, rare and legal."[46]

But we should do more as well. We should fight as inconsistent and self-defeating, the objections of the Christian Right to the dissemination among the young of information about birth control and access to effective contraception. Providing easy access to contraception increases individual rights. No embryos are desecrated because none are created. No rights are infringed, because contraception is merely offered, not imposed. It's the denial of that access that erodes freedom and needs to be resisted. In any event, to advocate abstinence rather than contraception is not a solution. Campaigning for sexual abstinence before marriage didn't prevent teenage pregnancies in the past and, in the sexually soaked culture of the modern

Carter saw in the new breed of fundamentalism within the church to which he remains so dedicated: "rigidity, domination and exclusion."[36]

Fundamentalists of all religious stripes seem reluctant to concede the necessarily conditional nature of true faith. We need to remind them that had they been born in a different time and place their religion would doubtless have been quite different, but no less true to them for that difference. We need to argue that the ultimate questions of the human condition cannot be "known" in any literal sense, and they certainly cannot be deduced from the textual evidence of a bible whose construction was a highly politicized process spread over a number of centuries. We need to insist that the quality of a religious faith is to be judged by the seriousness with which it's pursued, not by the dogmatism with which it's asserted. And we need to say that it's perfectly possible to lead a fully moral life without anchoring that moral code in any religious philosophy, and that many of us do just that. The humanistic values that shape civilized social practice in modern democracies are no monopoly of any particular church or of people of faith taken together. Those values have come down to us from the Enlightenment and are the common property of all democratic people, religious or otherwise, and they need to be understood and defended as such.

The limits of religious reductionism

There is something particularly frustrating in the propensity of the Religious Right to present themselves as a persecuted and ignored minority in a society that is overwhelmingly Christian and to have them explain the persistence of social ills as the product of that minority status. It's just so easy to look at the crime figures, the number of teenage pregnancies, and the spread of HIV/AIDS and the like, and to see them all as the inevitable consequence of a generalized retreat from religion in this country. Oh, if that were so. The solution would then be so easy. All we would have to do would be to go back to church. But church-going in the United States is already at a remarkably high level when set against the religiosity of other industrial democracies. Yet the United States remains much more prone than these other nations are to the set of social ills that so distress conservatives. The United States is a very religious society. It's also very crime ridden. By treating crime as the direct and unmediated consequence of dwindling religious values, the Christian Right blocks off the systematic analysis of any potential causes that are of a secular nature.

It's all very well for the Gary Bauers of this world to go into simple denial, insisting that "the horrifying violence in American life has little to do with the availability of guns and everything to do with our growing virtue deficit." They, too, are certainly at liberty to reduce everything back to abortion if they want to, as Bauer does.[37] But what the Christian Right is not at liberty to do is then to deny the legitimacy of other people ("liberals," no doubt) questioning and empirically testing the adequacy of so direct and unmediated a link between values and social behavior. After all, that link is not just a matter of assertion—of some blind statement of faith. There's real data out there that we need to look at and real questions that we need to ask. Might it be, for example, that gun crime in the United States is more common than elsewhere in the advanced industrial world because all Americans claim the right to bear arms and that we have more gun crime here because we have more guns? Might it be that criminality has increased since the 1960s because so too has income inequality in a society preoccupied with material wealth? And might the excessive sexuality of contemporary culture be a product, not of the perennial endeavors of Satan and the forces of darkness, but of the deregulation of the media industry in the wake of the Reaganite revolution? Those are certainly questions worth asking. But it's not possible to explore them in any systematic and open-ended way if, from the pulpit, each one of these assertions is immediately and entirely explained—Sunday after Sunday—by reference to the actions of a slothful congregation and a wrathful God.

"Forsaking all others for as long as you both shall live"

The Christian Right would have us believe that gay marriage threatens straight marriage and that homosexuality itself is proscribed by Scripture. Yet what is actually prescribed by Scripture, and what really threatens marriage in its traditional sense, is marital infidelity and divorce. The Bible is quite clear on that point, and many of us are guilty of that sin, including a significant number of leading figures in the Christian Right itself. By contrast, the New Testament is almost entirely silent on the issue of homosexuality—the Gospels entirely so, the Epistles only briefly—and although silence does not imply approval, it also does not imply condemnation. So, if biblical fundamentalists were really as concerned as they claim to be about the future of marriage in the United States, and if the adverse impact on children of parental separation was genuinely their number one worry, then the weight of their campaigning would surely be directed against adultery and divorce, in the manner of the far more traditional Catholic Church. But it's not.

Sexual orientation may be genetically transmitted, or it may be learned behavior. There's scope for dispute on that issue. But what's not in dispute is that adultery and divorce cannot be explained away genetically. There's no divorce gene. Yet it's homosexuality, not infidelity, that's singled out by the Christian Right for particular attention, and it's the legal rights and social recognition of gay couples, not divorced ones, that stand condemned. But gay couples, no less than heterosexual ones, set a high value on fidelity and stability in relationships over time. Children flourish well in stable gay households, just as they do in stable heterosexual ones.[38] So if stable relationships between loving adults are what a solid social order requires, the recognition of the rights of gay couples should be a paramount goal of

conservatives everywhere, rather than their prime target. As the conservative thinker Jonathan Raunch has rightly argued, communities everywhere have long "believed that marriage is a powerful stabilizing force: that it disciplines and channels crazy-making love and troublemaking libido." This "belief is a deeply conservative one, based on the age-old wisdom that love and sex and marriage go together and are severed at society's peril." So the question, then, boils down to this. Why, if that is true, as it undoubtedly is, "should homosexuals be the one exception?"[39]

"For richer or poorer, in sickness and in health"

Think about it. How can a gay relationship of a couple living privately down the road from you—as you live privately in your heterosexual relationship, if that's what you do—undermine yours by its mere existence? It can't, and it doesn't. What actually undermines marriages these days—heterosexual or otherwise—aren't private things like that. They're all the public ones—"toxic forces," Myers and Scanzoni call them[40]—that breed instability and stress in so much of modern life. Divorce rates are actually higher in the Bible Belt than they are in New England. So, too, are teenage pregnancies. That not only puts to rest many of the claims made about the importance of religious faith to family stability, but also it directs our attention to what else is higher in the Bible Belt than in New England: poverty, low wages, long working hours, alcoholism, and a culture of male patriarchy and sexual violence. Try tackling those, and family stability will no doubt grow as a by-product. Happy and contented people leave each other far less often than do those strapped for money, prospects, and hope. Marriages hung together in the 1950s not because they were happier but because divorce was so difficult. It was less a golden age of happy families than an age in which the agonies of failed marriages had to be privately endured. We don't want to go back to that. We want to go on, and we won't do that by developing some "domino theory" about gay marriage—that it's the thin end of a wedge that will destroy marriage in general. A wedge can be used to prop open a door or to seal it shut. Which consequence it has depends on where the wedge is placed, not on the wedge itself. We need to place it on the open side, the one that welcomes stable marriages, straight or otherwise.

By hounding gay couples as they do, members of the Religious Right help to destabilize the very private relationships and civil liberties that they claim to value most. You can't bash gays and protect civil liberties at one and the same time. It just isn't possible. You can't restrict marriage simply to heterosexual couples and still say that in this society "all men are created equal and are endowed by their Creator with certain unalienable rights, and th among these are life, liberty and the pursuit of happiness." How can " [wo]men" only mean "heterosexual [wo]men." It can't.[41] It can't, not eve you advocate different terminology: "marriage" for straights and "c unions" for gays. Separate but equal is not equal. Ask African Ameri

age, it won't do so again. Sexual activity rates among the American young are no higher than those among their Canadian and Western European equivalents. But the rate of teenage pregnancy is. The rate of teenage abortion is. The rate of sexually transmitted disease is. And it is because access by the young to contraception is significantly lower here. Leading figures on the Christian Right actually intensify the problem they respond to, by blocking secular solutions that offend their morality, and they need to stop. We have to equip the young to manage their own sexual practices in ways that prevent unwanted pregnancies and the transmission of sexual disease, rather than lecture them on the wickedness of premarital sexual activity. Management rather than repression, and condoms rather than sermons, should be the order of the day.

Suffer the little children to flourish, and their mothers, too

There are so many double standards at play in the arguments of the Christian Right that it's hard to know where best to begin. They're ferocious in their defense of the rights of unborn children, but of late they've been equally quick to condemn postpartum health care for the women who carry them.[47] They don't even show the same level of campaigning intensity for the children themselves, once born. We're still waiting for a right-wing Christian-inspired campaign against child poverty—although poverty is the main factor triggering abortions in the contemporary United States—or against the inadequacies of a health care system that leaves so many poor people (young and old) without adequate and equal coverage. True, the Christian Right has its own education agenda, but it's one about access to prayer and biblical studies, not about general standards or equality of access. Indeed, the social conservatism of the Christian Right invariably goes hand in hand with an economic equivalent that leaves the distribution of income to market forces and gaps in welfare provision to voluntary charity. The result is that, generation on generation, vast numbers of American children are born into social deprivation from which escape is progressively more difficult, but such social deprivation apparently does not offend the leading organizations of the Christian Right with anything like the intensity that abortion does. The poor are always with us, we're told. Like the weather, they're an inescapable fact of life. Why a God that loves us all should then leave some of us poor and others rich is not something that the Christian Right seem keen to discuss.[48] Unless they believe that income is an index of virtue—and that the poor deserve their poverty—then at the very least they ought to balance their defense of the interests of the unborn child with a parallel defense of the interests of the child once born. But they don't.

We should resist, too, the antifeminism that so often accompanies the attack on abortion and gay rights, and the reactionary nature of so much of the Christian Right's response to the possibilities opened up by contemporary medical research. Modern science has given women the capacity to

control their own fertility just as it has given men (and women) the ability
to avoid tuberculosis, polio, and a hundred other once-deadly diseases. The
human condition has been qualitatively improved by that science, and it will
be so again if research on embryos is allowed to continue. Leading figures
on the Christian Right are way too prone to fantasize about a golden age of
traditional family roles—before the "evil liberalism" of the 1960s—but that
golden age is a myth. Women have been liberated from much of the
misogyny and hidden domestic violence of the pre-pill period, and that set
of social freedoms must not be surrendered on the antiabortion altar. James
Dobson may want a world in which women obey their men—but we
shouldn't. Better he (and we) learn to live in equal partnership with those
we love. Adequate methods of birth control are an essential prerequisite of
that equal partnership, and we should say so.

Reframing the moral agenda

We need to challenge the *narrowness* of the moral agenda that the Christian Right pursues and to question the *adequacy* of the political party they've
anointed to deliver it.

We have to say to the Christian Right that homosexuality and abortion
do not exhaust the moral agenda of the modern world. Far from it. The
issues of life and death caught up in the abortion issue do demand moral
reflection—no sane person would deny that—but the private sexual practices of consenting adults most definitely do not. If those who want political
debate to be dominated by moral issues insist on restricting that debate to
questions of sexuality and sexual practice, then homosexuality is surely less
pressing a moral issue than say child pornography, or the sexual harassment
of minors, or domestic violence. And that agenda in its turn, unpleasant as
it is, has no claim to precedence over a whole range of other moral outrages
that also demand our response: genocide in Africa, slavery on a global scale,
massive poverty internationally and at home, environmental degradation,
and inadequate health care—the list is endless. So we must say to the Christian Right, if morality is your benchmark, come and join us in fighting all of
these moral issues. Indeed, sections of the Christian Right are now beginning to become so engaged. Even the new leadership of the Christian Coalition of America is attempting such a widening of its campaigning focus. But,
as it does so, it is noticeable that the more conservative elements within the
coalition are breaking away. Which raises the bigger question: Do the majority of Christian conservatives oppose homosexuality on moral grounds or
because they are acutely homophobic? If it's the latter, they should say so,
and drop the moralizing. We have to lift the moral debate up and away from
this prurient preoccupation with other people's crotches.

We also need to challenge the view that the only political party interested
in moral issues is the Republican one. Why not also others like the Democrats, whose record on "most of the great moral battles in our nation's

history—the fight for civil rights, a living wage, aid to the poor, disabled and homeless, health care, protection of the environment"[49]—is actually superior to its Republican alternative? "Am I the only person in America," Randall Balmer has written, "who finds it curious that," even with Republican control of the House from 1995, the presidency from 2001, and the Senate in 2003, "these conservatives have made no serious attempt to outlaw abortion, their stated goal?"[50] Could it be that they are playing politics with this question—using it as a wedge issue—keeping the prospect of reform alive (and therefore their base mobilized) by *not* outlawing it? It's surely significant in this regard that many liberal evangelicals are currently finding a home, not inside the Republican Party, but with the Democrats, and that a new generation of Democratic politicians is beginning to speak openly of its faith—Barack Obama for one—breaking with the party's older tradition of keeping politics and religion apart. A generation ago, it was enough for John Kennedy to say, "I do not speak for my church on public matters and the church does not speak for me." But, today, after two decades of activity by the Christian Right, that declaration is no longer enough. On its own, it only reinforces the conservative claim that Republicans alone are the party of God. So Democrats need to talk about the sources of their values and to make a virtue of those sources being, for many them, religious. The moral high ground in American politics is not automatically red. It can just as easily be blue, and we need to say so.[51]

Contrary to popular opinion, Jesus was probably not a Republican[52]

We would do well to remember that, for such a supposedly conservative man, Jesus Christ met an extremely unpleasant death at the hands of the Roman authorities. So perhaps Jesus wasn't a conservative after all. He certainly irritated the power structure of his day in ways in which Republicans in Washington haven't been doing lately. In fact, it's very hard to see the Republican and the conservative in the man who preached the Sermon on the Mount; just as it's also hard to see the logic of those with low incomes voting for a party that systematically denies them adequate welfare or a higher minimum wage. We need to say to poor, white evangelicals that they're being sold a bill of goods, fooled into voting for a party that won't help them, a party whose leaders apparently even privately roll their eyes at the excesses of the evangelical case.[53] Sunday after Sunday, evangelical congregations are being urged to attach more importance, when they vote, to social issues (of sexual orientation and abortion) that hardly touch their lives at all, instead of attaching that importance to economic issues (wages, health care costs, and pensions) that touch them directly. Where's the sense in that? Jesus taught that it was harder for a rich man to enter the Kingdom of God than it was for a camel to pass through the eye of a needle (Matthew 19:24) and that "if you want to be perfect, go, sell your possessions and give to the poor, and you will have treasure in heaven" (Matthew 19:21). So

whatever else He believed in, He visibly didn't believe in trickle-down economics. This man may have been many things, including the Son of God.
But an economic conservative? Never.

The Christian Right continually asserts that its social views encapsulate
the essence of a true Christian faith, as though it is not possible to be both a
proper Christian and a liberal. Yet, in reality, it is and always has been possible to combine a faith in Jesus Christ with a commitment to progressive
causes. There is a Christian Left as well as a Christian Right in contemporary
America, not to mention a very large—and politically very "soggy"—Christian
Center. According to the National Opinion Research Center, for example, "the
number of conservative Protestants who oppose abortion under all circumstances is a whopping 14 percent, less than the 22 percent who are consistently pro-choice." [54] The Christian community in the United States, like
the Christian community in the rest of the globe, is a *politically divided* one,
and from a democratic perspective, healthily so. And it is divided, as is secular America, by all the usual drivers of voting loyalty: race, class, education,
age, region, and gender. The typical (or perhaps more properly, stereotypi-
cal) white, southern, middle-class male evangelical Christian may be a rock-
solid Republican voter, but his black, northern, working-class female
equivalent most definitely is not;[55] even rock-solid support can and does
slip, as the Republican Party found to its cost in 2006.[56]

Even if you can somehow twist things about and interpret Jesus Christ's
instruction to "render unto Caesar the things that are Caesar's" as one of political quietude, there are clear inconsistencies in the wider message of the
Christian Right on which we need to dwell. With what sort of biblical
authority, for example, can the pro-life injunction to stop abortions not also
extend to the question of the death penalty? A consistent ethic of life would
say that if taking life is wrong, then surely it's always wrong. Cherry-picking
which lives can be taken, and which cannot, is just that. It's cherry-picking.
Selective literalism is still selective. At the very least, it requires an *active*
process of biblical interpretation. It's not that the Bible tells us so. It's that
leading figures on the Christian Right *choose* to give the Bible a conservative
spin—and if they can make that choice, then liberal Christians have exactly
the same right to interpret the Bible in the opposite direction. Too often the
leaders of the Christian Right hide behind their God. They put their words
into His mouth and then tell us that we must follow Him when they mean
that we must follow them. There's a profound dishonesty here. People have
the right to disagree on value issues and to engage in dialogue with each
other about those disagreements, but the leaders of the Christian Right
appear to want more than that. They want to stack the deck in their favor
by creating, not a level playing field between informed citizens, but a slip-
pery slope in which dissension is the work of the Devil. That shouldn't cut
any ice with any of us, whether or not we're religious. If the Christian Right
has a political case that stands up to examination in the normal way, then

let's hear it. Let them come down from the pulpit and move out onto the hustings. Let them keep God out of this. He's much too important to be used as anybody's cheerleader, no matter how good the intentions are of those who would use Him in that way—and we should say so.

Holy wars are always to be avoided—even ours!

The dangers of religious fundamentalism are real enough when all that's at stake are matters of public policy in the domestic arena: child care, health services, law and order, and the like. But they get really scary when fundamentalism and foreign policy interact, and they always have. Crusades, jihads, holy wars—think of how many people have been slaughtered in the name of one God or another. Religions become dangerous only when they become evil, and they become evil, following Charles Kimball's argument here, when they begin to talk the language of holy war.[57] Well, we're back into an era of holy wars, and this time not just with swords and scimitars. This time, the fundamentalists can—if they choose—fight each other with weapons of mass destruction. The fusion of fundamentalism and nuclear weapons is the new nightmare of the age.

This therefore is not the moment to fight fire with fire. Islamic fundamentalism poses new and genuine security issues for the United States—issues that we'll discuss in the next chapter. Those security threats are real. They're frightening, and they have to be addressed. But addressing them by matching them would be a disaster. A Christian jihad, even in response to an Islamic one—as canvassed by a number of U.S. military figures of an evangelical and fundamentalist predisposition—would still be a jihad. The world is currently so scarred by the legacy of previous religiously legitimated imperial projects that it hardly needs another. The Spanish, the British, even the Germans under Hitler—all of them rearranged other people's political furniture on behalf of a Christian God, and always at great cost to the people so rearranged. Regime change isn't a new element in the global political equation. It's what imperial powers do for a living—to others, of course, never tolerating it for themselves.

So now it's time to say: Enough. We don't need an American version of this old and worn-out tale. We have to insist repeatedly, to ourselves and to others, that this world will become safe again only when religious fundamentalism in all its forms—Islamic, Judaic, and Christian—begins to fade away. And not into an amorphous secularism, but into a genuine respect for the serious religious convictions of others: into what Charles Kimball has rightly called "a twofold mandate to love God and to love our neighbor."[58] He's always been puzzled and saddened, he tells us, "by people who make clear that they couldn't be very happy in heaven unless hell was full to overflowing with people who disagree with their particular theology,"[59] and so have I. We have a huge security interest, as well as a huge democratic one, in preaching the importance of tolerance, respect, and the pleasures of diversity. We can't preach that abroad if we don't practice it at home. Practicing and preaching go together, so let's all of us begin again to practice what we preach—freedom of conscience, freedom of speech, and freedom to disagree. Not fundamentalism with a capital *F*, but democracy with a lowercase *d*.

The Wisdom of the War in Iraq

Although more than five years have passed since the horrendous events of 9/11, Osama bin Laden remains alive and free and Saddam Hussein does not. We've yet to capture the man who orchestrated the attacks of that day, and we've yet to extricate our troops from a country whose government did not attack us, but which we overthrew anyway. It's one of the great paradoxes of the global order created in the wake of the attacks on the World Trade Center and the Pentagon—that the American and British military now find themselves so bogged down in post-Hussein Iraq that they lack the capacity to create for us a post–bin Laden al-Qaeda. It's a paradox of such importance that its politics quite rightly continue to divide us.

On the *lack* of a direct connection between Saddam Hussein and Osama bin Laden, the evidence is now unambiguously clear. Indeed that evidence was reconfirmed by the Senate Intelligence Committee as recently as September 2006, when they told us that "Saddam Hussein was distrustful of al-Qaeda and viewed Islamic extremists as a threat to his regime, refusing all requests from al-Qaeda to provide material or operational support."[1] And yet as late as March 2004, more than 50 percent of Americans polled continued to believe in the validity of the connection between the two, and in Saddam Hussein's involvement in the attacks of 9/11.[2] And they did so because—from leading figures within the administration and from their supporting cast of newspapers, radio programs, and blog sites—the impression was (and is) regularly given that Saddam Hussein and Osama bin Laden

were indeed comrades-in-arms and that, because they were, invading Iraq in
the pursuit of al-Qaeda made (and continues to make) perfect sense.

The conservative case in defense of the war in Iraq goes something like
this.

Iraq and terrorism

The invasion of Iraq was initially presented to the American people as an
essential step in the fight against al-Qaeda. The United States had been
attacked without warning or justification. The lives of innocent Americans had
been taken. A new kind of war had opened up between Islamic fundamentalists
and the United States: "not a voluntary war ... not an optional war ... a war
that was imposed upon us on 9/11," a war in which "we have to go wherever
we find a terrorist, wherever we think a threat exists."[3] Oceans no longer protect us, so we can't sit behind them, deciding whether or not to address threats
that are based far away. Now those threats come directly at us—they come invisible and unannounced—in a new kind of war in which preemptive military
action is vital to success. It's a war that leaves no room for neutrality, no space
to respect the territorial integrity of states sponsoring terrorism, and no place
for rogue states unwilling to abide by international law. Iraq under Saddam
Hussein was one such rogue state.

- It was a rogue state because of its own past practices and ambitions. Its
  regime was particularly vindictive toward its own people, particularly
  hostile to Israel, and particularly ambitious for regional power. The government of Saddam Hussein used chemical weapons against the Kurds. It
  had twice invaded its immediate neighbors without provocation. It had
  developed its own long-range missile capacity and associated weapons of
  mass destruction (WMD). It had systematically blocked UN inspection of
  its weapons programs, as mandated by the settlement ending the first
  Gulf War; and in 2002, it was refusing to allow full access to its facilities
  by the international inspectorate.
- The Iraq of Saddam Hussein was a rogue state because it had a record of
  direct senior-level contacts with known al-Qaeda militants. It was harbor-
  ing the worst of those militants—particularly Abu Musab al-Zarqawi. It
  allowed Islamic fundamentalists to undertake military training on its ter-
  ritory, and it welcomed and financed the killing of innocent Israeli citizens by Palestinian suicide bombers. Denials of such links, Colin Powell
  told the UN General Assembly in February 2003, were "simply not credible," such that the removal of Saddam Hussein from power would
  "remove an ally of al-Qaeda and cut off a source of terrorist funding."[4]
- These two features of its politics, taken together, then made Iraq a key
  member of a broader "axis of evil," a group of pariah states—Iran and
  North Korea as well as Iraq—that possessed stocks of lethal weapons in
  defiance of existing international agreements. Iraq was a particularly dangerous member of that axis because of its support of terrorists actively
  engaged in strikes against the United States, and because of the associated

likelihood that its WMD would fall into their hands. "Simply stated," the vice president told the Veterans of Foreign Wars in August 2002, "there is no doubt that Saddam Hussein now has weapons of mass destruction" and that "he is amassing them to use against our friends, against our allies, and against us."[5]

- The invasion of March 2003 was justified under the terms of international law and was made necessary by Saddam Hussein's refusal to comply with UN resolutions on the inspection of his weapon systems. In fact, military action against Islamic-inspired terrorism had been necessary since the first attack on the World Trade Center in 1993, and possibly even earlier than that. Had the Clinton administration been more decisive in 1998, bin Laden could have been taken out then, but that moment was lost through political weakness or worse.[6] George Bush, unlike Bill Clinton, did not waste the moment. He was a genuine war president who was prepared to act, and act decisively, *before* any further attack, firm in the knowledge that only through externally imposed regime change in Baghdad could the United States be made safe from further terrorist atrocities. Al-Qaeda had to be shown again, as it had already been shown in Afghanistan, that it had no place to hide.

Iraq and the fight for democratic freedoms

Those initial justifications have never been entirely abandoned, but they have been battered by subsequent events. When Iraq was invaded, no WMD were found, and when the archives were opened, it was the Iraqi regime's antipathy to al-Zarqawi and al-Qaeda that became clear, not its closeness to them. This new evidence has never gone unchallenged. There are still people out there arguing for WMD and the Iraqi link to 9/11. The original litany of justifications still pops up every now and then, and we still find administration figures conflating Iraq and bin Laden every time we reach September 11. But the way the Iraq War is now justified has definitely changed. Initially, the argument went *antiterrorism* first and freedom second. Now the order is normally reversed: *freedom* first, with antiterrorism as a fortunate by-product. When the president speaks about Iraq these days, in sharp contrast to the way he spoke about Iraq immediately before and after the invasion, the emphasis is less on the need to make us safe and more on the need to set the Iraqis free.

- So, for example, in London in November 2003, the president for the first time defended the Iraq War in the context of "three pillars of security" then said to be driving U.S. foreign policy. Pillar 1 and Pillar 2 required the international community to prevent the proliferation of WMD, if need be by the use of military force. They were entirely in tune with the original justifications for the invasion. But Pillar 3—the one on which he concentrated most when speaking in London—was not. Pillar 3 required a renewed commitment by the international community to the global expansion of democracy, starting with Iraq. "Our mission in Iraq is noble and it is necessary. Our coalition came to Iraq as liberators and we will depart as liberators," he told his London audience.[7] "Our aim is a

democratic peace,"[8] he said later, "a peace founded upon the dignity and
rights of every man and woman. . . . We have no desire to dominate, no
ambitions of empire." On the contrary, "this great Republic will lead the
cause of freedom."[9] The invasion of Iraq was now to be understood, that
is, less as an antidote to terrorism than as the trigger to a more general
democratization of the Middle East.

- The President's London audience was asked to understand that the
motives of the United States, in leading this great crusade for democracy,
were both altruistic and self-serving. Altruistic, because democracy
spreads freedom, but also self-serving, and legitimately so, because
democracy brings hope, justice, and progress to counterbalance the instability, hatred, and terror on which Islamic radicalism feeds. Soft power,
as well as hard power, was in play. "We cannot rely exclusively on military power to assure our long-term security,"[10] the president said in
2003. "Lasting peace is gained as justice and democracy advance." And
in the wake of 9/11, the stakes could not be higher. As the president put
it in London, "if the Middle East remains a place where freedom does
not flourish, it will remain a place of stagnation and anger and violence
for export. . . . No distance on the map will [then] protect our lives and
way of life." The spreading of democracy rather than the suppression of
rogue states—the "opposing of tyranny wherever it is found"—had
become America's best hope for its own national security; and it had
become that, according to the president, because the failure of democracy in Iraq would not only "throw its people back into misery," it would
also "turn that country over to terrorists who wish to destroy us."[11]

Iraq as the new battleground in the fight between democracy and fanaticism

Immediately after 9/11, the Bush administration made the critical decision
to frame the tragic events of that day in a broad way—not simply as the work
of a few misguided fanatics, but as a defining moment in a wider war on terrorism. The target thereafter was set both narrow and wide. It was set narrow:
either simply al-Qaeda or something slightly bigger, *Islamofascism*. It was also
set wider. It was set against *terrorism in general*—against any antistate group
willing to use unannounced violence in the pursuit of its political ends, including Hamas and Hezbollah, groups engaged in armed struggle against Israel. By
2004, the great claim for the war in Iraq was that that country was now the
central front in both this narrow and this wider conflict.

- It was the central front in the narrow conflict, in that the administration
was convinced that the continuing insurgency in Iraq drew its strength
from the arrival there of foreign fighters, keen to engage in jihad. "They
attacked us not for what we've done wrong, but for what we do right"
became the standard conservative explanation of the events of 9/11.[12]
"Better we fight terrorists far from home, so that we don't have to face
them on our own streets" became the administration's response to those
who accused them of creating the insurgency by invading a country
unconnected to the events of 9/11. And "better we win than lose,

regardless of why we went in" became the standard argument against those who persisted in questioning the wisdom of the original invasion. In London in 2003, the president was gracious enough to admit that there could be "good-faith disagreements . . . over the course and timing of military action." But whatever had "come before," he said, "we now have only two options: to keep our word or to break our word." It was his intention to keep his: "to meet our responsibilities in Afghanistan and in Iraq by finishing the work of democracy we have begun,"[13] starving the fundamentalists of the social and economic fuel they needed to recruit and prosper.

- Iraq is also the central front in a wider battle between tyranny and freedom, a genuine clash of cultures with the defense of Israel as a key additional element. It is not a clash of entire religious cultures. Only extreme elements on the Christian Right label the entire Muslim world, or Islam as a religion, as inherently anti-Semitic and hostile to freedom. The Bush administration does not. It defines the problem not as one of an entire religion, but as "the perversion by the few of a noble faith into an ideology of terror and death."[14] The president presents the war in Iraq as a fight between civilized and uncivilized people and as a fight between democrats and fanatics. He regularly says that the terrorists are inspired by beliefs and goals that are clear and focused, evil but not insane. He also talks regularly of their genuine hatred for America and for freedom, a hatred that was not triggered by any specific act on our part or grievance on theirs—the ones they list he dismisses as simply excuses for the violence they're determined to inflict on us—and thus a hatred that cannot be appeased away by concessions or bribery. What's at stake in the ongoing battle to stabilize post-Hussein Iraq, so the argument goes, is not the presence or absence of American troops. What's at stake are modern values against premodern tyrannies: democracy against theocracy, the rights of women against the rulings of the Shari'a, and religious pluralism against Islamic orthodoxy.

- Al-Qaeda sees itself engaged in a holy war to sweep the entire Muslim world free of western institutions and practices; the Bush administration, in countering that, occasionally also talks the language of religion and war. The president even said on one occasion that God told him to invade Iraq.[15] But more normally, administration figures talk the language of universal values under threat. They tell us that we're engaged in "the decisive ideological struggle of the 21st century."[16] They present the fight in Iraq as one designed to strengthen moderate Arab forces in their struggle with fundamentalism. They characterize the insurgents as Islamic fascists, united by a desire to kill Jews and damage America[17]—as "thugs and gangsters who seek to intimidate through violence and through terror."[18] They present the enemy as one that views the whole world as its battlefield, one intent on winning regional power in the Middle East in order later to threaten and intimidate the entire non-Muslim world. Vice President Cheney calls it "their dark vision."[19] And so he and the president present the fight in Iraq not "as a clash of civilizations" but as "a struggle for civilization" itself: a fight "to maintain the way of life enjoyed by free nations," so that "good and decent people across the Middle East can raise up societies based on freedom and tolerance and personal dignity."[20]

Iraq as a success story, slowly unfolding

Until very recently at least, senior figures in the Bush administration also presented the fighting in Iraq as a slowly unfolding story of success.

Initially, the administration announced major combat operations successfully over in May 2003, when they still equated the defeat of Saddam Hussein's army in the field with success in the invasion itself. They expected—and told the American people to expect—that coalition troops would be "greeted as liberators," that the entire exercise would be a "cakewalk," and later (when it was not) that even so, "they're in the last throws, if you will, of the insurgency."[21] Senior administration figures even initially anticipated a smoother ride, post-Hussein, than the UN peace-keeping mission had experienced in the Balkans. This anticipation came on the premise that, to quote Paul Wolfowitz a month before the invasion, "there's been none of the record in Iraq of ethnic militias fighting one another that produced so much bloodshed and permanent scars in Bosnia."[22]

- It didn't work out that way, of course, and leading members of the administration were soon obliged to alter their timescale and to moderate their claims. By June 2005, Donald Rumsfeld, was talking about an insurgency that could go on "five, six, eight, ten, twelve years."[23] But even then he was still insisting—as administration figures continued to do thereafter—that slowly the United States and its internal Iraqi allies were winning the war in Iraq. To say otherwise is "flat wrong," the secretary of defense told NBC. "We are not losing in Iraq."[24] On the contrary, in less than two-and-a-half years, as he earlier testified to the Senate and House Armed Forces Committees, the U.S. military had enjoyed unprecedented success in the war on terror. American arms had overthrown two terrorist regimes, liberated 50 million people, captured Saddam Hussein and the majority of his senior aides, hunted down thousands of terrorists, disrupted terrorist cells on most continents, prevented a number of terrorist attacks, and captured or killed close to two-thirds of all known senior al-Qaeda operatives.[25] As late as October 2006, the president was still insisting that "absolutely, we're winning."[26] It was only in December 2006 that he, and his new defense secretary, both publicly conceded for the first time that the war in Iraq was actually *not* being won. Even then, they made that admission of previous failure only to justify an increase in U.S. troop levels that would bring, they claimed, future success.
- We have been consistently told by senior figures in the Bush administration that things are also going well in the war against terror in the United States itself. The latest major example of this came in September 2006, when the president released an updated "National Strategy for Combating Terrorism," in which he and his team took stock of progress on

homeland security to date. Their conclusion—widely cited at the time—
was that America is safer now than it was in 2001, but that we're not yet
fully safe. We're safer because "we have made substantial progress in
degrading the al-Qaeda network, killing or capturing key lieutenants,
eliminating safe-havens, and disrupting existing lines of support."[27] But
we remain unsafe because, as the president said on an earlier occasion,
in a very real sense the war on terror can never fully be won.[28] Liberty
from terrorism, like liberty on so many other things, requires eternal vigilance. It is, however, we are regularly told, a vigilance made easier in
this case by much of the indirect fallout from the continuing demonstration of U.S. military determination in Iraq—not least, the coming to heel
of Libya and the isolation of Syria (two of the region's other rogue states),
the freezing of terrorist assets in bank accounts worldwide, and the widespread recognition in terrorist circles that, unlike in the 1990s, the
United States would this time stay the course and see the business done.

Iraq is a beacon of liberty from which we must not cut and run

The only way we can lose this thing, the Bush people insist, is by not staying the course. And the only thing that undermines our military stance in Iraq,
and hence our security at home, is criticism from political opponents in the
United States, criticism that carries with it the hidden message that we will
eventually "cut and run."

- To do so would be a disaster. It would embolden Islamic fundamentalism
  across the entire Muslim world, reinforcing their view of western weakness. It would undermine the staying power of secular and moderate
  Islamic forces in the Middle East. It would expose Israel to even higher
  levels of terrorist attack. It would shift power and influence within the
  region toward Iran. It would leave key oil fields under the control of fundamentalist regimes that are ideologically opposed to the United States,
  and it would provide Islamic terrorist groups with new havens of support
  and finance. Far from bringing U.S. troops home as a way of increasing
  domestic security, pulling them back from forward positions abroad
  would actually endanger that security in the middle and long term.
  We've seen appeasement before. We saw in the 1930s and the dreadful
  consequences that followed. Appeasing fascists only delays the moment
  of confrontation. It doesn't avoid it. It just makes it worse when it has to
  be faced, and it weakens those who have to face it. Terrorists kill, and
  they kill indiscriminately. They kill "because they're trying to shake our
  will."[29] They know what they're about, and we need to know it too.
  "They're trying to drive free nations out of parts of the world,"[30] and we
  mustn't let them. In fact, we have no choice: "the dream of some," as
  Condoleezza Rice put it, "that we could avoid this conflict, that we do
  not have to take sides in this battle in the Middle East, that dream was
  abolished on September the 11th."[31]
- Setting arbitrary dates for troop withdrawal is defeatist. It's also "dangerous, reckless, and shameless."[32] As Rush Limbaugh regularly reminds his

listeners, it just isn't possible to support the troops without also supporting the mission. To question the original reasons for the invasion of Iraq is to say, to those who've lost loved ones because of that invasion, that their family members died in vain. To talk of Iraq as another Vietnam, as so many critics of the war now do, is simply to give hope and succor to the insurgents. It tells them that, if they bomb and maim enough American soldiers, they'll get what they want—that is, a destroyed Iraq within which they can build a fundamentalist Islamic regime, and from which (down the line) they can launch attack after attack on a United States without backbone or character. The 2006 antiwar campaign of Ned Lamont in Connecticut, for example, sent exactly the wrong message from America to Iraq. It "encouraged al-Qaeda types,"[33] according to the vice president. Joe Lieberman's view was that it would "be seen as a tremendous victory by the same people who wanted to blow up ... planes."[34] It played politics at home while brave men and women died abroad. It put party before country and short-term advantage before principle. "For the sake of our security," the vice president has argued, "this nation must reject any strategy of resignation and defeatism in the face of determined enemies."[35] "We cannot fall prey to pessimism about how this will come out," Condoleezza Rice has said, "the really devastating problem for the world would be if America loses its will."[36]

A LIBERAL RESPONSE

So with troops in the field and emotions running high, how best to respond to all of that? This way, at least.

First, recognize that we have a genuine dilemma

The dilemma is this: It is difficult to support the troops without supporting the mission. Rush Limbaugh is quite right on that. It can be done, of course, and ultimately it has to be done. Ultimately, we have to insist that the best way to support the troops is actually to bring them home. We have to say that it wasn't liberal America that initially put them in harm's way, so it's no good on the part of the administration leaders to pretend that it's their critics who are now the greater threat to military lives. This was a hole dug for military families, and for the rest of us, by George W. Bush and his neocon advisers. American troops shouldn't be under attack in Iraq because they shouldn't be there. They shouldn't be killed or injured in a vain search for WMD or in some belated attempt to create western democratic institutions in a society riddled with ethnic and religious tensions. Those deaths and injuries aren't making us safer or lessening the recruitment pool for al-Qaeda. On the contrary, every day we stay in Iraq that pool is being reinforced by our presence there, and we need to say so.

But the question is how. How to be a responsible and legitimate opposition in the middle of a war, even if that war was one of choice rather than of necessity? That's not an easy question to answer, because it's true that by criticizing the mission, we're also saying to the families of the fallen that the lives of their loved ones have been given in vain, and that's not something that most of them want to hear. Cindy Sheehan is the exception among grieving military mothers, not the norm—a woman of remarkable sagacity, whose work we should and must support. But she, and we, are still vulnerable to two of the administration's most powerful counterarguments, and we're vulnerable to them because they contain a solid core of truth. Our critique of the war must to some degree embolden the insurgency. It must make the insurgents think that, with a different administration, troops will be withdrawn—so that it makes sense to intensify the fight against those troops now. And any rapid withdrawal must create a power vacuum into which Islamic fundamentalist forces will move, with all the possible Armageddon scenarios that the conservative blog sites regularly paint for us. So we can't just cut and run from this war, no matter how much we'd like to, and no matter how strongly we feel that the invasion of Iraq was a blunder of monumental proportions. George Bush has trapped all of us in a terrible quagmire, one in which—on his logic—"we must kill all the terrorists we are creating" and "American soldiers must keep dying because American solders have [already] died."[37] What we have to say, is not that we will cut and run, but that we must get away from that logic. We must say, first and foremost, that the war in Iraq has become a killing field out of which George Bush can't lead us, but out of which a more liberal administration must.

We need to recognize that opposition to the war crosses party lines

There is a conservative as well as a liberal critique of this war, and we need to say that. It simply isn't the case, as is so often implied by the manner in which antiwar protesters are described, that all patriotic Americans stand foursquare with the president on this. They don't. Indeed, by January 2007, very few of them did. By January 2007, only 26 percent of Americans polled approved of the president's handling of the war, and only 16 percent supported his "surge" in the number of U.S. troops deployed in Iraq. His poll numbers had been higher earlier in the war, but by 2007 majority support was definitely with those who wanted this war over and behind us.

Not that all that opposition is in total agreement. It isn't. A significant strand of conservative opposition objects to the administration's prosecution of the war because that prosecution is insufficiently tough and decisive for their tastes. The Michael Savages, Bill O'Reillys, and Rush Limbaughs of this world want even more aggressive policies to get the insurgents' attention: martial law for O'Reilly, "shock and awe" for Limbaugh, even a bit of carpet bombing in Savage's case.[38] More mainstream conservative voices—William Kristol at the *Weekly Standard* being among the more vocal—long wanted

Donald Rumsfeld's head on a plate because of his insistence on a lean and small military presence to win and subdue Iraq.[39] "Our core problem in Iraq," as they put it, remains his decision "to invade Iraq on the cheap."[40] Conservative critics, including a string of retired generals, then add to that critique a litany of disastrous postinvasion decisions (not least the disbanding of the Iraqi army). The Powell doctrine—of invading only with overwhelming force—is visibly alive and well in sections of the American Right. But so, too, is the argument from isolationists like Pat Buchanan, that staying out of foreign wars is by far the best defense of American national security, and the argument from the Libertarian Right, that being in Iraq is counterproductive to the fight against al-Qaeda.[41] It's not simply liberal voices who draw parallels between Iraq and Vietnam—Pat Buchanan's "Big Muddy"—or who decry American impotence in the face of intensified threats from North Korea, Iran, or even Hezbollah. Many Republicans do so, too, and over time the number and centrality of these Republican critics of the war has increased significantly.

Senators like Chuck Hagel and representatives like Christopher Shays of Connecticut are not alone in their recantation of earlier prowar positions and votes. Certain well-known and widely respected neoconservative intellectuals and journalists are also now among their number. Two in particular— Andrew Sullivan and Francis Fukuyama—have recently jumped ship in a thoughtful and very public way. Andrew Sullivan has written at length about "what I got wrong about the war," criticizing himself and his kind for overoptimism in relation to democratic change, for overgeneralizing lessons learned from the fall of Communism, and for deafness in the face of constructive criticism. Sullivan has admitted to a "real sense of shame and sorrow that so many have died because of errors made by their superiors and by writers like" himself.[42] Francis Fukuyama, once a signatory of the famous letter to President Clinton demanding regime change in Iraq, has now abandoned his support for defining features of the Bush doctrine developed after 9/11: particularly for "preemption, regime change, unilateralism and benevolent hegemony." He's even on record as rejecting "democracy and modernization in the Middle East" as "a solution to jihadist terrorism," putting his faith instead in the empowering of existing Muslim communities.[43] *Mea culpa* is definitely the fashion of the hour among many thinking conservatives these days, with the result that those of us in liberal circles, long unhappy with this war and unpersuaded from the outset by the arguments used to justify it, are no longer alone. On the contrary, we're now in very respectable company.

This was a war of choice—it was just a very bad choice

No matter how often major figures in the Bush administration say otherwise, the invasion of Iraq in 2003, *unlike* that of Afghanistan in 2001, was not a war of necessity. It was a war of choice. It was a war chosen by this administration and justified by a set of claims that no longer stand up to public scrutiny.

- We were told that invading Iraq (and at such speed)—remember the rush, going to war in March 2003 when the UN weapon inspectors were asking for a delay of only several months and the Iraqis were desperately seeking a last-minute deal—was vital because Iraq had WMD that it would either use or hand over to terrorists. Colin Powell put that argument to the General Assembly in February 2003, but he was wrong.[44] Iraq had no such weapons. No such handover ever occurred or had been contemplated.[45] North Korea did have such weapons, of course, and Iran was also said to be developing them; but, again, it was Iraq alone of the "axis of evil" states that was singled out for invasion.
- We were told that invading Iraq was essential because of links between Saddam Hussein's regime and leading members of al-Qaeda. But, in truth, no such links existed, direct or otherwise. On the contrary, the evidence quickly emerged that relationships between the prewar Iraqi government and Islamic fundamentalists were antagonistic and mutually suspicious. Evidence built up, too—even more shocking in its way—that U.S. security agencies were aware of those antagonisms and suspicions *before* the invasion, but they did not pass on that information. What was widely known at the time, however, and was definitely passed on, was the extent of Saudi funding of Islamic fundamentalism and of Pakistani support for the Taliban. Yet it was Iraq, not Saudi Arabia or Pakistan, that then received the full force of U.S. and U.K. military might.
- We were told that that invasion was justified under existing UN resolutions, because of Iraqi noncompliance with those resolutions, and therefore it was essential to the maintenance of the United Nations' credibility. Yet we set no such requirement on Israel as it regularly defied other UN resolutions. The United Nations itself felt that it was the invasion, not the Iraqis, that undermined its credibility—to the point, indeed, that by September 2004 the UN secretary-general was prepared to declare the U.S. and U.K. action illegal under international law.
- We were told that invading Iraq was vital to save Iraqi citizens from the wrath of a dictatorial regime and to spread democracy there. Yet clear evidence quickly emerged of a double standard in U.S. foreign policy on Arab democracy over time.[46] It was conveniently forgotten in Washington that Saddam Hussein had committed most of the atrocities used to justify the invasion when he was actually an ally of the United States against Islamic fundamentalism in Teheran. As a central architect of the war, Donald Rumsfeld had readily met with him as late as 1983, immediately after the Iraqi regime had used, and was known to have used, chemical weapons against the Iranians and the Kurds. The first Bush administration stood idly by as Saddam Hussein butchered Kurdish and Shia opposition to his rule in the wake of the first Gulf War, and the current administration remained fully in support of authoritarian regimes elsewhere in the region (from Saudi Arabia to Pakistan) even as it preached the cause of democracy for Iraq.

- Finally, we are regularly told that ultimate responsibility for the continued potency of Osama bin Laden lay at the feet of the Clinton administration—who had blown the opportunity to kill him in 1998. Yet evidence quickly emerged of similar Bush administration failings: a steady stream of warnings about an attack to come that failed to produce a response from the Bush people in the days and weeks before 9/11.[47] We were led to believe that the invasion of Iraq was triggered by those events. Yet we now know that there was no Iraqi involvement in either the planning or the execution of the attacks on the World Trade Center and the Pentagon that day. We also know that—in key sections of the administration—the desire to invade Iraq predated the attacks of 9/11.[48] Paul Wolfowitz, one of those enthusiasts, even conceded later that Iraq's WMD had been singled out for emphasis only because the administration judged it likely to be the best argument they could use to win popular support for an invasion to which they were committed, WMD or not.[49]

There can be no doubt that this was not a war of necessity. It was a war of choice, one designed to meet a goal—that is, regime change in Baghdad—long wanted by key figures within the administration.[50] Given 9/11, the United States had to go after the Taliban. It did not have to go after Saddam Hussein, and yet it did.

They know it, really—read the small print and find the admissions of error

When reflecting on the appropriateness of its invasion of Iraq, key figures in the Bush administration still glide over this gap between justification and reality whenever they can. The president was still indirectly linking 9/11 to Iraq in his memorial address some five years later. The vice president regularly lists legitimate responses to 9/11, and places the invasion of Iraq high on that list. When challenged, however, key spokespeople for the administration don't just glide in that fashion. They also do one or more of five other things. They assert the primacy of the "democratizing Iraq" objective, as though that had been the dominant driving motive from the outset. They place the blame for the lack of fit between claim and evidence squarely back on the shoulders of faulty intelligence, saying that everyone believed that intelligence at the time. They talk of a world made safer by Hussein's fortuitous removal from power and downplay the current relevance of any of the arguments originally used to justify his removal. They then ask us if we would be safer, or less safe, if a future Iraq was ruled by men intent on the destruction of the United States.[51] And, most terrifying of all, they try to move us on—shifting the focus of fear onto Syria and Iran—framing the next phase of their crazy neocon drive for U.S. military dominance in the Middle East by replaying their old arguments on a new enemy.[52]

To which our response needs to be twofold. The first response has to be *skepticism bordering on irritation*. After all, governing is all these people do for a living, and if they can't get vital information right before launching a major invasion, perhaps they ought to stand aside and let more competent people govern us instead. They certainly need to be reminded that extensive doubts existed well before the invasion regarding the validity of the intelligence used to justify the rush the war. Those doubts were both public and private. Public doubts came not least from the chief UN weapons inspector and from a range of major governments, including the Russian and the French. And private ones including those doubts widely disseminated inside the State Department, the Central Intelligence Agency (CIA), and other security agencies in both the United States and the United Kingdom. The United Kingdom's joint intelligence committee even warned Tony Blair in February 2003 that the threat posed by al-Qaeda "would be heightened by military action against Iraq."[53] It was a warning he chose to ignore. For what's clear now is that in the critical months leading up to the invasion, the hawks in the administration leaned on the security services—and leaned heavily—to give them the information they required. What's also clear is that those hawks gave disproportionate weight to information from émigré groups with their own political agendas, information that turned out to be particularly inaccurate. And not just hawks in the U.S. administration. The U.K. government, too, was accused of "sexing up" some of the data it published in the buildup to the invasion. Those data were then recycled in Washington to further justify the rush to war, as senior administration figures began to use tactics to discredit their critics that would later land some of them in court.[54] If those who governed us in both Washington and London in 2003 were misled by inadequate intelligence, as they now claim, then they were foolish to be so. If they distorted that information to cover up a decision already made, as they now deny, then they were treacherous. "Knaves or fools" appears to be the only choice here—and what an impoverished choice it is.

The other response has to be one of *disclosure*. For all the implied Iraq–9/11 linking they still make in their set speeches, many of the key players in this drama have quietly conceded, when pushed, that the original justifications that took them to war were false. Condoleezza Rice did it in 2006, admitting that Saddam Hussein, "as far as we know, did not order September 11, may not even have known of September 11."[55] Colin Powell did it, too, telling reporters in January 2004 that he had seen "no smoking gun, concrete evidence about the connection" of Iraq to al-Qaeda. He later called his February 2003 UN speech "a lasting blot on his record" and his neocon colleagues in the Bush cabinet "fucking crazies."[56] When Tim Russert asked the vice president in 2006 if "we have any evidence linking Saddam Hussein or Iraqis" to 9/11, he said simply, "no ... we've never been able to confirm any connection between Iraq and 9/11."[57] Both George Bush and Tony Blair eventually conceded that they'd been misinformed about Iraq's WMD.[58] President Bush even tried to make a joke of it in March 2005, lampooning himself, pretending to look under pieces of furniture in the Oval Office for

WMD,[59] and he had this remarkable exchange with a reporter as late as August 2006. When asked "what did Iraq have to do with the attack on the World Trade Center?" he immediately said, "nothing. . . . nobody has ever suggested that the attacks of September the 11th were ordered by Iraq."[60] Really? Nobody? Not even Donald Rumsfeld, who famously announced just 15 days after the attack that he had "bulletproof evidence of ties between Saddam and al-Qaeda."[61] Bulletproof evidence. 15 days. Really? No suggestion at all? No slam-dunk evidence at all? Amazing.

Wars like this are both self-fulfilling and self-defeating

Invading Iraq was a terrible mistake. It was a blunder of monumental proportions, and we need to say so. It wasn't just any old policy mistake. It was, and is, a catastrophe, under whose shadow we'll all have to operate for decades to come. The lives of our children will be threatened by this idiocy because its most likely outcome will be the emergence of exactly the world that it was designed to avoid. Policy failure doesn't get more total than that.

At the very least, invading Iraq dissipated the huge amount of global support and goodwill evident after 9/11. Conservatives like to remind us of Palestinians cheering in the street as the towers fell and of Saddam Hussein's official approval of the attack. But they were the exceptions, not the rule, in the immediate aftermath of the collapse of the Twin Towers. World anger at al-Qaeda was general in September 2001. Seventeen countries willingly sent troops to fight alongside the United States in Afghanistan, and 70 more sent logistical support. But not any more. Now world opinion has shifted massively against America. All that goodwill has been lost. All the fine words about reconstructing Afghanistan have been betrayed, as energies, focus, and resources have moved south to Baghdad. In Iraq, the U.S. military has actually done al-Qaeda's work for it: overthrowing a secular modernizer despised by Islamic fundamentalists and laying the ground for the emergence of a theocratic Iraq that al-Qaeda alone could never have delivered.

In Iraq, the presence of U.S. troops recruits support for terrorism faster than those troops can kill or capture the terrorists so recruited. Tragically, the invasion has created the very phenomenon that the Bush administration claimed was there before but that was not. Iraq *is* now is a terrorist haven. It wasn't before, but it is now. George Bush and Tony Blair made it so, by invading a country unconnected to 9/11, and by redirecting resources away from military action and social reconstruction in the one country— Afghanistan—that was. The invasion of Iraq in March 2003 put in place the very things to which it was supposed to be a response. It *created* the link between Saddam Hussein's supporters and Islamic jihadists that it was supposed to destroy,[62] and it *created* the danger against which the administration now warns us—that is, if we pull out, Iraq will fall into the hands of men bent on our destruction. As Al Gore put it, the president "planted the seeds of war" and is now "harvesting a whirlwind."[63]

So what is that harvest? For Iraq, sadly, it's likely to be a failed attempt at western democracy. No matter how many times President Bush tells us that democratic stability there will eventually prevail, the depth of the insurgency triggered by the invasion is—and will remain—a huge roadblock to that stability. The Bush administration talks endlessly these days of democratic progress in Iraq, but it lives in a self-delusionary bubble that it shares with less and less of the rest of us. Its key ally—Tony Blair—is now on record as admitting the invasion to have been "pretty much of a disaster."[64] Its own ambassador to Baghdad recently conceded that the invasion had "opened a Pandora's box of sectarian conflicts" that made "Taliban Afghanistan look like child's play."[65] Even its senior generals now admit to the proximity of civil war in Iraq, as the death toll among Iraqi civilians continues to soar.[66] Many thousands more are already dead there than died on 9/11 here, and there's no end in sight to the death and injury yet to be endured.[67] American soldiers die. Iraqi civilians die. And whole areas of supposedly "liberated" Iraq are now governed by, and subject to, the very Islamic fundamentalism that characterized Afghanistan under the Taliban, and which gave al-Qaeda succor.

Invading Iraq hasn't completed the job begun by invading Afghanistan. It's negated it, and we need to say so. American soldiers and Iraqi civilians are being slaughtered for no good purpose—in fact, for a bad one. They're dying to set the scene for the consolidation of a caliphate that stretches from Teheran to the borders of Israel itself. For what else is to be expected from an invasion begun with so much ignorance of the complexity of local conditions, and so little preinvasion planning on the problems of democratic nation-building? And what else is to be expected from a military presence, now largely restricted to huge base areas, that has surrendered real control of much of Iraq to insurgent forces? George Bush may see himself as political Islam's greatest opponent. The reality is that he's nothing of the kind. He's actually their star "recruiting sergeant."[68]

We can't become safer at home by growing terrorists abroad

In the process of digging the U.S. military deeper and deeper into an Iraqi hole, President Bush is also digging the mainland United States into a hole that is *less* safe rather than more. If you doubt that, try asking the British—after their 7/7, the London bombings on July 7, 2005—whether the presence of U.K. troops in Iraq has increased the safety of U.K. citizens on the street.[69] Or ask the commuters in Madrid a similar question. This war is costing precious U.S. lives. It's also costing precious U.S. dollars: lives and dollars that could be better spent on genuine and extensive security at home.[70] You don't put out a fire by pouring oil on it. You don't make yourself fireproof by shipping your best fire-fighters overseas. You don't protect yourself from a ring of potential enemies by picking off the weakest and allowing the others to flourish, and you don't strengthen your capacity for rapid response by bogging down the bulk of your military capacity in a quagmire of your own making. If Hurricane Katrina taught us anything about preparedness, it was that U.S. readiness to deal with a major disaster— natural or terrorist-made—is woefully underdeveloped. We need to argue, and argue strongly, that bringing the troops home is not only the best way to keep them safe, but also the best way to keep us safe. And it would do so by lowering the capacity of U.S. arms (by their very presence abroad) to stimulate the flow of young disaffected Arab men into the ranks of fundamentalist Islam and by increasing the presence of U.S. soldiers back here in the United States, who then would be able to defend in depth our borders, our air space, and our food supplies.

The evidence is now overwhelming that by invading Iraq the Bush administration increased the threat of terrorism and fueled Islamic radicalism worldwide. Their own intelligence agencies told them this as recently as September 2006.[71] So it's worth asking: Why does the president continue to leave the impression in the mind of the American public that Saddam Hussein's regime was in some manner linked to al-Qaeda and that its fall weakens the terrorist network? Is it because he can't admit that his policies have actually created the links that they were designed to destroy? Is it because he can't admit that his determination to overthrow Saddam Hussein predated 9/11? Or, is it because he can't admit what his intelligence agencies now privately tell him, namely, that the invasion of Iraq has actually strengthened the radical Islamic forces that it was designed to weaken? Whichever it is, it's surely time to argue that invading Iraq without UN approval was exactly the *wrong* response to the terrorist attacks launched on us in September 2001. It's time to recognize that, if winning the war on terrorism was the real goal of U.S. foreign policy in March 2003, invading Iraq in so unilateral a manner actually made winning that war harder. It's perhaps even time to see that, if reducing the threat posed by radical Islam to U.S. homeland security was the aim, no policy could have been invented that was less likely to succeed in the long term than that of using predominantly U.S. troops to depose an Arab dictator. By invading Iraq, the Bush administration made a monumental mistake, and we need to say so.

There's an element of "blowback" in play, whether or not we like it

Nothing justifies 9/11. Liberals were as outraged by the events of 9/11 as were conservatives, and the Right must not be allowed to monopolize the flag on this issue. The invasion of Afghanistan was entirely legitimate and necessary, and we need to keep saying so. We need to keep saying, too, that liberals are as determined as conservatives to see al-Qaeda finished, and that they as committed to homeland security and core American values as is the Bush administration. But although nothing justifies what happened on 9/11, certain things do help to explain the terrible events of that day. In that explanatory mix, there is unfortunately an important role for "blowback"—that is, for problems created for us today by foreign policy decisions made long ago. We need to understand that, so that we may better eradicate any features of our current policy and practices that could feed a similar blowback in the future.

Conservatives like to tell themselves, and us, that we were attacked on 9/11 not for what we've done wrong but what we've done right. Oh, that it was that simple. But it's not. We need to understand why Islamic fundamentalists hate us. We also need to understand how what we do now, unless we're very careful and principled in our foreign policy, can fuel that hatred. Islamic fundamentalists hate the United States because America is a presence in their region, one that sustains institutions and states to which they take principled objection. They object to the state of Israel and to its treatment of the Palestinians (and now of the Lebanese). They object to the religiously moderate and invariably *undemocratic* Islamic regimes that American money sustains, and they object to the presence of U.S. military personnel on Arab soil. The United States cannot and must not abandon Israel, but the slowness and character of Tel Aviv's response to genuine Palestinian grievances only feeds anti-American sentiment in the region, as well as anti-Semitism there. We have a powerful interest in resetting our relationship with Israel, to speed the creation of a viable Palestinian state, and we have a powerful interest in pursuing the democratization of Arab governments in Egypt and in Saudi Arabia. We cannot apply one rule to Israel and another to the rest. Nor can we have one political imperative for Iraq but another for coalition partners willing to fight the insurgency with us. When the United States explodes militarily outside its borders in search of terrorists, it gives the green light to Israel to do the same. When the Bush administration treats repressive regimes in the Islamic part of the former Soviet Union as allies, because of the military bases they provide, it sends out a signal that what really matters to Washington is regional control, not democratic development. None of those messages make us safer. They just grow support for al-Qaeda.

Which is why, at the very least, how we comport ourselves in the contemporary Middle East must not add to this existing stock of grievances. The shame of Abu Ghraib, the holding of enemy combatants at Guantánamo Bay, the rendition of terrorist suspects to secret CIA jails, the use and defense of questionable "interrogation techniques," the choice of allies who themselves regularly torture and murder their opponents—none of these help the American case. They simply attract criticism from nongovernmental organizations like Amnesty International and even the United Nations, and rightly so. "Water-boarding" is an unacceptable technique of interrogation, whether administered by the intelligence services of dictators or those of democracies, and we must say so. Colin Powell and John McCain were correct to insist in 2006 that the administration's willingness to bend the Geneva Conventions only puts the lives of U.S. military personnel further at risk, because it robs the United States in the Middle East of the moral high

ground that it needs to retain.[72] And by the same logic, the uncritical and
rapid dispensation of support for the Israeli invasion of South Lebanon was
equally destructive of the long-term security of U.S. personnel in the entire
Arab region. It was destructive because, as in Iraq, the excessive use of military force only fueled further fanaticism, and it was destructive because it
provided yet more ammunition to those who argue that U.S. policy in the
region operates on a blatant double standard—one that is generous to Israel
but not to its Arab neighbors.[73]

A progressive way forward

We need to remember that retreating from an impossible position takes
not cowardice but courage, and that repeating folly is idiocy, not state craft.
We need, as a matter of urgency, to reframe this debate from one of *win or
lose* in a war between good and evil—the Bush framing of our choices that is
now costing us so much—to one of *how best to contain the damage* done by
the Iraq war to the global struggle between moderates and fundamentalists
in the Islamic world. No matter how often the administration tells us otherwise, you don't defeat fanaticism by force of arms. You contain it by eternal
vigilance, and you stunt its growth by identifying and eradicating the conditions that recruit for it. Being simultaneously tough on terrorism and tough
on the causes of terrorism requires a sophistication of policy that appears to
be literally beyond this administration to comprehend, let alone deliver. It's
a sophistication that a more liberal administration must develop and deploy.

The way forward has to be twin-tracked: back to the war on terrorism
and out of Iraq.

- We do live in new times, and the Bush administration must not be the only
  voice saying so. For the first time, we do face groups of determined men and
  women, willing to sacrifice themselves in what they understand as a holy
  cause, willing to hit western targets (and especially American ones) without
  warning or mercy.[74] Dreadful weapons are available for them to use, weapons
  genuinely capable of mass destruction. We therefore have an overwhelming
  security interest in locating and disarming those people. We also have an overwhelming security interest in locating and containing the dissemination of
  those weapons. And, we have an overwhelming security interest in doing both
  those things with the full support and cooperation of others. Why in cooperation with others? Because local sources invariably have better knowledge of
  homegrown radicals than do external sources. Because international agencies
  are better at regulating WMD than are individual nation-states, however
  powerful. And because the greater legitimacy of multilateral action is bound to
  lessen the adverse fallout—in new radicals recruited—whenever a terrorist cell
  is located and captured. We clearly need a consistent, sustained, and broadly
  based "war" against any organization that is planning acts of violence directed
  at us, and at us alone. But what we don't need is a widely diffused and unilater-
  ally implemented "war" against any state or nonstate actor that we happen not

to like. Well-funded homeland security, plus action abroad focused on proven terrorists, and action implemented with broad international support—the Afghan model—is still the best way forward. Inadequately funded homeland security, unilateral overseas action against potential threats, and action implemented by ad hoc coalitions of the rough and the willing—the Iraq model—visibly is not.[75]

- Which is why we need to begin a phased withdrawal of U.S. and U.K. troops from Iraq. As John Murtha rightly said, "we cannot win this militarily . . . our military has done everything that has been asked of them. It is time to bring them home."[76] We already have more than enough evidence that "the militarization of this struggle largely benefits the radical Islamic movements"[77] that it's designed to quell—to the point indeed that, if "staying the course until the time is right or completing the mission means creating a multi-party, multi-faith liberal democracy in Iraq," then we might be talking about a course so long as to be "a quandary not just for us but for our grandchildren."[78] After all, it didn't take U.S. arms this long to defeat Hitler, so something is clearly going wrong. We have to get out—not to cut and run, but certainly to internationalize and pull back. We have to set dates for withdrawal. We have to redeploy troops back into Afghanistan. We have to pull the United Nations and all the regional powers, especially Islamic ones, into a negotiated settlement of the Iraqi insurgency, and we have to redirect the bulk of our diplomatic energies to a rapid and full settlement of the dispute between Israel and Palestine that so fuels contemporary Arab anti-Americanism. We need to stand shoulder to shoulder with those who argue that we can support the state of Israel without supporting its occupation of the West Bank.[79] We need to stand alongside those who say that with more U.S. and Israeli flexibility, the major problems of the region can be solved diplomatically rather than by force of arms, and we need to stand foursquare with those who argue that the route to peace in the Middle East lies through a focus on the achievement there of global development goals rather than U.S. (or even Israeli) military ones.[80]

The president likes to talk about his three-pronged strategy for victory in Iraq: establishing democracy, rebuilding the economy, and training Iraqi security forces. But, currently none of those things is going very well. The writ of the democratically elected government doesn't stretch out much beyond the Green Zone. The economy remains paralyzed by sectarian violence, and the training of reliable Iraqi troops in still painfully slow. We should therefore counter with a three-pronged strategy of our own. A political settlement must be negotiated through a Dayton-style conference of internal players and regional powers. Economic reconstruction must be internationalized under the auspices of the United Nations, and the training of an adequate security force should be handed over to a multinational peace-keeping presence in which the soldiers of major Islamic nations play a significant role. The United States and the United Kingdom claimed to be acting as the agent of the United Nations as they invaded. That claim was specious then, but needs to be made real now. After all, the United Nations has been exploring its own internal reform and the development of a new mandate: the "responsibility to protect." Now would be a good time to test that mandate in practice.

The best defense against another 9/11 is not Michael Savage's carpet bombing of insurgents. And it's not President Bush's more humane cycling and recycling of U.S. troops in and out of Iraq. The best defense against another 9/11 is the creation of strong international institutions and a prosperous Middle East in which Israelis and Palestinians have settled their differences—one, moreover, in which the United States is neither so visible nor so unilateral a player. Getting there won't be easy—and, in the meantime, we will need eternal vigilance at home and progressively strengthened institutions and laws abroad. But getting there is possible. It's just not possible the military way. The road to safety at home lies through justice and cooperation beyond our borders. So it's justice that we need, not war—soft power, not hard. We need *homeland security plus global justice*, starting with an internationally negotiated settlement in the Middle East. There's a defense policy that's genuinely worth fighting for—fighting for at the ballot box, that is, and fighting for right now.

_____ **10** _____

Is Prosperity Safest in Republican Hands?

I n the thick of the electoral campaigning in the run-up to the midterm elections in 2006, President Bush's standard stump speech had two recurrent themes. One of these themes was a defense of his Iraq policy, with an associated claim that a Democratic Congress would reverse course, weakening America's security as it did so. We've just discussed the issues raised by that claim. But there was another theme—that a tax-and-spend Democratic Congress would imperil America's economic strength, not just its military one. The claim was that the economy was safest in Republican hands. It's a claim that's often made and generally goes something like this.

The U.S. economy is robust under Republican leadership

There are signs of economic strength everywhere, evidence of the superiority of Republican stewardship. In October 2006, Treasury Secretary Paulson pointed to a series of economic indicators that made him "feel good about the economy." Economic growth was running at an annual rate of more than 3 percent. There had been 38 straight months of job growth, with 470,000 new jobs created in the previous three months alone. Unemployment, at 4.4 percent, was still going down, and tax revenues were still going up, as output and spending increased. The productivity of U.S. labor was rising steadily, at an annual rate of more than 3 percent since 2000. Real after-tax income for the average American was up 9.8 percent since the Republicans recaptured the

White House. The budget deficit, though large, was at last beginning to fall. Even gas prices spent most of 2006 on their way down. "The U.S. economy is strong and getting stronger," under Republican leadership, Paulson's Treasury announced immediately before the 2006 midterm elections. "Since the President signed the Jobs and Growth Act in 2003," the banner headline on its press release read, "the U.S. economy has made a remarkable recovery."[1]

The standard claim made repeatedly by members of the Bush administration is that everything is now going well and that the basic economy is strong. President Bush regularly explains his optimism for the future in this fashion. "We're an innovative society," he's said, "and there are a lot of really capable, smart people continuing to make sure we remain innovative ... on the leading edge of change."[2] The government's doing its part too: lowering its discretionary spending, simplifying the tax code, terminating low-priority and low-performing government programs, and seeking a line-item veto to better eradicate waste in public spending. "The American economy remains the envy of the world," the president told his radio audience in July 2006. And no wonder: "18 straight quarters of growth," tax cuts that "have left nearly $1.1 trillion in the hands of American small business owners, workers and families," 6.6 million new jobs created since 2003, and the real prospect that the rising tax revenues produced by economic expansion will enable the administration to hit its goal of halving the federal deficit by 2008, a full year ahead of schedule.[3]

The economy's strong because it's free of government regulation and taxation

Why are things going so well? When Henry Paulson's predecessor as Treasury Secretary John Snow was asked that question in November 2005, he tied it to Republican policies on markets and taxation. "We have adopted," he told his radio audience, "on a scale beyond that of any other country, a reliance on market forces." "Markets work. We let markets work. The market is a marvelous mechanism for high gross domestic product (GDP) growth, high job creation and high wages." Which is why the president is so keen to "put in place a low tax-rate environment," he said, it's only that kind of environment that "encourages capital investment and job creation ... by giving incentives ... to people to invest, and to establish new businesses and to take risks."[4] His boss agreed. "I'm optimistic," the president later told reporters, "that we have good policy in place that will encourage the entrepreneurial spirit. And I firmly believe, so long as this is an entrepreneurial-oriented country, America will remain the economic leader we want it to be."[5] "Cutting your taxes worked."[6]

Both the treasury secretary and the president were speaking directly out of the basic Republican handbook. Economies flourish, according to that canon, only when the players inside them are left free to pursue their own ambitions and goals. Everyone knows that governments govern best by governing least. The trick is to take as little as possible out of private hands and private pockets, rewarding enterprise and effort, energy and skill. The Republican tax cuts of President Bush's first term, we're regularly told, did exactly that, triggering spectacular economic expansion. Those tax cuts are scheduled to run out in 2010, so the best guarantee of continued prosperity is to make them permanent. The other best guarantee is to leave economic activity as free as possible—to cut back on regulations and red tape—to "trust the people to make the decisions on how to save, to spend, or invest," as the president is prone to put it.[7] The Republicans are doing that. The Democrats would not. That's why Republican leadership of the economy is vital to its continued success.

The economy will grow stronger still as those freedoms are extended globally

The key front for political leadership in economic matters is not at home. It's overseas. The key job is to open more and more markets to U.S. goods by chipping away at protectionist barriers, by insisting on the proper valuation of foreign currencies, and by negotiating wider and wider free trade areas. Previous Democratic administrations have been far too prone to subject the U.S. economy to onerous international obligations—particularly environmental ones. But not this administration. It has refused to buy into the Kyoto Protocol. It's defended American commercial interests inside the World Trade Organization (WTO). It's working with foreign governments—particularly the Chinese— to prevent the systematic undervaluing of their currencies, and it's negotiated wider free trade areas both in Central America (through the Central American Free Trade Agreement, CAFTA) and the Middle East (principally with Jordan). That's 124 million new consumers for American goods. It's all part of the administration's determination to open increasing numbers of global markets to American exports, under rules that ensure a level playing field for American products abroad. Given that level playing field, it's the president's stated belief that "the American worker, entrepreneur and farmer can compete with anybody, any time, any place."[8]

The general reasoning at play here is this: 95 percent of all potential U.S. customers live outside its borders. Free trade with these customers helps everyone. Protectionist policies do not. "Millions of American jobs are supported by exports, including one in every five factory jobs," the president told the Detroit Economic Club in 2006, and because they are, "here in America … economic isolationism would mean economic disaster."[9] Deregulation at home and free trade abroad are the key requirements of long-term economic success for the United States. The Republican Party knows that in its bones. The Democrats do not, which is why long-term prosperity is something the Republicans, and only the Republicans, can be relied on to deliver.

The American model is the envy of the world

American living standards are the envy of the world, and the economic as well as political freedoms on which they rest make the United States *the* model to which other nations aspire. After all, people flock in the millions into this country. Very few people want to leave it, and this pattern of migration speaks to the way in which American economic practices give expression to the basic human desire for liberty. That pattern also reflects, according to the White House, the superior performance of the U.S. economy relative to other possible societies to which immigrants might turn. The U.S. economy in 2005 grew "faster than any major industrialized economy" and its job creation record since August 2003 exceeded that of "Japan and the European Union combined."[10] Little wonder then that many Republicans are prepared to insist that "America is the greatest, freest and most decent society in existence" and that "American life as it's lived today [is] the best life that our world has to offer."[11]

Of course, there was a time—in the recent past—when other leading industrial countries challenged the United States for global leadership and as a
model for the future. Japan and Western European welfare economies did so in
the 1980s. For a time, as they caught up with U.S. technology and living standards, they seemed to offer a better way forward: more state-led economic
growth in the Japanese case, more generous welfare settlements and workers'
rights in the European. But not any more. Now they're all backpedaling,
realigning their economic institutions on American lines. Japan has been stuck
in economic recession since 1992. Growth and employment rates in Western
Europe have stagnated in similar fashion. Only the United States experienced
the 1990s as a period of sustained growth. Only the United States has met the
challenges of globalization by creating more employment, not less. Japan and
Western Europe no longer constitute viable alternative models. The future is
American: Future economic prosperity everywhere depends on less regulation,
not more; on more competition, not less; and on less welfare, not more.

The only thing that can damage American prosperity is intervention by the Democrats

Which is why handing over the management of the U.S. economy to the
Democrats would be such a disaster. Democrats don't understand how an economy works. They would increase taxes, eating away at the private enterprise
and individual ambition that are the keys to American success. They would
immerse successful U.S. companies in a string of new regulations and externally imposed environmental constraints. They would shift the emphasis of
public policy toward the protection of old industries rather than the development of new ones. And they would increase the minimum wage at the cost of
American jobs. Under the Democrats, policies that have failed in Europe and
Japan will be introduced wholesale here, and fail again. Tax cuts are essential
to long-term economic health, and yet if the Democrats have their way, taxes
will automatically go up again as we hit the 2010 expiration date on the Bush
tax cuts. There's only one party whose record on tax cuts can stand detailed
investigation by anyone with any intelligence at all. It's the Republicans. As
Vice President Cheney put it in October 2006, "our party has a clear record on
taxes and so do our opponents. When we cut taxes in 2001, most Senate Democrats and nearly 85 percent of House Democrats voted against it."[12] It doesn't
come much clearer than that.

A LIBERAL RESPONSE

To these arguments, we need to say the following.

The Republicans are not as keen on deregulation as they like to claim

The Republicans like to present the strongest sections of the U.S. economy as "government free," with themselves as the great defenders of that
freedom; in reality, however, those sectors are often strongest precisely

because they're *not* government free, and the Republicans know it. Large numbers of American engineering firms rely on demand from the Pentagon for their profits, and you can't get closer to government than that. Large agribusinesses and a swathe of small independent farmers rely on extensive farm subsidies, and a significant number of congressmen and women—from both parties—pride themselves on the amount of "pork" they bring back to their particular constituencies. The Bush administration hasn't retreated from the economy, no matter what it claims. It's actually practiced big government *military Keynesianism*—deficit spending that's primarily beneficial to the military-industrial complex. The American corporate sector spends billions of dollars each year on lobbying and puts huge amounts of money into party coffers whenever an election looms.[13] It does that not simply to keep government regulation at bay, but also to generate regulations that suit American companies and orders that keep them in business. Whatever else the U.S. economy may be, free of government it is not, and no Republican Party will make it so—or even wants to—no matter what the Republican leadership says at the top of each election cycle.

President Bush may well insist that "open trade is not just an economic opportunity, it is a moral imperative,"[14] yet that didn't stop him from imposing a 30 percent tariff on imported steel in the run-up to a 2002 midterm election in which Republican candidates in "rust belt" states needed his help. He may believe in his heart-of-hearts that economies work best when regulated least, but the social fallout from the collapse of big companies is just too enormous for even free-market Republicans to ignore entirely. Imagine, for example, internal travel in an America without United, Delta, and Continental Airlines. Immediately post-9/11, that was a real possibility, until public money flowed into the airline industry to ease the blow, and rightly so. The conservative free-market mind-set is entirely out of date, on this as on so much else, clinging to economic dogmas that were appropriate (if ever they were appropriate) only in that early stage of industrial capitalism in which small firms, and small firms alone, competed on a level playing field for market share. The U.S. economy has long since left that stage behind. Big companies stride across each sector of economic activity. The largest of them, Wal-Mart, employs almost one American in every hundred. Giants of this kind are too powerful to be left without regulation. Both their immediate and their long-term impact on both the social and natural world is too enormous to be left to their management alone, driven as their decisions have to be by short-term profit-making criteria. What's good for General Motors is not always good for America, no matter how often we're told it is, and we need to say so.

Selective deregulation is a form of class war

When Republicans talk about deregulation, they normally mean one of two things: (1) removing blockages on the ability of corporate America to make quick and easy profits, or (2) removing regulations that are protective of the American worker. The Bush administration has systematically extended deregulation on both fronts: putting Bush loyalists in charge of regulatory agencies, whittling away existing Occupational Health and Safety Administration (OSHA) standards, blocking new regulations, and cutting funding for the inspection of existing ones.[15] Under the euphemism of "reforming OSHA," the Republicans in Congress used their monopoly of power in Washington between 2004 and 2006 to replace compulsory regulations with voluntary codes of practice that eroded labor standards and made litigation in defense of them progressively more difficult to win. The normal argument used was that regulations erode the capacity of managers to manage, but what they actually do is oblige managers to manage better. They block off sweatshop routes to easy profits, acting as a spur—a beneficial constraint[16]—and obliging U.S. companies to compete on the basis of their technical efficiency alone. Strong labor market regulations encourage managers to draw on the expertise and commitment of those they manage, rather than to treat them simply as factors of production whose cost must be minimized. Amid the increasingly sophisticated technology of modern production, there is a competitive advantage to be had from a secure and flexible labor force and from management practices that gather knowledge by sharing it. The Germans lifted themselves to industrial greatness by making their workers secure. The Japanese did it by extensive use of quality circles. American management has generally been slow to see the need for these more "trust-based" forms of competitive strength, and the Republican Party clearly doesn't buy into this model at all.[17] But the future doesn't lie with super-alienated labor forces. It lies with more humane forms of capitalism, and we need to say so.

Even to use the term "deregulation" to cover the removal of responsibilities from companies and rights from workers obscures the asymmetries of power at play. Companies need regulating, whether they like it or not, to ensure that the externalities they generate (the social consequences of what they do) are figured into their calculations of costs. Such corporate regulation is essential to protect long-term public interests. But, for workers, regulation has a more immediate and direct function. Labor market regulation is necessary, in the short term as well as in the long term, to protect individual workers from excessive exploitation and danger. An individual worker facing a large employer has little power of his or her own. Regulations bring the government in on the worker's side, ensuring adequate minimum standards of pay, working conditions, and human rights. Republicans talk the language of deregulation, but they're normally reluctant to withdraw subsidies and special favors from the corporations that fund them. They're characteristically less restrained, however, when stripping away protective regulations from the people those companies employ. "One rule for capital but another for labor" is very much the Republican way. Such selective deregulation is a class project. It's reactionary and unnecessary, and we should say so.

This is no time for an "antitrade union" bias

It's time again to give credit where credit is due. The typical Republican argument about markets does not differentiate between markets for commodities and markets for labor, and that's a serious error. Labor markets are special things. People and baked beans are not the same. You can't buy and sell them in quite the same way. The Conservative Right seems to understand that when considering senior and professional compensation packages. There's no sustained right-wing critique of the workings of professional organizations like the American Medical Association or of salary compensation committees fixing (yes, "fixing") the money flowing to chief executive officers (CEOs).[18] But with trade unions and ordinary workers, it's different. There's a genuine class bias in the degree of venom directed at them—venom that ignores the critical role played by trade union pressure in the creation of America's postwar prosperity,[19] and venom that ignores the critical role played now, in America's continuing economic strength, by the skills and diligence of ordinary workers. We need to remember, and honor, those who actually make the cars—not just the people in the suits but also the men and women working the assembly line. Too often in Republican rhetoric the only "producers" we hear about are entrepreneurs. The only people with rights at work are those with the right to hire and fire. The rest of us seem to enter the picture only as consumers—our interests restricted to low prices (and taxes, of course), our motivations no wider than the perpetual desire to buy. But we don't just consume, we also work. Our rights and needs at work need to enter the equation. Because if they don't, as the Republicans pile on tax cuts for the few, we're going to remain stuck where most of us are now—on that treadmill of long working hours, stagnant wages, diminishing benefits, and perennial job insecurity, which is, for so many people, the actual reality of daily life in George Bush's much-vaunted economy.

Strong trade unions are good things. They're a voice for the underprivileged. They win basic security, and dignity at work, for those for whom they bargain. They block off sweatshop routes to competitiveness. They bring rights to Americans as workers to parallel the rights they enjoy as voters.[20] There's plenty of evidence that people work better in conditions of security and trust.[21] Ask lawyers—they do—so why should less credentialized workers be any different? There's a Costco model of economic effectiveness to set against the Wal-Mart one, and we need to push for it.[22] Indeed there's something genuinely offensive in the speed with which trade unions, long the champions of the low paid, are now condemned as generators of *inequality* by the very Republicans who would cut taxes on the rich as their way of helping the poor. If America is really to flourish in today's global economy, U.S.-based companies need to mobilize the skills and potentialities of all the people they employ, not just of those at the top. There's only so much extra motivation you can extract from an underpaid labor force by giving ever greater largesse to the man in the big office. A stronger labor movement, and not a richer boardroom, is the key requirement for long-term American employment and income security—not tax cuts for the privileged few but labor rights for the hard-working many. And we need to say so, over and over again.

This economy is not as strong as the Republicans would have you believe

Republicans normally justify their whittling away of trade union rights and worker protection by pointing to external competitive pressures. The U.S. economy is strong, they tell us, because its costs are low. And yet, for all the lowness of those costs, the economy is not strong. It's certainly not strong in international competitive terms. It used to be. In the 1950s and 1960s, U.S. manufacturing performance led the world, but not any more. Since 1990, the United States current account with the rest of the globe—the value of what we sell abroad compared with what we buy from overseas—has been *negative*; with the deficit normally growing larger as a percentage of GDP with each successive year.[23] Indeed, "over the past 15 years, U.S. imports at constant prices [have grown] at a trend rate of 8.3 percent a year while exports grew at 5.1 percent," trends which if they continue could leave the current account deficit as high as 17 percent of GDP by 2016.[24] Certainly, by 2005, the United States was selling abroad only $0.53 worth of goods for every $1 it spent on imports, bridging that vast gap only by selling stocks, bonds, and equities to foreign capital holders on a gigantic scale. It's not just that the United States is overly dependent on foreign sources of oil. That overdependency, and the vulnerability it brings, is recognized on both sides of the aisle. It's also that living standards in the United States are overly dependent on the willingness of foreign governments and private investors to lend the foreign currency that U.S.-made goods no longer earn abroad. Whether or not the Bush administration likes it, "the United States has once again entered a period of large external imbalances," imbalances that this time are even bigger than they were when Ronald Reagan presided over an equivalent period of indebtedness.[25] In 2005, the U.S. *trade deficit* increased by $200 billion in the last three months of the year alone, to stand at an alarming 7 percent of GDP.[26] To finance an imbalance of this scale, the U.S. economy has accumulated some $3 trillion dollars of foreign debt since 1999. It's a Rake's Progress that one day soon could culminate in a traumatic moment of reckoning.

If that were not bad enough, consumption in the United States remains as high as it currently is only by individual Americans running a similar level of personal debt. The total of U.S. household debt was only 70 percent of total disposable personal income in 1980. It's now 130 percent, with debt service payments absorbing 20 percent of all American disposable income. The U.S. economy survives with an average personal savings rate of only 1.5 percent of personal income. The long-term average used to be

7.4 percent, but the 2005 figure was actually negative, at -0.5 percent. What's in play here is not just personal debt, but a large and growing level of government debt as well. It's not just that the United States lives on borrowed money from abroad. It also lives on money borrowed at home, money brought forward in time from rounds of production and pay yet to come. People buy now, and pay later. Governments spend now, and tax later. Wages remain stagnant, so demand is sustained only by working longer hours and drawing on credit cards whose subsequent clearance (at rates of interest pushed up by government borrowing) eats ever further into real living standards. U.S. consumers pulled the world out of recession in 2004, but only by mortgaging their own future. The whole edifice of the U.S. economy, that is, now rests on *debt*—external, internal, and governmental—and debt on that scale is a precarious foundation for the long-term health of an economy that the Republicans continue to describe as safe only in their hands.

It's the absence of key public policies that explains this growing weakness

This move from a position of leading world economy to leading world debtor did not happen overnight. Nor was it accidental. It was a decline that was allowed to happen—partly through government neglect, partly through mistaken public policy.

Partly it has been a matter of neglect. The preoccupations of successive U.S. administrations—Democratic as well as Republican—have been elsewhere. They've focused on maintaining U.S. military and diplomatic dominance in both a Cold War world and post–Cold War world. The United States is an imperial power, and, like previous ones—the Spanish and British both—pays an enormous *internal economic price for that position of world leadership*. For far too long, U.S. governments allowed and encouraged the export of American capital to strengthen frontier democracies in the standoff with Russian communism, capital that might otherwise have been invested at home. For far too long, U.S. governments spent precious overseas reserves maintaining an extensive overseas military presence and fighting a series of regional wars, ultimately flooding the global economy with dollars that nobody wanted. For far too long, U.S. governments allowed U.S. engineering companies to go soft on easy Pentagon-based contracts acquired without significant competition—what we might call the Halliburton effect—and they set and reset exchange rates to prevent economic collapse within the capitalist half of the global order, even when domestic manufacturing requirements would have had those exchange rates set otherwise. These are all the standard consequences of Great Power status. Political classes elsewhere saw the need for economic competitiveness to generate international strength, and pursued it accordingly. The postwar U.S. political classes took economic competitiveness for granted and allowed their exercise of international strength to take precedence over their protection of their industrial base.

Of course, being the dominant power with the reserve currency allowed U.S. policy makers to get away with things for years that lesser mortals (smaller nations) never could. Foreign direct investment has flowed into the United States in great volume, to compensate to some degree for excessive capital export by American firms and financial institutions. But a tipping point always comes in that pattern of capital import and export, a point at which the local manufacturing base becomes too small, and too foreign owned, to give the local economy the competitive edge that its long-term prosperity requires. There is always a point at which downsizing and *de-industrialization* go too far—a moment at which local "capital" begins to do well although local "industry" does not. In the last decade, the U.S. economy has crossed that tipping point. Whole industries have been allowed to collapse, with their production centers relocated overseas and their domestic market colonized to greater and greater degrees by firms based and owned abroad. Some 2.5 million U.S. manufacturing jobs were lost in the first three years of the Bush administration alone. The clothes we wear, the cars we drive, the electrical goods we use, the chairs and beds on which we sit and sleep are increasingly "made abroad," especially in China. By the end of 2005, the U.S. trade deficit with China was two and a half times larger than it had been in 2000, and at the end of 2006, China's foreign exchange reserves topped $1 trillion for the first time. That's "pretty compelling evidence," as Senator Dorgan put it, that "something has to change."[27] The right-wing of the Republican Party worries about the number of immigrants coming into the United States. What it really ought to worry about is the number of American jobs going out. Once, the United States was the great exporter of manufactured goods, and American workers were the world's highest paid. But not any more, and yet the Republicans still tell us that "the economy is strong." Their friends on Wall Street may be, but the rest of us? I wonder.

Running hard just to stand still

Those millions of ordinary Americans who don't work on Wall Street are finding it harder and harder to live the American Dream. The figures capturing that struggle are everywhere. We've already seen the data on wage stagnation. The real wages of American workers actually fell in the 1980s and early 1990s, before briefly reviving in the last years of the century, only to stagnate again as the economy stalled. "Real median family income fell every year from 2000 to 2004. It increased [in 2005]," but in 2006, it was "still lower than it was in 2000."[28] Falling real wages were met by more than rising credit card debt. They were also met by an increase in *working hours*. Over the three decades that now divide us from the Vietnam War, American workers on average have come to put in an extra 160 hours of work a year.[29] That's equivalent to working four more 40 hour weeks every year. The Republicans will point to rising U.S. labor productivity, and tell us that American labor is still more productive than labor elsewhere in the advanced industrial world. And they're right, it is. It's more productive because it works longer. German workers put in 370 fewer hours a year than we do, and the Swedes put in 230 fewer hours. Even the Japanese—long the great workhorses of the postwar industrial world—now only work as many hours a year as Americans.[30] When you look at productivity *per hour*, the U.S. lead entirely vanishes. Yet it is output per hour that determines standards of life. U.S. workers no longer monopolize the world's highest living standards. They now share that status with workers in northern and western Europe, particularly with the Scandinavians and the Swiss.[31]

The U.S. economy came out of recession in 2002, but initially only into a jobless recovery. Fully one-third of those made redundant in 2000–2001 were still workless three years later, and by then an additional 13 percent had found only part-time jobs.[32] By 2006, unemployment was officially down again—to 4.6 percent—a figure that obscured just how many of those made redundant had given up the search for work entirely. Had they not, the unemployment figure would still be closer to 8.7 percent.[33] Although new jobs were available by then for the majority of those still actively seeking employment, the new jobs coming on stream paid less—on average 17 percent less, according to the Bureau of Labor Statistics.[34] Job insecurity, bouts of unemployment, and diminished earning potential are the true prospects facing many Americans in today's tarnished labor markets—prospects made no easier to manage by the Republican Congress's refusal in 2003 to extend the length of state-provided unemployment benefits. Hardly the stuff on which to live out a viable American Dream.[35]

Insecure and low-skilled work is this economy's Achilles' heel

In fact, the U.S. labor force is increasingly splitting in two, with a small high-paid, high-skill top strata and a large—indeed, very large—low-paid and low-skilled base.[36] In that low-skilled base of non-college-trained workers, low wages go hand in hand with high levels of *job insecurity, industrial accidents, stress-related illness,* and *family breakup.* The American model looks great on the television—nothing but glamour, dynamism, and affluence. But, for increasing numbers of Americans over time, the reality is otherwise. It's not for nothing that Wal-Mart has become the largest employer in the United States; its cocktail of low wages, poor benefits, and cheap imported goods speaks to the central weakness of the modern U.S. economy. More and more American-based industries can no longer compete with the rising tide of particularly Chinese competition, and they can't because China's endless pool of displaced rural labor enables it to manufacture consumer goods at a fraction of the cost of producing them in U.S. factories paying U.S. wages. So those factories close or those wages fall, and people redeploy to the service sector where Chinese competition cannot reach. More and more American workers find themselves caught up in a globally generated "race to the bottom," obliged to turn to companies like Wal-Mart for the shoddy goods they need and the shoddy wages they alone still provide. U.S. labor is going backward, and still the Republicans tell us that the economy is strong. Which economy do they mean? This one, or China's? It's very hard to say.

The Wal-Mart dimension to the present trajectory of the U.S. economy needs to be understood and challenged. Wal-Mart claims repeatedly that its big-box buying power brings real gain to the American consumer and real job growth to the U.S. economy. But the reality is more complex than the claim. The impact of Wal-Mart on prices and employment is often over-stated. Independent researchers suggest a price gain of less than 2 percent,[37] and the creation of Wal-Mart jobs is more than offset by the loss of other jobs in the retail sector caused by Wal-Mart's presence within it. A Wal-Mart opens, and small retailers close, the *You've Got Mail* effect, for those who know their Tom Hanks films. Wal-Mart's low wages pull down local wages with them. Its antiunion stance weakens organized labor. Its limited welfare benefits leave Medicaid picking up the tab, and Wal-Mart's vast buying power not only deindustrializes America, it also holds down wages in China. Even the great textile giants like Hanes are so dependent on Wal-Mart for their sales that they are driven on their own crazy global treasure hunt: obliged to relocate their production first south of the Rio Grande, and then west of the Pacific Ocean, in order to meet the company's perennial demand that prices fall. Indeed, with so much of Wal-Mart's output now outsourced, it's easier to see the company as China's export tool rather than as the cham-pion of the American consumer. Little wonder then that, by 2006, speaking out against Wal-Mart began to earn Democrats votes.

Free trade ratchets down, fair trade ratchets up (we want to go up)

Free trade in these circumstances is less a recipe for prosperity than for disaster—and a company like Wal-Mart is a key player in that developing tragedy. It and other companies like it are the mechanisms by which wage costs abroad are also kept low. Indeed, recently, when the Chinese govern-ment (hardly, after all, a bastion of democracy) moved to strengthen workers' rights out of fear of industrial unrest, it was American firms operating in China that were apparently among the most vocal opponents of the change of line.[38] The CEOs of such companies, ever watchful of the quarterly returns and the associated stock price, need that cost-containment, but the rest of us do not. The American Federation of Labor–Congress of Industrial Organizations (AFL-CIO) currently reckons that if the Chinese government merely enforced its existing set of health and safety regulations, production costs in China would rise by 44 percent.[39] But the Chinese government won't, of course, and it is under no pressure to do so unless the United States and the European Union, the major buyers of its goods, make such labor standards a precondition for continued access to their home markets. And they should, because we all stand to benefit from a rise in Chinese (and

Mexican) wages. If wages rise there, so too will demand, and the space will open again for the reconstruction of a broadly based and high-paying U.S. manufacturing sector. The great trick of international economic policy is to set in motion a logic that *ratchets up* wages, demand, and living conditions, rather than ratchets them down. It's a trick that can be achieved under international trading rules that are genuinely fair but not under trading rules that are only ostensibly free. Free and unfree people cannot trade fairly. We need fair trade rules that can trigger freedom everywhere, not free trade rules that erode freedom even at home.

There is an immense amount of nonsense talked about the benefits of unregulated free trade.[40] Most Republicans seem to forget that protectionism was crucial to the original American growth story, that the party of Lincoln came to power urging people to "vote yourself a farm, vote yourself a tariff."[41] Open markets made sense from an American perspective only much later, when American-made goods had become the best in the world. When that was so, between 1945 and 1973, employment and prosperity here were enhanced not just by the opening of foreign markets to U.S. goods, but also by the export of American currency and capital. Foreigners in Europe and Japan brought that money immediately back to the United States to purchase the technologies and consumer goods they could not generate themselves. But those days are gone. Reverse engineering has done its work. Major overseas economies now produce their own high-skilled engineers, marketing people, and accountants. Capital is now genuinely mobile: it will go wherever it can to make the profits it needs. What does not move with anything close to the same ease is labor itself. Labor forces now have to compete with each other to attract investment and jobs to their part of the global economy. Their education and skill levels therefore become a key differentiator between them, and so, too, do the wages and working conditions under which they operate.[42] The International Labor Organization (ILO), we should remember, reported in 2004 that in 2003 2.8 billion people were employed globally—a doubling of the number employed from a generation earlier—but that 1.4 billion of these workers were still earning less than $2 a day. $2 a day? No American worker can compete with that, and none should be expected to, which is why a full U.S. recovery requires not free trade but *fair trade*. We need a trade policy that pulls up wages abroad, not one that pulls them down at home, which is why we also urgently need a new Marshall Plan to put purchasing power into the hands of the world's poorest workers, the establishment of global labor standards, and the spread of human rights—so that those workers can develop trade unions and improve their own conditions of life.

There is a better way

A global "race to the bottom" doesn't need to be the only policy show in town. There is a better way, one linking a different foreign economic policy to a new set of internal initiatives that can ratchet up living standards rather than ratchet them down. The result would combine the enhanced national security promise of a multilateralist foreign policy with the greater economic security of a managed economy and trade. Republicans claim that only their policies will strengthen America and make it more secure. We need to say that the claim is false. Republican policies actually weaken America and make it more vulnerable. Progressive policies, and progressive policies alone, can reverse that weakening. Domestically, they can do this by developing industrial policies to strengthen the manufacturing base and by establishing social policies to tackle embedded inequalities in income and access to essential services. Abroad, they can do this by military disengagement and the negotiation of a fairer global trading system. None of that resetting will be easy. None of it will be quickly achieved. But nor will any part of this more desirable trajectory even come into view unless we make a sharp break from prevailing Republican policies.

That break will require, at the very least, the following:

1. A significant increase in the national minimum wage and in the existing system of earned income tax credits[43]
2. The replacement of recent tax cuts on the rich by a genuinely progressive tax code[44]
3. A new industrial policy to reinvigorate the manufacturing base[45]
4. New labor laws to give workers a voice in corporate governance[46]
5. Extensive public funding of job creation programs, not least in internal security and the construction of public housing[47]
6. A lessening of the gradient along which welfare payments are cut as work is taken
7. A significant increase in the quality and remuneration of teachers[48]
8. A significant extension in systems of industrial training
9. Proper family-friendly policies that include adequate child care for working mothers, parental leave, and rights for part-time workers[49]
10. Reforms to the health care system to give secure and reliable access to services regardless of ability to pay
11. Resetting of the social insurance system to protect workers against catastrophic drops in their income—at childbirth, during unemployment, and for retraining[50]
12. The trading of agricultural subsidies for a new system of strong internationally mandated labor standards[51]
13. The establishment of model trade agreements with safeguards for workers and independent producers in *both* countries[52]
14. The systematic and incremental reduction of government and overseas debt
15. A complete withdrawal from Iraq as part of a return to a multilateralist foreign policy

Steps to a Better Future

R. H. Tawney once gave the British Labour Party a piece of advice that we could still use today. Crushed by a conservative landslide in 1931, reeling on the ropes of electoral defeat, plenty of people within that party were ready to throw in the towel. But not R. H. Tawney. Don't panic in the face of resistance, he told the party. Expect it. It's going to come anyway. Don't dodge the opposition by compromising principles and promising smooth things. "Support won by such methods is a reed shaken by every wind."[1] Instead, get up and fight for what you believe in. You can't negotiate on your knees. Explain your aims with complete openness and candor and prepare for power by mobilizing behind you "a body of conviction as resolute and informed as the opposition" you face.[2] Don't encourage your adherents "to ask what they'll get from a [progressive] Government, as though a campaign were a picnic, all beer and sunshine." Ask them rather "what they will give." "Make them understand that [your return to power] is merely the first phase of a struggle, the issue of which depends on them."[3]

That was good advice in 1932, and in the wake of the 2006 midterm election, it's good advice today. That election broke the Republican stranglehold on power in Washington. It gave the Democrats a chance to recapture the political agenda, and it threw into stark relief the tensions currently dividing the Republican coalition. The election results in 2006 made clear that voters in general are more progressive than the conservative lobbyists in Washington would have us believe. They certainly are less overwhelmingly concerned with social issues than is the Christian Right, less willing to dismantle social security than are the Libertarians, and more concerned with health care than with immigration. So there is a space—an opportunity again—for progressive politics. But political spaces always close, and close quickly, if they're not taken—particularly spaces like this one. This is a space that is likely to be fiercely contested by conservatives outraged at so unexpected a loss of power, conservatives who are convinced that they were "thumpered" out of their Congressional chairmanships in 2006 not because George Bush was too right-wing, but because he was not right-wing enough.

Conservative forces have been shaken, but they will regroup. So if the progressive moment is not to be lost, liberals will need to respond as Tawney did long ago. The question is "how?" This way, at least.

Calling the conservative bluff

If conservatives think that poverty and social injustice can be solved without government help, and that economic recovery requires only tax cuts and free trade, we should invite them to try it on a personal basis. We should invite them to settle in a rundown part of some northern city; deny themselves education, good social contacts, and subsidized housing; take on the care of two or three small children; and face a job market of unskilled, low-paid work. Then we should invite them to go live the American Dream, and if they find that they can't, then we should also invite them to admit that what they can't do, others can't be expected to do either. We should invite them to recognize that circumstances make people, and people make circumstances too, and that if we want people to prosper, we must act on their circumstances. The flourishing of individual rights, so important to American conservatives, requires a politics of equal starting points. There can be no genuine equality of rights, generation on generation, if vast income differences in one age group produce huge inequalities in life chances for the next. Children cannot be held responsible for the poverty (or indeed affluence) into which they're born, and because they can't, it's time to reassert the importance of level playing fields. It's time for liberals to say that when playing fields are as unequal as they are now, individual self-help and an active voluntary sector will never be enough to give everyone an equal chance. Level playing fields have to be built. Building them requires public programs. It requires a strong and assertive Liberalism.

The liberal voice needs to be very clear, too, on some very basic points of political philosophy: clear on freedom and clear on democracy. Freedom and license are not the same thing, and formal freedoms must have substance to be real. Proper political freedoms have to be matched by equivalent economic and social freedoms. Other advanced democracies know that. They even write basic social rights into their constitutions. We don't, but we're still subject to the same truth. If significant numbers of Americans can't get proper health care or face destitution if they lose their job, then their freedom is impaired, no matter how solid is their right to vote. That voting power too must be real as well as formal. Where is the real democracy when unregulated lobby money buys so much influence? Where is the real democracy when politicians are subject to vast no-go areas—no regulating companies, no giving American workers job protection, no managing markets? Conservatives are quick to tell us how much unnecessary taxation we pay. They're not so quick to tell us how much unnecessary expenditure we make to the private suppliers of our health care. But what's good for the goose is good for the gander. We need to ask why people are "freer" if they hand over money to the private companies that they don't elect than to the politicians whom they do. We need to say that markets can be effective allocators of resources and can be genuinely sensitive to people's real preferences, but only if everyone operating freely within them has the same amount of purchasing power and the same amount of money to spend. To the degree that they don't—to the degree that incomes and property rights are significantly unequal—then to that degree, too, unregulated markets become flawed. Markets in unequal societies respond to those with money. Democracies respond to people with votes. Everyone has a vote, but not everyone has money. It's time for the collective interests of the people with votes to prevail over the self-interest of the people with money.

Valuing intellectual endeavor

It's a striking feature of so much conservative commentary on the state of modern America today that the sophistication of their problem specification is never matched by a parallel sophistication in the solutions canvassed. Conservative America is full of woe about our modern condition: too much regulation from the Libertarians, too much moral decay from the Religious Right, too many immigrants, too many foreign wars. The list of woes is potentially endless. But not the solutions. They always come quick and short. Build a wall. Stop a gay marriage. Cut a tax. Get people off welfare. Leave it to the private sector. Set the people free. And if the problems persist, even when you've done all that freedom setting, blame liberals for their continued interference with the wonders of the free market, and then carry on much as before. Build a higher wall. Create a lower tax. Bring the limits on welfare even further forward. But whatever you do, don't pause and don't think. Just spot a problem, grab a cliché, and charge ahead!

That cannot be the progressive way. We have to say that the social ills of contemporary America have such complex roots, and are so stacked one upon the other, that the last thing they'll respond to are quick and simple solutions. In fact, so complex and intertwined are the issues here that the conservatives often have a point: Even well-intentioned progressive solutions can sometimes make things worse. Things are so interlocked and mutually reinforcing in the contemporary crisis of the American welfare state, for example, that moving forward on one front often does equate to moving back on another. Raising the age of retirement to ease the burden of payroll tax on the young may look desirable from one perspective, but not necessarily from all of them. It's a great solution if you're white, young, and affluent; but because on average the poor die younger than the rich, and a greater proportion of black Americans than white Americans are poor, it's not so great a solution if you happen to be old, poor, and African American. Conundrums of that kind are always there for the advocates of free markets to exploit. Just leave everything to the interplay of supply and demand, they say. Don't interfere. If you move on one front, you'll only make the other front worse. But how ludicrous is that? Complex and interlocking social problems aren't solved by the quick fix of doing nothing. Interlocking social problems are only solved by joined-up policy initiatives that address each element of the conundrum simultaneously. This isn't the moment for economics 101. Advocating market solutions for every social problem is either lazy or self-indulgent. Either way, a faith in unregulated markets is fast becoming the leading nonsense of the age. Unregulated markets reproduce and amplify inequalities. Well-regulated markets don't, and we should say so.

Consolidating power

Between now and 2008, the big *defensive* task facing the Democratic Left is wedge-issue control. Time and again, conservatives go into electoral battle prioritizing issues that divide progressive politicians from significant elements in their potential voting base. It's no accident that a Republican Party that's actually committed to tax cuts, income inequality, and two-tier health systems doesn't present itself in that way. There are no votes to be had in telling potential supporters in working-class communities that a vote for the Republicans is a vote for the rich. It makes more sense to play to the social agenda—to go for the three Gs (Gays, Guns, and God)—and to narrow down the economic agenda to a question of tax burdens and the adverse effect of immigration on wages and jobs. The task of the Democratic Left is to block that reactionary strategy—by widening the economic agenda and by repositioning the social agenda into its proper secondary place. Taxes are only burdensome if wages are not rising. Immigration only threatens employment if jobs are scarce. And, economic liberals are as free as conservatives to disagree about the pros and cons of abortion and gay marriage. It's up to liberal politicians to expose the hypocrisy and double standards tucked away in so much of the right-wing, antigovernment rhetoric. It's up to liberals to point out the heavy subsidization of corporate America hidden behind the Republican's program of deregulation, and to highlight the contradictions between the Sunday-morning moralizing of the Christian Right and the daily reality of the world that the Republicans offer—corruption in high places and destitution in low ones.

The *offensive* task of the Democratic Left is one of progressive agenda-setting. We need to say that the real social issues of the day are not the three

Gs but the three Hs (Health, Happiness, and Hope). Real freedom, we need to say, requires real resources in the hands of real people—education, skills, job security, health care, and prosperity in old age. It's not enough to have the freedom to compete. A civilized society must also give people the capacity to cooperate. America is at a genuine crossroads, we should say, and we should insist that now is the time to turn away from programs and parties that pit us against each other in an unregulated struggle to survive. This is no time to duck the economic agenda, because the electoral data are largely on our side. Class, not culture, still shapes the modern electorate, no matter how hard social conservatives work to make it otherwise. As Matthew Yglesias has written, "Poorer people vote for the Democrats, richer ones for the GOP, and the battle lines are drawn in the middle of the income spectrum, just where you'd expect."[4] Which is why the Democratic Party should take Thomas Frank's advice, and stop "making endless concessions on economic issues, on welfare, NAFTA, Social Security, labor law, privatization, deregulation, and the rest of it."[5] For as he's written, only a party retreating from issues of that kind is "vulnerable to cultural wedge issues like guns and abortion and the rest whose hallucinatory appeal would ordinarily be far overshadowed by material concerns."[6] The Republicans talk about class in a coded way. The Democrats don't talk about it at all—and that needs to change. We have to get away from an electoral world in which a Kansas voter "tired of everything being wonderful on Wall Street and terrible on Main Street" actually voted Republican.[7] That's as crazy as chickens voting for the sauce in which they will be cooked, and we should say so.

Recapturing the narrative

Political journeys are always long ones, and electoral coalitions are not just things to build. They're also things to sustain. I suspect that the real reason that the Republican Right rails so loudly against academia and the liberal media is that they know the importance of ideas and their dissemination, and they sense that a careful examination of many of their ideas will only expose their flaws. What is true for them is true for us as well. Progressives have a powerful interest in the funding of extensive and rigorous social research. Facts can only help to demonstrate where policy is needed and what that policy should be. And progressives have a huge interest is ensuring that awareness of their research is widely and effectively spread. The imbalance of resources between the think tanks of the Right and those of the Left is one of the great progressive weaknesses of the age. The paucity of liberal media outlets relative to conservative ones is the other great weakness. At least the shortage of center-left think tanks is now being corrected, if only incrementally and slowly, as liberals begin to grasp the nature of the conservative *movement* they face and to understand the need to match that movement by one of their own. That correction cannot come soon enough. In truth, it's long overdue and still inadequate in scale.[8]

The best way to build a movement is to play effective counterhegemonic politics. That involves creating in the public mind both *a great divide* between what we stand for and what Republicans in practice offer, and a clear sense of the *principles* underpinning our progressive program. Democrats will only' create that sense of division if they talk openly and confidently again about morality and vision—emphasizing the importance of equality and justice, individual liberty based on positive rights, and real freedom rooted in economic and social security. The role of the Left as a moral force must be to make decency, compassion, and care respectable again. We must talk not only about individualism and self-help, but also about responsibility to others. And we must insist that the trinity of equality, compassion, and community constitutes *the* route to prosperity and progress, and not—as our political opponents would have it—prosperity's greatest barrier.[9]

In and of itself, that trinity will not be enough, however, for ultimately the only way to recapture the dominant narrative in American politics is actually to assert one, and you can't assert what you don't possess. Unfortunately, Michael Tomasky is quite right when he says, "the Democrats still don't have ... a philosophy, a big idea that unites their proposals and converts them from a hodgepodge of narrow and specific fixes into a vision for society."[10] The party desperately needs an overarching narrative: another version of the New Deal and Great Society assertion that America has a heart as well as a wallet and that people help themselves best by also helping others. Perhaps progressives can use Jared Bernstein's telling acronyms, contrasting the Republican's YOYO society with the Democrat's WITT, and framing the choice before the American people as one between a "You're On Your Own" society and a "We're In This Together" one.[11] Or maybe the Democratic Party could repackage itself as offering not just a New Deal but also a New Security: physical security, through multilateralism; personal security, through developed social programs; and economic security, through labor reskilling and managed trade. At the very least, the party ought now to repackage itself as proudly liberal again—that's Liberal with a capital *L*—as a party unabashedly engaged in the pursuit of social justice.

I, for one, am with Douglas Massey:

> Damned right I'm a liberal and this is what I stand for. I believe that government should invest in people by seeing to their health and education, for people are the ultimate resource in society. I believe that markets are not states of nature, but human inventions with imperfections and fallibilities, and that government must work to ensure they function for the good of the many rather than the benefit of the few. I believe it is the obligation of government to make sure that needed markets exist, that competition within them is fair, that transactions are transparent, and that competition is accessible to everyone. I believe that because markets are fallible, and that they can and do break down from time to time, government must create public institutions to protect

people from periodic market failures. Finally, I believe that government must ensure equal civil, legal and political rights for all citizens regardless of background.[12]

Recaging the dogs

Progressives were in the past, and must become again, authors of their own fate. Democratic Lefts always get the Conservative Rights that they train. These days, European Conservatives—British Tories, French Gaullists, German and Italian Christian Democrats—are all liberals in American terms. They are because they have to be, if they're to win support from electorates that are seeped in the values and institutions of European social democracy. But not here. Here it's the Conservative Right that sets the electoral tone, and it's the New Deal coalition that lies fractured and broken. The ultraconservatism of the contemporary American Right is testimony, not to something unique in the American character, but to the postwar failure of Liberalism to hold the center ground in American politics. It's only the weakness of the Democrats that has allowed Republican rottweilers to run so free for so long. Recaging the dogs, recapturing that center ground, and obliging the American Right to reeducate itself in the electoral potency of liberal Republicanism are currently the central tasks facing progressive forces in the United States. Hopefully, books like this will make some small but positive contribution to this vital if enormous enterprise.

Notes

CHAPTER 1

1. The imagery here is Paul Krugman's, writing in "Things Fall Apart," *The New York Times,* October 2, 2006. On the perennial tension between libertarians and social conservatives within the Republican coalition, see Ryan Sager, *The Elephant in the Room* (Hoboken, NJ: John Wiley, 2006).

2. To read more, and to see in detail the primary sources used as basic data here, see the blogsite linked to this volume at http://www.liberaltoolkit.blogspot.com.

3. Robert Reich, "The Lost Art of Democratic Narrative," *The New Republic,* March 21, 2005.

4. Stuart Hall, "The Great Moving Right Show," in *The Politics of Thatcherism,* eds. Stuart Hall and Martin Jacques (London: Lawrence and Wishart, 1983), p. 39.

5. For a fascinating discussion of the importance of getting the words right, see Geoffrey Nunberg, *Talking Right* (New York: Public Affairs, 2006).

CHAPTER 2

1. Bill O'Reilly, *Culture Warrior* (New York: Broadway Books, 2006), pp. 26–27. His target is people he labels "secular progressives." I guess that would include me.

2. Lest anyone think this an overstatement, try for size the campaign around David Horowitz's "Academic Bill of Rights" and the associated naming of left-wing academics. On this, see David Horotwitz, *The Professors: The 101 Most Dangerous Academics in America* (Washington, DC: Regnery Publishing, Inc., 2006).

3. The construction of this section draws heavily on books, newsletters, and Web sites created by, among others, Rush Limbaugh, Bill O'Reilly, Ann Coulter, Sean Hannity, Mark Levine, Tammy Bruce, and Michael Savage.

4. So, for example, this from Michael Savage: "at many of our colleges—which are often nothing more than houses of porn and scorn—pro-terrorist professors like Ward Churchill at the University of Colorado at Boulder spew speeches that

transcend the treacherous. For example, ensconced in his twisted Lilliputian world, Churchill told Fox News that 'Bush, at least in symbolic terms, is the world's leading terrorist' . . . Listen to this lunatic, a spokeschick for the Fish Empathy Project, a new . . . initiative to harass business. She explained, 'Fish are so misunderstood, because they're so far removed from our daily lives. They're such interesting, fascinating individuals, but they're so incredibly abused.'" Michael Savage, *Liberalism Is a Mental Disorder* (New York: Nelson Current, 2003), pp. xxiii–iv, 94–95.

5. "I remember an America that was beautiful, free and safe. Sure, some of the politicians may have been just as corrupt as now. But somehow you could tell they still loved America. That's the difference I've discovered over time. There has always been a tension between Democrats and Republicans, but there were no traitors like there are today: it was unheard of." Michael Savage, *The Enemy Within: Saving America from the Liberal Assault on our Schools, Faith and Military* (Nashville, TN: WND Books, 2003), p. 21.

6. "The emergence of an international social liberalism, which is at its core soft-communism, is a very real threat to the sovereignty of our nation. Forces from within and without our country continue to try to tell us that we are out of step with the rest of the world. The 'sophisticated' Europeans laugh at us for our naïveté and our clinging to religion and family values. . . . Our children are being inculcated with the international-socialist credos from crib to college. They are being taught that European socialist leaders are men of superior brains who must triumph over the ignorance, the stupidity, and the short-sighted selfishness of the American masses . . . in other words, under the soft Marxism of Bill Clinton, America was weakened—morally, militarily and spiritually" (Michael Savage, *Liberalism Is a Mental Disorder,* pp. xiii, xiv, 200).

7. Mark Levine, *Men in Black: How the Supreme Court Is Destroying America* (Washington, DC: Regnery Publishing, Inc., 2005), p. 10.

8. "Granted, true Democrats, the so-called blue-America, probably consider themselves just as patriotic (if not more so) than the residents of so-called red-America (the Republicans). But in their zeal to help the unfortunate, they are now largely espousing the tenets of socialism, not democracy" (Michael Savage, *Liberalism Is a Mental Disorder*).

9. "Extreme liberalism is a mental disease. It's a destructive contagion more deadly than any force this country has ever faced. . . . Modern distorted liberalism is the Enemy Within" (Michael Savage, *The Enemy Within,* p. 14).

10. Rush Limbaugh, to the Heritage Foundation, November 2004.

11. "So when people call up and tell me you can't make it in America—or that it takes welfare or a bunch of government handouts—I tell them they're crazy. *Of course* you can make it. If I'm doing it, you can. You don't have to make it big—that often takes breaks beyond one's total control. But you can make it and do quite well, if you're wiling to invest the effort." Sean Hannity, *Let Freedom Ring* (New York: HarperCollins Publishers, 2002) p. 282.

12. "The conservative movement is dead. I take no pleasure in making that observation. Let's face facts. . . . When I first voted for George W. Bush, I didn't think I was getting Bill Clinton-Lite" (Michael Savage, *Liberalism Is a Mental Disorder,* pp. xi, 89). The case is argued far more carefully and fully in Bruce Bartlett, *Impostor: How George W. Bush Bankrupted America and Betrayed the Reagan Legacy* (New York:

Doubleday, 2006); and in Pat Buchanan, *Where the Right Went Wrong* (New York: Thomas Dunne Books, 2004).

13. "In the major media, if you're a lib, you're protected. If you're a conservative, you're crucified. Case in point. . . . I was fired from MSNBC" (Michael Savage, *The Enemy Within,* pp. 217–219).

14. For balance, we should note here that Ann Coulter has an equivalent set of what she calls "pointers," for conservatives to use against liberals. They are: don't surrender out of the gate; you don't need to be defensive; you must outrage the enemy; never apologize; never compliment a Democrat; never show graciousness towards a Democrat; never flatter a Democrat; do not succumb to liberal bribery; prepare for your darkest secrets to become liberal talking points; and always be open to liberals in transition." Ann Coulter, *How to Talk to a Liberal (if you must)* (New York: Three Rivers Press, 2004), pp. 11–19.

15. The case for the importance of a reframing of the debate is at its clearest in George Lakoff's, *Don't Think of an Elephant: Know Your Values and Frame the Debate* (River Junction, VT: Chelsea Green Publishing, 2004). For a more light-hearted demonstration of the same truth, see Katrina vanden Heuvel, *Dictionary of Republicanism* (New York: Nation Books, 2005).

16. In the interest of balance, it should be noted that Ann Coulter makes a similar criticism of liberals, accusing them of "hate speech," not least in their regular habit of attaching the adjective "stupid" to the proper noun "George W. Bush." Ann Coulter, *Slander* (New York: Three Rivers Press, 2002), p. 43.

17. Ann Coulter, *How to Talk to A Liberal,* p. 16.

18. Michael Savage, *Liberalism Is a Mental Disorder,* p. xxiii.

19. The term is Kevin Mattson's, in his "The Book of Liberal Values," *Prospect,* February 2006, p. 32.

CHAPTER 3

1. See, for example, Polly Toynbee, "Taxes Are a Moral Good, and Avoiding Your Fair Share Is a Moral Disgrace," *The Guardian,* September 15, 2006.

2. Dean Stansel, *The Hidden Burden of Taxation,* The Cato Institute, Policy Analysis No. 302, April 15, 1998.

3. Senator Rick Santorum, "It's Time to Kill the Death Tax," www.townhall.com, June 8, 2006.

4. Sean Hannity, *Let Freedom Ring* (New York: HarperCollins, 2004), p. 206.

5. The president's radio address, April 15, 2006.

6. Ibid.

7. Daniel Mitchell, "A Benchmark for Assessing the Recommendations of the President's Tax Reform Panel," The Heritage Foundation, Web memo no. 890, October 24, 2005.

8. Chris Edwards, *Business Tax Cuts Crucial in a Slowdown,* Cato Institute Web site, October 5, 2001.

9. Bill O'Reilly, "Working for a Living," www.BillOReilly.com, August 11, 2005.

10. Daniel Mitchell, "The President's Tax Agenda," Heritage Foundation, Web memo no. 992, February 7, 2006.

11. Jim Gilmore, chair of the Republican National Committee, quoted in Hannity, *Let Freedom Ring*, p. 211.

12. The term was invented by David Stockman, Ronald Reagan's budget director, the theory being that tax cuts would create budget deficits and so induce cuts in programs, ultimately pulling government back to a 1920s level of activity.

13. Mitchell, "The President's Tax Agenda."

14. This list is normally pure Adam Smith; *The Wealth of Nations*, Book V, Chapter XI.

15. See Steve Forbes, *Flat Tax Revolution* (Washington, DC: Regnery Publishing, Inc., 2005).

16. Such a flat tax would avoid the standard four "costs" normally attributed by conservatives to the complexity of the tax code: the army of tax consultants it sustains; the barriers to efficient corporate and personal decision-making it creates; the invasion of privacy with which it is associated; and the extent of noncompliance it induces. On these, see Chris Edwards, *The Simple Tax Life*, Cato Institute Web site: www.cato.org, April 17, 2006.

17. O'Reilly, "Working for a Living."

18. The *Cato Handbook on Policy* put the case against high taxation this way. "The most obvious cost is that Americans are left with less money to meet their needs for food, clothing, housing and other items, and businesses are left with fewer funds to invest and build the economy. In addition the tax system imposes large compliance burdens and 'deadweight losses' on the economy. *Compliance burdens* are the time and administrative costs of dealing with the tax system's rules and paperwork. *Deadweight losses* are created by taxes distorting the market economy by changing relative prices and altering the behavior of workers, investors, businesses and entrepreneurs" (2004, p. 118).

19. Rush Limbaugh, "Top 20% Pay 80% of Taxes," *Welcome to Rush 24/7*, August 13, 2004.

20. Dick Cheney, speaking at the Harley-Davidson plant in Kansas City, January 6, 2006.

21. George W. Bush, quoted in Jonathan Weisman, "Bush Hill Republicans Agree to Extend Expiring Tax Cuts," *The Washington Post*, May 3, 2006.

22. For a Reaganite argument that the result of the Bush administration's 2001 tax cuts was *slower* growth than the U.S. would have enjoyed if no tax cuts had passed at all, see Bruce Bartlett, *Imposter* (New York: Doubleday, 2006), p. 55.

23. If by total public spending you mean spending on social programs, the U.S. figure—at 14.6 percent of GDP—is less than all but Ireland in the top 18 Organisation for Economic Co-operation and Development (OECD) economies in 2001, and by some margin. The Italian figure was 23.9 percent of GDP, the Swiss figure was 27.5 percent, the U.K. figure was 21.5 percent, and even the Japanese figure was 16.6 percent. Jonas Pontusson, *Inequality and Prosperity* (New York: Century Foundation, 2005, p. 145).

24. The two periods in question being 1974–1978 and 1979–1983. This from Greg Anrig, Jr. *Why It's Good to be Rich—and Getting Better All the Time* (New York: Century Foundation, 2004).

25. For this argument, see Daniel Mitchell, *State of the Union 2006: A Mixed Message on Tax Policy*, The Heritage Foundation, Web memo no. 981, February 1, 2006.

26. Jill Barshay, "The Labor versus Capital Debate," *CQ Weekly*, February 6, 2006, p. 4.

27. For these percentages, see Bernard Wasow, "Myth 1: The rich deserve most of the tax cuts because they pay most of the taxes," *Class Warfare Fact and Fiction* (New York: Century Foundation, 2004).

28. Hutton estimates the rate of inequality in the United States as *twice* that in Japan, Germany, and France. Will Hutton, *A Declaration of Independence* (New York: W.W. Norton, 2003), p. 130.

29. Edward N. Wolff, *Top Heavy: The Increasing Inequality of Wealth in America and What Can Be Done About It* (New York: The New Press, 2002), pp. 8–9.

30. Paul Ryscavage, *Income Inequality in America: An Analysis of Trends* (New York: M. E. Sharpe, 1999); and Lawrence Mishel, Jared Bernstein, and Sylvia Allegretto, *The State of Working America* (Ithaca, NY: ILR Press, 2005), pp. 39–105.

31. Data in *The Financial Times*, July 25, 2006.

32. This, after a similar pattern through the 1983–1998 period when, "to put it succinctly, the top quintile received a little less than 90 percent of the total increase in income and over 90 percent of the increase in wealth" (Wolff, *Top Heavy*, pp. 37–38).

33. It fell back to a mere 237:1 in 2001 as stock values fell, and stood at 262:1 in 2005. See Ian Dew-Becker and Robert Gordon, *Where Did the Productivity Growth Go?* National Bureau of Economic Research working paper no. 11842, December 2005.

34. This calculation is based on data from the Luxemburg Income Study, reported in *The New American Economy: A Rising Tide that Lifts Only Yachts* (New York: Century Foundation, 2004), pp. 7–9.

35. Mishel, Bernstein, Sylvia Allegretto, *The State of Working America*, p. 3.

36. "Recent analysis suggests that ... far from disappearing in three generations, as earlier work optimistically suggested ... income differences based on family background are likely to persist for many generations." Bernard Wasow, "Myth 4: Over the course of their lifetimes, Americans are highly likely to enjoy upward economic mobility," *Class Warfare Fact and Fiction* (New York: Century Foundation, 2004). For data suggesting that social mobility might actually be higher in certain industrial societies abroad—not least Finland, Sweden, Canada, and Germany, see Heather Bouchey and Christian Weller, "What the Numbers Tell Us," in *Inequality Matters*, eds. James Lardner and David Smith (New York: The Free Press, 2005), pp. 35–36; and Bernard Wasow, *Rags to Riches: The American Dream is Less Common in the United States than Elsewhere* (New York: Century Foundation, 2004).

37. The classic study is Sheldon Danziger and Peter Gottschalk, "Do Rising Tides Lift All Boats? The Impact of Secular and Cyclical Changes on Poverty," *AEA Papers and Proceedings*, May 1986, 76(2): pp. 405–410.

38. A rise of less than $2 on the minimum wage by June 2007 would directly benefit 7.2 million American workers, and indirectly benefit some 8 million more. Economic Policy Institute, *Minimum Wage: Facts at a Glance*, January 2006.

39. The Employment Policy Institute comes to mind most readily. See, for example, their press release, "Labor Day 2005: Five Reasons Not To Increase the Minimum Wage," September 2, 2005.

40. For a recent survey of the debate and the evidence, see "Minimum Wage," CQ Researcher, December 16, 2005; also see Liana Fox, "Minimum Wage Trends," Economic Policy Institute briefing paper no. 178, October 24, 2006.

41. One consequence of the 2006 midterm election results is that President Bush now appears to agree with the Democratic majority in Congress on the importance of raising the minimum wage.

42. Edwin Feulner, *Flat-Out Smart*, The Heritage Foundation, Press Commentary, October 25, 2005.

43. Will Hutton, "One Tax the Rich Will Love," *Observer*, September 11, 2005, p. 24.

44. Michael Tomasky, "The Real Tax Test," *The American Prospect*, June 2006, p. 3.

45. Dan Morgan, "Farm Program Pays $1.3 Billion to People Who Don't Farm," *The Washington Post*, July 2, 2006.

46. The more sophisticated of the conservative theorists often quietly concede that point. This from Daniel Mitchell: "contrary to what both political parties argue, there does not seem to be a strong relationship between the budget deficit and interest rates. Nor is there much reason to believe that lower interest rates, by themselves, will have a pronounced effect on investment." *Taxes, Deficits and Economic Growth*, Heritage lecture #565 (www.heritage.org/Research/Taxes/hl565.cfm), May 14, 1996.

47. For the remarkable scale of this "pork" in the Republican-controlled 109th Congress, see Robert Reich, "An Economy Raised on Pork," *New York Times*, September 3, 2005; and Ryan Sager, *The Elephant in the Room* (Hoboken, NJ: John Wiley, 2006), p. 102.

48. Notebook and Numbers. *Time*, June 12, 2006, p. 21.

CHAPTER 4

1. Welfare policies in the United States are means-tested policies, unlike social insurance policies of the Social Security kind. To qualify for the former, you have to demonstrate *need*. For the latter, you only have to demonstrate *contributions*. In 2005, the U.S. welfare system had more than 70 means-tested aid programs providing cash, food, housing, medical care, and social services to low-income persons.

2. For a scholarly if idiosyncratic challenge to this assertion, see chapter 1 of Christopher Howard, *The Welfare State Nobody Knows* (Princeton, NJ: Princeton University Press, 2007). Yet even he ultimately concludes that his (larger) welfare state "does not do much to lift the poor out of poverty, or to close the gap between rich and poor" (p. 209).

3. Robert Rector and Kirk Johnson, "Understanding Poverty in America," Research, Welfare, The Heritage Foundation, January 5, 2004.

4. Kirk Johnson, "The Data on Poverty and Health Insurance You're Not Reading," Research, Welfare, The Heritage Foundation, August 27, 2004.

5. Ibid.

6. Rector and Johnson, "Understanding Poverty in America."

7. For the claim that "low IQ continues to be a much stronger precursor of poverty than the socioeconomic circumstances in which people grow up," see Richard Herrnstein and Charles Murray, *The Bell Curve: Intelligence and Class Structure in American Life* (New York: The Free Press, 1994), p. 127.

8. Robert Rector, "Poverty and Inequality," in *Issues 2006: The Candidate's Briefing Book* (Heritage Foundation, 2006), p. 110.

9. Bill O'Reilly, "Katrina and the Poor," September 8, 2005.

10. In his 1935 State of the Union Address.

11. Michael Tanner, "The Poverty of Welfare," Cato Institute, 2003, p. 158.

12. Quoted in Robert Rector, "The Good News About Welfare Reform,' Research, Welfare, The Heritage Foundation, September 20, 2001, p. 9.

13. Charles Murray, *Losing Ground* (New York: Basic Books, 1984), p. 9.

14. Charles Murray, *In Our Hands* (Washington, DC: The AEI Press, 2006), pp. 3–4.

15. The imagery is that of Monica Charen, *Do-Gooders* (New York: Sentinel, 2006), p. 26.

16. Michael Tanner, "The End of Welfare," Cato Institute, 1996, p. 88.

17. Robert Rector, before the Sub-Committee on Human Resources of the Committee on Ways and Means, House of Representatives, February 10, 2005.

18. Robert Rector, "The Effects of Welfare Reform," Research, Welfare, The Heritage Foundation, March 15, 2001, p. 1.

19. This, in Rector, "The Effects of Welfare Reform," p. 4.

20. Rector, "Poverty and Inequality," p. 109 (italics added).

21. Senator Daniel Patrick Moynihan called it "the most brutal act of social policy since Reconstruction."

22. Rector, "Welfare Reform," p. 114; Robert Rector and Patrick Fagan, "The Continuing Good News About Welfare Reform," The Heritage Foundation Backgrounder, Executive Summary No. 1620, February 6, 2003.

23. Rector, "The Good News About Welfare Reform," p. 3.

24. Such rules were implemented by the Bush administration in June 2006.

25. Rector and Johnson, "Understanding Poverty in America," p. 14.

26. Michael Tanner, "Welfare Reform Less Than Meets the Eye," Policy Analysis No. 473, Cato Institute, April 1, 2003, p. 23.

27. The idea is Charles Murray's, initially a $10,000 a year basic income, and *no* other federal or state program benefiting some citizens but not others. See his *In Our Hands*, pp. 8–14.

28. Cato Handbook for 105th Congress, "Welfare Reform," Cato Institute, p. 4.

29. Tanner, "Welfare Reform Less Than Meets the Eye," p. 1.

30. Her story is told in John Cassidy's "Relatively Deprived: How Poor Is Poor?" *The New Yorker*, April 3, 2006.

31. On rent as a problem for the poor, see Barbara Ehrenreich, "Earth to Wal-Mars," in *Inequality Matters*, eds. James Lardner and David A Smith (New York: The Free Press, 2005), p. 53; and Jason DeParle, *American Dream* (New York: Penguin, 2004), p. 11.

32. The EPI credibly defend this "twice the poverty threshold" as corresponding "closely to more rigorously defined measures of a family's ability to meet its basic needs" (Lawrence Mishel, Jared Bernstein, and Sylvia Allegretto, *The State of Working America 2004/2005* (Ithaca, NY: ILR Press, 2005), p. 310).

33. Ibid., p. 313.

34. This, from Howard Berkes, "A Rural Struggle to Keep the Family Fed," National Public Radio, November 21, 2005.

35. Lee Rainwater and Timothy Smeeding, *Poor Kids in a Rich Country* (New York: Russell Sage Foundation, 2003), p. 22.

36. United Kingdom, Spain, and Italy (Ibid., p. 45).

37. Mishel, Bernstein, and Allegretto, *The State of Working America 2004/2005*, p. 411.

38. Jonas Pontusson, *Inequality and Prosperity: Social Europe versus Liberal America* (Ithaca, NY: Cornell University Press, 2005), p. 171.

39. Amartya Sen's 1999 data, cited in Cassidy, "Relatively Deprived: How Poor Is Poor?"

40. David Shipler, *The Working Poor: Invisible in America* (New York: Alfred A. Knoff, 2004), p. 287.

41. Sharon Hays, *Flat Broke With Children* (New York: Oxford University Press, 2003), p. 231.

42. In 2004, the Women, Infants, and Children (WIC) program run by the Department of Agriculture helped feed 7.9 million more—6 million of them children in poor families.

43. It was only briefly in the early 1970s, for example, that the rate of benefit increase outstripped that of wages. The value of the typical welfare check fell by 40 percent over the next two decades.

44. Gary Burtless, "Public Spending on the Poor: Historical Trends and economic Limits," in *Confronting Poverty*, eds. Sheldon H. Danziger, Gary Sandefur, and Daniel Weinberg (Cambridge, MA: Harvard University Press, 1994), p. 51.

45. James K Galbraith, *Created Unequal* (New York: The Free Press, 1998), p. 20.

46. Ibid., p. 16.

47. Christopher Jencks, Scott WInship, and Joseph Swingle. "Welfare Redux," *The American Prospect*, March 2006, p. 37. It was noticeable, too, that, as the case-loads fell, the proportion of those still on them who were long-term welfare recipients increased. Even the Cato Institute people have commented that "those remaining on the rolls are a hard-core of long-term unemployed and difficult-to-place recipients" (Tanner, "Welfare Reform Less Than Meets the Eye," p. 61).

48. Domestic violence is a huge hidden issue here. For details, see Demie Kurz, "Women, Welfare, and Domestic Violence," in *Whose Welfare*, ed. Gwendolyn Mink (Ithaca, NY: Cornell University Press, 1999), pp. 132–151.

49. Tanner, "Welfare Reform Less Than Meets the Eye," p. 80. Hence, his overall conclusion follows: "if welfare reform has not been the disaster claimed by critics, neither has it been quite the success claimed by supporters" (p. 56).

50. As Ronald Reagan put it in his 1986 State of the Union Address, "how often we read of a husband and wife both working, struggling from paycheck to paycheck to raise a family, meet a mortgage, pay their taxes and bills. And yet some in Congress say taxes must be raised. Well, I'm sorry; they're asking the wrong people to tighten their belts. It's time we reduce the Federal budget and left the family budget alone. We do not face large deficits because American families are under-taxed; we face those deficits because the Federal Government overspends."

51. The existence of the welfare poor beneath them only hurts them to the extent that welfare-to-work programs create an even bigger supply of people in pursuit of their low-paid jobs. As the 1996 Act was first being implemented, Nobel Laureate Robert Solow estimated that, to get even a 1 percent increase in demand for labor to increase to absorb them, wages would have to fall by 2 or 3 percent in real terms, with most of that fall hitting already employed low-wage workers. See Robert Solow, *Work and Welfare* (Princeton, NJ: Princeton University Press, 1998). p. 31.

52. Galbraith, *Created Unequal*, p. 10.

53. These figures in J. Schwarz and Thomas Volgy, *The Forgotten Americans; Thirty Million Working Poor in the Land of Opportunity* (New York: W.W. Norton, 1993), p. 14.

54. Galbraith, *Created Unequal*, p. 20.

55. If a notion of the "welfare state for the rich" shocks, consider this: "we have in place today not one but two competing welfare systems. One is the private one disproportionately for the rich, based on the ownership of financial assets. The other is a public one, mainly for the retired population, with dribs and drabs for the younger poor. Both are financed mainly by working Americans, who pay taxes to the state and interest to their creditors, and then try to live on the remainder" (Galbraith, *Created Unequal*, pp. 13–14).

56. Cited in Jonathan Alter, "The Other America: An Enduring Shame," *Newsweek*, September 19, 2005, p. 42.

57. To give credit where it is due, Charles Murray for one does recognize that work and welfare will have to go together unless we're willing to let a lot of children starve. On this, see his "Can We Replace Welfare With Work?" in *Reducing Poverty in America*, ed. Michael Darby (Thousand Oaks, CA: Sage, 1996), p. 81.

58. Hays, *Flat Broke With Children*, p. 278.

59. Thomas Sowell, among others, denies that, claiming that "the black family, which had survived centuries of slavery and discrimination, began rapidly disintegrating in the liberal welfare state that subsidized unwed pregnancy and changed welfare from an emergency rescue to a way of life" (Thomas Sowell, *A Painful Anniversary*, www.townhall.com, August 17, 2004). But the sources of fragility here are deeper and older than that. If they weren't, welfare could not have been so caustic. Discussing them used to be taboo on the Left—remember the reaction to the leaked report in the 1960s by the young Daniel Patrick Moynihan. But no longer. The interplay of racism and its legacies on the one side, and urban decay and welfare support on the other, has produced a new form of social exclusion with its own *internal* motor of reproduction, particularly hostility to learning among young African American males in families on low income. But it's not just internal. There's not space here to discuss all the external forces in detail, but a full analysis would need to factor in such things as commercial sport as a new form of athletic sharecropping and the commercialization of rap music.

60. Shipler, *The Working Poor*, p. 27.

CHAPTER 5

1. Social Security's formal name is Old Age, Survivors, and Disability Insurance: a scheme that provides pensions and insurance to workers and their families in the event of disability and death.

2. Peter J. Ferrara and Michael Tanner, *A New Deal for Social Security* (Washington, DC: Cato Institute, 1998), p. 1.

3. The chairman of the Trustee's Panel, quoted in the *Winston-Salem Journal*, May 2, 2006, p. A7.

4. Laurence Kotlikoff, quoted in Mary H. Cooper, "Social Security Reform," *CQ Researcher*, September 24, 2004, 14(33): p. 4.

5. Michael Tanner, "Signs of Crisis are Clear," *USA Today*, February 1, 2005 (reproduced on The Cato Institute Web site). See also Laurence Kotlikoff and Scott Burns, *The Coming Generational Storm* (Cambridge, MA: MIT Press, 2004).

6. Ferrera and Tanner, *A New Deal for Social Security*, p. 111.

7. Ibid.

8. Edward H Crane, "Securing Reform: The Simple Rules for Transforming Social Security," The National Review Online, October 19, 2004, at www.national review.com/nrof_comment/crane200410190831.asp.

9. Ferrara and Tanner, *A New Deal for Social Security*, p. 82.

10. George McGovern, *Social Security and the Golden Age* (Golden, CO: Fulcrum Publishing, 2005), p. 2.

11. Not to mention the even earlier Civil War pension scheme, with half a million men on its rolls by 1910, almost one in three of all men then over 65 in the United States. That pension scheme paid about 30 percent of average wages, at a time when the fledgling German pension scheme—Bismarck's—was paying about 17 percent. See E. Amenta and T. Skocpol, "Taking Exception: Explaining the Distinctiveness of American Public Policies in the Last Century," in *The Comparative History of Public Policy*, ed. F. Castles (Cheltenham, UK: Edward Elgar, 1999), p. 297.

12. Employment Policy Institute, *Social Security: Facts at a Glance* (Washington, DC: EPI, May 2005).

13. Interview with Mara Liasson, "Morning Edition," National Public Radio, May 25, 2001.

14. The figures are Dean Baker's and Mark Weisbrot, in their *Social Security: The Phony Crisis* (Chicago: University of Chicago Press, 1999).

15. It all depends on which projection you take. The Social Security trustees' "intermediate" scenario in their 2005 report had the Fund in surplus right through to 2041. Their more optimistic low-cost scenario had the surplus still intact in 2080.

16. Given that wages by 2040 will be at least 30 percent higher than now, even if payroll taxes then have to be slightly increased, "it will take a great deal of imagination to perceive this as some sort of highway robbery by tomorrow's senior citizens against the youth of today" (Baker and Weisbrot, *Social Security: The Phony Crisis*, p. 2).

17. If the Fund earns less on its investments than is normal among private pension fund managers, then the solution seems obvious. Do what they do. The Brookings Institute's Barry P. Bosworth and Gary Burtless regularly canvas this as a more effective and immediate to any "problem" deemed to be looming by the Fund's conservative critics (see, for example, Gary Burtless's evidence to the Senate Committee on the Budget, January 19, 1999). For a similar argument, see Nancy Altman, *The Battle for Social Security* (Hoboken, NJ: John Wiley, 2005), p. 305.

18. Taking away the cap ought to be the one to go for first; because its removal would, at a stroke, improve Social Security's capacity slightly to redistribute income from the rich to the poor. It would also release into the Trust Fund much needed tax revenues to offset any shortfall thought to be looming. The percentage of total payroll now escaping taxation—because it's over the $90,000 cap—has risen from 10 percent to 15 percent since 1983, which is in line with the growing inequality of income and wealth in the United States. Raising the cap would therefore be entirely in line with the original goals of the Social Security program.

19. Mary H. Cooper, "Social Security Reform," *CQ Researcher*, September 24, 2004, 14(33): p. 4.

20. Which, accordingly, has itself been pushed unto deficit: reportedly some $23 billion by 2005.

21. 2005 State of the Union Address.

22. Baker and Weisbrot put it as wide as 11 percent to 13 percent (*Social Security: The Phony Crisis*, p. 13). The administration of the current Social Security system takes only 0.8 percent of total revenues.

23. I am dependent here on Baker and Weisbrot's calculations (*Social Security: The Phony Crisis*, pp. 8–9). But there are many others, equally sanguine about future stock price growth.

24. "A safe retirement based on a 401(k) account requires decades of discipline, something many people don't have. A recent study by Hewitt Associates, the employee benefits research firm, found that 45 percent of workers cashed out their 401(k)s when leaving a company, instead of leaving the money in the plan or rolling it over into a new one. And some workers cannot or do not participate in the retirement plans available to them" ("The Pensions Deep Freeze," editorial, *New York Times*, January 14, 2006).

25. Economic Policy Institute, *Social Security: Facts at a Glance* (Washington, DC: EPI, 2005).

26. National Organization of Women, "Talking Points about Women, Social Security and Privatization," Washington, DC, March 4, 2005.

27. Henry J. Aaron, "Privatizing Social Security: A Bad Idea Whose Time Will Never Come," *The Brookings Review* 21(2003): pp. 16–23.

28. On this, see John Myles and Paul Pierson, "The Comparative Political Economy of Pension Reform," in *The New Politics of the Welfare State*, ed. Paul Pierson (Oxford, UK: Oxford University Press, 2001), pp. 305–315.

29. See, for example, The Century Foundation Report, *Chile's Experience with Social Security Privatization: A Model for the United States* (on its Web site www.tcf.org; accessed on March 10, 1999); or Manuel Riesco, *Private Pensions in Chile, A Quarter Century On* (CENDA, Santiago, Chile, available at www.cep.cl). It is significant that the Chilean reform, introduced under the Pinochet dictatorship, did not extend to either the military or the police. They remained in their state-financed scheme.

30. Cited in Richard Lapper and Adam Thomson, "The Chilean Model Runs out of Road," *The Financial Times*, November 28, 2005, p. 11.

31. "Any debt owed *by* future generations will also be owed *to* future generations, because each generation that pays interest on the national debt pays that money to members of the same generation who own the Treasury bonds" (Baker and Weisbrot, *Social Security: The Phony Crisis*, pp. 17–18).

32. Employment Policy Institute, *Social Security, Frequently Asked Questions*, Washington, DC, EPI, 2005.

33. On this, see Robert Eisner, *Social Security: More Not Less,* Century Foundation/Twentieth Century Fund Report (New York: Century Foundation Press, 1998), pp. 4, 41–42; and Heidi Hartmann and Catherine Hill, *Strengthening Social Security for Women* (Washington, DC: National Council of Women's Organizations, 1999).

34. Jacob Hacker, *The Great Risk Shift* (Oxford, UK: Oxford University Press, 2006), p. 38.

CHAPTER 6

1. Rush Limbaugh, "Health Care and Automobiles," *Welcome to Rush 24/7*, August 30, 2004. For a similar argument, see Michael Savage, *The Enemy Within* (Nashville, TN: WND Books, 2003), p. 55.

2. The OECD average for health expenditure as a percentage of GDP in 2001 was 8.3 percent, with the United States at the top of the range, Switzerland next at 10.9 percent, Germany at 10.7 percent, Canada 9.7 percent, France 9.5 percent, Sweden 8.7 percent, and Japan and the United Kingdom both 7.6 percent [*Towards High Performing Health Systems* (Paris: OECD, 2004), p. 78]. That translated into per capita spending on health care in the United States of $5,267, Canada $2,931, and France $2,736.

3. Both these from Michael Cannon, "Hilary's Worse Nightmare," Cato Institute Web site: www.cato.org, May 9, 2004.

4. Michael Cannon, "Kerry Prescribes More Government-Run Health Care," Cato Institute Web site: www.cato.org, April 23, 2004.

5. Michael Cannon, "Medicare and Medicaid," in *The Cato Handbook on Policy* (Washington, DC: The Cato Institute, 2004), pp. 85–86.

6. Cannon, "Medicare and Medicaid," p. 86.

7. Michael Cannon, "Welfare Reform's Unfinished Business," Cato Institute Web site: www.cato.org, May 26, 2005.

8. Ibid.

9. Hence the president's proposal, in his 2007 State of the Union Address, to, as he put it, "level the playing field for those who do not get health insurance through their job" by providing tax breaks to help low-income people buy health insurance and tax increases for workers whose health plans cost significantly more than the national average.

10. Cited in Cannon, "Medicare and Medicaid," pp. 86–87.

11. John Cogan, R. Glenn Hubbard, and Daniel P. Kessler, *Healthy, Wealthy and Wise* (Washington, DC: The AEI Press, 2005), p. 2.

12. Christopher J. Conover, "Health Care Regulation: A $169 Billion Hidden Tax," Cato Institute, Policy Analysis No. 527, October 4, 2004.

13. Savage, *The Enemy Within,* p. 55.

14. Cannon, "Hilary's Worse Nightmare." p. 1.

15. National Center for Policy Analysis, "A Single-Payer Health Care System for California," *Daily Policy Digest,* June 26, 2006.

16. Michael Cannon, "Eight Reasons to Delay the Imprudent Drug Program," Cato Web site: www.cato.org., November 14, 2005. Bruce Bartlett later called the Medicare drug bill "the worst piece of legislation ever enacted," *Imposter* (New York: Doubleday, 2006), p. 80.

17. Allen B. Hubbard, assistant to the president for economic policy, *New York Times,* April 3, 2006.

18. Michael Cannon, *Medicaid's Untallied Costs,* Cato Institute Web site: www.cato.org, July 1, 2005.

19. Cannon, "Hilary's Worse Nightmare," Cato Institute Web site: www.cato.org.

20. President Bush, quoted in *The New York Times,* January 29, 2006.

21. Tom Miller, "Private Health Care," in *The Cato Handbook for Congress: Policy Recommendations for the 108th Congress* (Washington, DC: The Cate Institute, 2004), p. 283.

22. Ibid., p. 293.

23. Michael Cannon and Michael Tanner, *Healthy Competition* (Washington, DC: Cato Institute, 2005), pp. 27–30.

24. OECD, *Towards High Performing Health Systems*, p. 44.

25. Paul Krugman, "Death by Insurance," *New York Times*, May 1, 2006.

26. The Census Bureau figures for 2005 show an increase of 6.8 million in the number of the medically uninsured since 2000. The total includes 8.3 million children—more than 1 American child in 10—the first increase in that number since 1998.

27. Broadly speaking, three equally sized groups are currently uninsured in the United States: young healthy adults on more than $50,000 a year; Medicaid-eligible poor who don't take up private insurance; and workers earning more than the poverty level but less than $50,000 a year—the group referred to in chapter 4 as the "twice-poor" (this, from Cogan, Hubbard, and Kessler, *Healthy, Wealthy and Wise*, pp. 18–21).

28. OECD, *Towards High Performing Health Systems*, p. 51.

29. Leif Wellington Haase, *A New Deal for Health* (New York: The Century Foundation Press, 2005), p. 22.

30. Tom Miller, "Rising Health Costs," The Cato Institute Web site: www.cato.org, August 13, 2002.

31. The most serious attempt to address access issues from a market perspective can be found in Cogan, Hubbard, and Kessler, *Healthy, Wealthy and Wise*, p. 72, where they estimate tax changes could reduce the uninsured by between 6 and 20 million (i.e., up to half). The best Cato has come up is this: "For low income individuals lacking access to health insurance, the better policy solutions include safety net reforms that strengthen state high-risk pools and encourage charitable contributions to provide health services through nonprofit intermediaries. ... In the long run, improving the quality of education that lower-income individuals receive, expanding their personal control of healthcare decisions [sic!], and reversing regulatory policies that increase the cost of their heath care will yield even greater returns in improved health outcomes" (Miller, *The Cato Handbook for Congress*, p. 291).

32. Susan Giaimo, "Who Pays for Health Care Reform?" in *The New Politics of the Welfare State*, ed. Paul Pierson (Oxford, UK: Oxford University Press, 2001), p. 357.

33. "Low-wage workers are about half as likely as high-wage workers to have employer-provided health insurance from either their own employers or a family member's; and women among the low-paid are twice as likely to be without such cover as are low-paid men" (Heather Boushey and Mary Murray Diaz, "Heath Insurance Data Briefs #1: Improving Access to Health Insurance," Center for Economic and Policy Research, April 13, 2004, p. 2).

34. Emergency room visits nationwide increased by 20 percent between 1992 and 2001, although the total number of emergency departments fell by 15 percent in the same period (Haase, *A New Deal for Health*, p. 22).

35. "A recent study by the Urban Institute estimated that 43 percent of low-income workers and 31 percent of middle-income workers would be unable to afford

alternative coverage should they lose their employer benefits" (Haase, *A New Deal for Health*, p. 9).

36. On the Tennessee cutbacks, see Julie Rovner, "Tennessee Health-Care Cuts Roil Poor Community," NPR, July 5, 2006.

37. Paul Krugman, "Health Economics 101," *New York Times*, November 14, 2005.

38. Haase, *A New Deal for Health*, pp. 13–14.

39. Virtually the entire growth of Medicare spending is on patients with five or more conditions; many triggered by or associated with obesity. So there are lifestyle issues to discuss on the "demand" side of the medical equation, similar in kind to those surrounding smoking and cancer treatment (see Kenneth Thorpe and David Howard, "The Rise in Spending Among Medicare Beneficiaries," *Health Affairs*, August 22, 2006).

40. This is not to say that it's inefficient. Charles Morris' writings regularly stress the *rising* productivity of U.S. medicine. Procedures are now often quicker and cheaper than ever before. As he says, "it is not falling productivity that is driving costs ... but the expanding basket of effective interventions—both for diseases doctors have always treated, and for a growing list of conditions previously beyond our reach." Charles Morris, *What's Right With Health Care* (New York: The Century Foundation, March 3, 2006), p. 1.

41. Chris Giles, "Healthcare Costs Rising Faster than GDP: OECD," *Financial Times*, June 27, 2006, p. 4.

42. David Williams and James Lardner, "Cold Truths About Class, Race and Health," in *Inequality Matters*, eds. James Lardner and David A Smith (New York: The New Press, 2005), p. 103.

43. Ichiro Kawachi, "Why the United States Is Not Number One in Health," in *Healthy, Wealthy and Fair*, eds. J. Morone and L. Jacobs (New York: Oxford University Press, 2004), p. 20.

44. The details are at NPR, May 3, 2006, and in the corresponding issue of the *Journal of the American Medical Association*.

45. Paul Krugman, "The Health Care Crisis and What to Do About It," *New York Review of Books*, March 23, 2006, 53(5): 1–14.

46. The description of the system is that of J.D. Kleinke, cited in Haase, *A New Deal for Health*, p. 24.

47. Americans for Health Care and Center for American Progress, "If It's Broke, Fix It," Washington, DC, no date.

48. In the 110th Congress, this prohibition is likely to be removed.

49. Charles Morris, *Falling Apart at the Seams* (New York: The Century Foundation, 2006), p. 51.

50. On this, see Krugman, "The Health Care Crisis," p. 4.

51. Lawrence Jacobs, "Health Disparities in the Land of Equality," in *Healthy, Wealthy and Fair*, eds. Morone and Jacobs, p. 59.

52. This was 90 million patients in 1990, but 114 million in 2003.

53. The Kaiser Foundation reported that the cost to companies of providing health care to employees rose 12 percent in 2004, five times the rate of increase of wages.

54. "The gap between work and health coverage is [now] widening. Twenty million working Americans lack health insurance, or about one in every ten workers,"

and "four workers in every ten with benefits now expect to lose them at some point in the future" (Haase, *A New Deal for Health*, pp. 9–10). Nearly 4.5 million fewer Americans under 65 had employer-provided coverage in 2005 than in 2000.

55. Leif Wellington Haase, "Universal Health Coverage: The Problem with Individual Mandates," The Century Foundation Web site, www.tcf.org, February 14, 2003.

56. Ibid.

57. This, on page 116 of the remarkably valuable essay by Mark Schlesinger, "The Danger of the Market Panacea," in *Healthy, Wealthy and Fair*, eds. Morone and Jacobs, pp. 91–134.

58. Not everyone argues it that way. For the entirely opposite argument, see Krugman, "The Health Care Crisis," p. 13.

59. Center for American Progress, "Progressive Prescriptions for a Healthy America," Washington, DC, no date.

60. Charles Morris, *Falling Apart at the Seams*, pp. 57–60.

61. Haase, *A New Deal for Health* (Washington, DC: Century Foundation Press, 2005), p. 5.

62. *DLC Blueprint Magazine*, July 22, 2006.

63. An injunction beloved by all fans of *The Godfather* movies.

64. Center for American Progress, "Progressive Prescriptions for a Healthy America," Washington, DC, p. 11.

CHAPTER 7

1. The estimates do vary, and the numbers are controversial. The Immigration and Naturalization Service put the figure at 7 million for 2003; the U.S. Census Bureau at 8.7 million for 2000; the Pew Hispanic Center estimates 11.5 to 12.0 million; Bear Stearns Asset Management has it at 20 million (figures from Rush Limbaugh, *Welcome to Rush 24/7*, May 22, 2006).

2. Michael Savage, *Liberalism is a Mental Disorder* (New York: Nelson Current, 2003), p. 60.

3. Robert Rector, "Amnesty and Continued Low-Skill Immigration Will Substantially Raise Welfare Costs and Poverty," The Heritage Foundation Backgrounder No. 1936, May 16, 2006, p. 2.

4. Robert Rector, *Senate Immigration Bill*, The Heritage Foundation, Web memo no. 1076, May 15, 2006. The Cato Institute, by contrast, dismisses these numbers as not even passing the "laugh test." Cato's argument is that the Heritage Foundation is exaggerating the numbers of temporary workers who will stay and draw relatives after them (for the disagreement, see the Cato Web site: www.cato.org, May 30, 2006, and the Heritage Foundation Web site: www.heritage.org, June 5, 2006).

5. Limbaugh, *Welcome to Rush 24/7*, April 4, 2006.

6. Savage, *Liberalism is a Mental Disorder*, p. 60.

7. See, for example, Roy Beck, *The Case Against Immigration* (New York: W.W. Norton, 1996), pp. 136–155.

8. Pat Buchanan calls it "La Reconqista." See his *The Death of the West* (New York: Thomas Dunne Books, 2002), p. 123.

9. Peter Duignan and Lewis Gann, *The Debate in the United States over Immigration* (Stanford: Hoover Institution Press, 1998), p. 38.

10. Limbaugh, *Welcome to Rush 24/7*, March 31, 2006.

11. The key source here is academic rather than popular: Samuel Huntington, *Who Are We? The Challenge to America's National Identity* (New York: Simon & Schuster, 2004).

12. Leonard Zeskind, "The New Nativism," *American Prospect*, November 2005, p. A15.

13. Tom Tancredo, *In Mortal Danger* (Nashville, TN: WND Books, 2006), pp. 82, 157.

14. J. D. Hayworth, *Whatever It Takes: Illegal Immigration, Border Security and the War on Terror* (Washington, DC: Regnery Publishing, Inc., 2006), p. 28.

15. Tancredo, *In Mortal Danger*, p. 165, citing the research data of Madeleine Pelner Cosman.

16. Savage, *Liberalism Is a Mental Disorder*, pp. 61–62.

17. La Shawn Barber, reviewing J.D. Hayworth's, "Whatever It Takes," townhall .com, February 21, 2006.

18. This in Robert D. Novak, "Immigration and Terrorism," townhall.com, July 6, 2006.

19. Limbaugh, *Welcome to Rush 24/7*, May 5, 2005.

20. On this, see Beck, *The Case Against Immigration*, chapter 8.

21. Tancredo, *In Mortal Danger*, p. 163.

22. BillOReilly.com, May 4, 2006.

23. Savage, *Liberalism is a Mental Disorder*, p. 71.

24. Ibid., p. 84.

25. Limbaugh, *Welcome to Rush 24/7*, April 12, 2006.

26. Limbaugh, *Welcome to Rush 24/7*, May 26, 2005.

27. Limbaugh, *Welcome to Rush 24/7*, April 3, 2006.

28. Limbaugh, *Welcome to Rush 24/7*, June 21, 2006.

29. Savage, *Liberalism is a Mental Disorder*, p. 84.

30. Buchanan's "crucial steps" are these: "Build a fence along the 2,000-mile border to stop the flood. End welfare benefits to illegal aliens, except emergency medical treatment. Vigorously prosecute employers who hire illegals. Cease granting automatic citizenship to 'anchor babies' of illegals who sneak across the border to have them. Take care of mother and child; then put them on a bus back home. Turn off the magnets, and the illegals will not come. Cut off the benefits, and they will not stay. In five years, the crisis will be over" (Patrick J. Buchanan, "The Stealth Amnesty of Rep. Mike Pence," WorldNetDaily: www.worldnetdaily.com, June 13, 2006).

31. Quoted on *BBC News*, December 17, 2005.

32. The Bush quotations in this paragraph and the next are from the president's Address to the Nation on Immigration Reform, May 15, 2006.

33. Quoted in Lee P. Butler, "It's Amnesty Only if We Say It's Amnesty," Opinion Editorials.com, June 28, 2006.

34. Michael Bloomberg, quoted in *The Washington Post*, July 6, 2006.

35. *The Cato Handbook for Congress* (Washington, DC: The Cato Institute, 2004), p. 638.

36. Quoted in *The New York Times*, July 20, 2006.

37. Data from a speech to the Cato Institute by U.S. Commerce Secretary Carlos M. Guitierrez, August 1, 2006.

38. David Brooks, "Immigrants to Be Proud Of," *New York Times*, March 30, 2006.

39. On this, see Luis Frega and Gary Segura, "Culture Clash? Contesting Notions of American Identity and the Effects of Latin American Immigration," APSR, *Perspectives on Politics*, June 2006, 4(2): pp. 281–283.

40. James Lindsay and Aubrey Singer, *Changing Faces: Immigrants and Diversity in the Twenty-First Century* (Washington, DC: Brookings Institution, 2003), p. 232.

41. Richard Alba, "Mexican Americans and the American Dream," APSR, *Perspectives on Politics*, June 2006, 4(2): p. 291.

42. The title of Jared Diamond's prize-winning book, first published by W.W. Norton in 1997.

43. "From 1616 to 1619 what may have been bubonic plague introduced by European fishermen in modern Maine spread south along the Atlantic seaboard ... killing as many as 90 percent of the region's inhabitants. Portals of coastal New England that had once been as densely populated as Western Europe were suddenly empty of people." Nathaniel Philbrick, *Mayflower* (New York: Viking, 2006), p. 48.

44. Jared Diamond, *Guns, Germs and Steel* (New York: W.W. Norton, 2005), p. 78. See also Charles Mann, *1491* (New York: Knopf, 2005), pp. 100–104.

45. "Indian populations were falling almost everywhere: European diseases and European disruptions did deadly work, and a population estimated at 4 to 5 million before 1492 was tumbling towards half a million by the end of the eighteenth century." Colin Calloway, *The Scratch of a Pen: 1763 and the Transformation of North America* (New York: Oxford University Press, 2006), p. 24.

46. This was the figure cited to the 108th Congress by the Cato Institute, *The Cato Handbook for Congress*, p. 632.

47. Between 2000 and 2005, according to estimates from the Pew Hispanic Center, there were more than 1.4 million unauthorized workers in the construction industry, and 1.2 million in leisure and hospitality. Agriculture had 110,000 ("The Labor Force Status of Short-Term Unauthorized Workers," Fact Sheet, April 13, 2006). Unauthorized migrants made up 24 percent of all agricultural workers in 2005, 17 percent of all cleaners, 14 percent of all construction workers, and 12 percent of all those employed in food preparation. Collectively, unauthorized migrants made up 4.9 percent of the civilian labor force in March 2005, some 7.2 million workers out of a total of 148 million (Ibid., March 7, 2006). An earlier study published by the Pew Hispanic Center of Washington, DC (Philip Martin, "Guest Workers: New Solution, New Problem?" March 21, 2002) put the number of unauthorized workers in agriculture much higher: at 1.2 million, or 47 percent of all wage-earners in the industry (Lindsay Lowell and Robert Suro, *How Many Undocumented?* www.pewhispanic.org). Either way, the evidence suggests a big dependency in certain industries on undocumented labor, which then affects costs in a way that is beneficial to consumers—for example, lowering housing costs in North Carolina by an estimated 10 percent (Robert Craver, "Building Lives: Hispanics Keep Cost of Construction Down." *Winston-Salem Journal*, January 10, 2006, p. 1).

48. "Thousands of new jobs each year for low-skilled workers ... in retail sales, food preparation, cleaning and janitorial services ... agriculture, construction, and landscaping and grounds-keeping" (Daniel Griswold, "America Needs Real Immigration Reform," Cato Institute Web site: www.freetrade.org/node/333, May 18, 2006).

49. The latest findings here are in David A. Jaeger, "Replacing the Undocumented Work Force," Center for American Progress, March 2006.

50. See George Borjas, *Heaven's Door: Immigration Policy and the American Economy* (Princeton, NJ: Princeton University Press, 1999); and George Borjas and Lawrence Katz, "The Evolution of the Mexican-born Workforce in the United States," National Bureau of Economic Research, Working Paper No. 11281, April 2005.

51. Sources Tito Boeri, Gordon Hanson, and Barry McCormick, *Immigration Policy and the Welfare System* (Oxford, UK: Oxford Univeristy Press, 2002): pp. 192–204; Alan B. Krueger, "Two Labor Economic Issues for the Immigration Debate," Center for American Progress, April 4, 2006; and "Do Immigrants Really Hurt American Workers' Wages?" *Economist*, April 8, 2006, p. 76.

52. This of course would be a huge change of policy. The U.S. economy has more than 6 million workplaces. In 1999, 417 employers were fined for hiring undocumented workers. In 2004, that number was down to three.

53. Speech by Commerce Secretary Gutierrez to the Cato Institute, August 2006.

54. For details, see Lindsay Lovell and Roberto Suro, "The Improving Educational Profile of Latino Immigrants," Pew Hispanic Center, 2006.

55. See Ronald Mize, "Mexican Contract Workers and the U.S. Capitalist Agricultural Labor Process: The Formative Era 1942–1964," *Rural Sociology*, March 2006: 71(1).

56. See Rosa Maria Aguilera-Guzman, V. Nelly Salgado de Snyder, Martha Romero, and Maria Elena Medina-Mora, "Paternal Absence and International Migration: Stressors and Compensators Associated with the Mental Health of Mexican Teenagers of Rural Origin," *Adolescence*, Winter 2004, 39(156): pp. 711–724.

57. NAFTA phased out tariffs on agricultural produce between the United States and Mexico over a 15-year period, ending in 2008. Agricultural exports grew during those years in both directions, doubling in a decade in the Mexican case, but increasing by more than 15 percent a year on the American side. Rice, cattle, pigs, corn, dairy, and fruit products have gone south in such volume that, by 2001, Mexico's agricultural trade deficit with the United States was running at more than $4 billion a year (Geri Smith, "Mexico's Farmers Are Getting Plowed Under," *Business Week*, November 18, 2002). Corn imports, for example, from the United States into Mexico increased a staggering eighteen-fold between 1994 and 2002, affecting three million Mexican farmers and triggering rural unemployment.

58. These figures, and those later in this paragraph on rural unemployment, are from Bill Weinberg, "NATFA At Ten: Tragic Toll for Mexican Maize," *Native Americas*, June 2004, XXI(2): 52.

59. John Judis, Immigration Confusion: Illegal Substance," *The New Republic Online*, April 6, 2006.

60. Those subsidies cover crops such as cotton, corn, rice, and soybeans. The U.S. farm program paid growers an average of $15.3 billion a year between 1996 and 2001 and $23 billion in 2005 (C. Ford Runge, "Agrivation: The Farm Bill from Hell," *The National Interest* 72, Summer 2003). By contrast, Mexican farm subsidies totaled only about 6.8 billion pesos in 1996, running at about one-third the Organisation of Economic Co-operation and Development (OECD) average for agricultural support (*OECD Observer*, June/July 1997).

61. See the Pew Hispanic Center report, "Unauthorized Migrants: Numbers and Characteristics," June 14, 2005.

62. Michael Dukakis and Daniel Mitchell, "Raise Wages, Not Walls," *New York Times*, July 25, 2006.

63. The Pew Hispanic Center estimate that "40 to 50 percent of the total [unauthorized migrant population] entered the country through legal ports of entry"—that is, are overstayers on visitor and student visas, or on temporary work permits ("Modes of Entry for the Unauthorized Migrant Population," Fact Sheet, May 22, 2006).

64. The Congressional Budget Office estimated that the building and maintenance of 870 miles of fencing would cost $3.3 billion (Jonathan Weisman, "Cost of Senate Immigration Bill Put at $126 Billion," *Washington Post*, August 22, 2006, p. A01).

65. The Center for American Progress estimates the cost of deporting 10 million illegal immigrants over a five-year period at $206–230 billion, or at least $41.2 billion annually. That's twice the current cost of military operations in Afghanistan, and half the annual cost of the war in Iraq (see David A. Jaeger, "Deporting the Undocumented: A Cost Assessment," July 2005).

66. The big six are California, Texas, Florida, New York, Arizona, and Illinois. New Jersey and North Carolina are also big recipients of Mexican migration, and the diaspora is now countrywide (see William Frey, "Diversity Spreads Out," Washington, DC: The Brookings Institution, March 2006).

CHAPTER 8

1. Dan Wakefield, *The Hijacking of Jesus* (New York: Nation Books, 2006), p. 16.

2. Ryan Sager, *The Elephant in the Room* (Hoboken, NJ: John Wiley and Sons Inc, 2006), p. 146.

3. There is immense complexity here, difficult to capture in a short chapter, and one huge anomaly—namely, that African American conservative Protestants vote overwhelmingly for the Democrats. Our focus here is on the arguments of organizations and leaders claiming to speak for conservative Christians. For what conservative Christians in contemporary American actually think, see Andrew Greeley and Michael Hout, *The Truth About Conservative Christians* (Chicago: University of Chicago Press, 2006).

4. John Winthrop, "City Upon a Hill," sermon, 1630.

5. Quoted on the Web site of People for the American Way, under the entry for the CWA, www.pfaw.org.

6. Concerned Women for America, "About CWA," www.cwfa.org/about.asp.

7. Traditional Values Coalition, "Traditional Values Defined," www.traditionalvalues.org/defined.asp.

8. Kevin Philips, *American Theocracy* (New York: Viking, 2006), p. 102.

9. Pat Buchanan, *The Death of the West* (New York: Thomas Dunne Books, 2002), p. 179.

10. Cited in Joseph L. Conn, "The Christian Coalition Born Again?" *Church and State*, 2002, 55 (10).

11. Gary Bauer, "Why We Always Lose," American Values Web site: www.amvalues
.org, February 20, 2004.

12. It was at Jerry Falwell's church in October 2005 that the Rev. Franklin Graham
reportedly responded to Hurricane Katrina by saying of New Orleans, "there's been
satanic worship. There's been sexual perversion. God is going to use that storm to
bring revival. God has a plan. God has a purpose" (This in Robert Keyes, "Franklin
Graham Sees Hurricane Katrina as Judgment of God," www.americanchronicle.com
/artices, September 27, 2006).

13. Robert Knight, "Iraq Scandal is 'Perfect Storm' of American Culture," Concerned Women for America, May 12, 2004.

14. Jerry Falwell reacted to the attacks on 9/11 by saying to Pat Robertson on his
700 Club that "I really believe that the pagans and the abortionists, and the feminists,
and the gays and the lesbians who are actively trying to make that an alternative lifestyle, the ACLU, People for the American Way, all of them who have tried to secular-
ize America. I point the finger in their face and say 'you helped this happen.' " He
later retracted his statement to this degree at least—confirming that the hijackers
alone bore direct responsibility for the attacks, but remaining of the view that the
ACLU and others "have removed our nation from its relationship with Christ on
which it was founded" and so "created an environment which possibly has caused
God to lift the veil of protection which has allowed no one to attack America on our
soil since 1812" (on the CNN Web site www.cnn.com; September 14, 2001).

15. Some of them are very homophobic—indeed Jerry Falwell once went so far
as to describe the AIDS epidemic as "the wrath of a just God against homosexuals,"
such that "to oppose it would be like an Israelite jumping into the Red Sea to save
one of Pharoah's charioteers," cited in Clint Willis and Nate Hardcastle (eds.), *Jesus
Is Not a Republican* (New York: Thunder's Mouth Press, 2005). It's interesting in this
regard that the 2006 scandal of Mark Foley's solicitation of young pages was treated
by many Christian Conservatives primarily as a scandal about homosexuality within
the higher reaches of the Republican Party, rather than as a scandal about the sexual
exploitation of the young and vulnerable. It was the fact that Foley was gay rather
than predatory that seemed to give offence.

16. www.operationsaveamerica.org/misc/misc/purpose.html.

17. Traditional Values Coalition, "Traditional Values Defined."

18. This, from the Rev. Mark H. Creech, on the Web site of the American Family
Association, www.afa.net., October 4, 2006.

19. Traditional Values Coalition, "Traditional Values Defined."

20. Janice Shaw Crouse, "Post-Modern Thinking: How It Has Betrayed American
Women," *Data Digest*, Beverly LaHaye Institute, April–May 2005, VI(2): 2.

21. Cited on the Web site of People for the American Way, under the section on
"Family Research Council," www.pfaw.org.

22. Louis Sheldon of the Traditional Values Coalition, at a hearing on the
National Education Association, April 1991.

23. The Rev. Mark H. Creech, www.afa.net.

24. Bill Press, *How the Republicans Stole Christmas* (New York: Doubleday, 2005),
p. 27.

25. Interviewed by Deborah Caldwell in an article headed "A Double Attack
Against the Name of Jesus Christ," at www.beliefnet.com/story/111/story_1117.html.

See also Stephen Zunes, "The Influence of the Christian Right on U.S. Middle East Policy," Foreign Policy in Focus Report, June 28, 2004.

26. For a representative sample of comments of this kind, from Jerry Falwell, Franklin Graham, and Pat Robertson among others, see the Web site of the Ontario Consultants on Religious Tolerance, www.religioustolerance.org/reac_ter2.html.

27. In 1971, delegates to the Southern Baptist Convention actually adopted a resolution calling "on Southern Baptists to work for legislation that will allow the possibility of abortion under such conditions as rape, incest, clear evidence of severe fetal deformity, and carefully ascertained evidence of the likelihood of damage to the emotional, mental and physical health of the mother." Randall Balmer, *Thy Kingdom Come* (New York: Basic Books, 2006), p. 12.

28. "The IRS threat to segregated schools was what initially enraged the Christian Community," Randall Balmer quotes Paul Weyrich as saying (Ibid., p. 16). Paul Weyrich has long been a major figure on the American Right.

29. Jerry Falwell, for example, opposed civil rights in the 1960s, and a decade later visited South Africa and denounced Nelson Mandela as a communist.

30. Randall Balmer argues that the claim that the movement began as a reaction to *Roe v. Wade* is the real "abortion myth" (*Thy Kingdom Come*, pp. 11–14). Ed Dobson, Falwell's colleague in the Moral Majority, is quoted by Blamer as saying, "I frankly do not remember abortion ever being mentioned as a reason why we ought to do something" (*Thy Kingdom Come*, p. 16).

31. Greeley and Hout, *The Truth About Conservative Christians*, p. 2.

32. Cited in Willis and Hardcastle, *Jesus Is Not a Republican*, p. 240.

33. This wonderful image is not mine. It's shamelessly borrowed from David G. Myers and Letha Dawson Scanzoni, *What God Has Joined Together: The Christian Case For Gay Marriage* (New York: HarperCollins, 2005), p. 135.

34. In his *Our Endangered Values* (New York: Simon & Schuster, 2005), President Carter calls on Christians to resist the rise of fundamentalism within their own ranks, and to "encompass people who are different from us with our care, generosity, forgiveness, compassion and unselfish love" (p. 31).

35. The clearest and most powerful recent statement of this argument can be found in my Wake Forest colleague Charles Kimball's *When Religion Becomes Evil* (San Francisco: HarperCollins, 2002).

36. Carter, *Our Endangered Values*, p. 34.

37. ". . . of course back in the '50s and early '60s we had not yet seen the undermining of the sanctity of human life that was unleashed in the early '70s by *Roe v Wade* . . . there are consequences when you tell young women they have a 'right' to take innocent human life. Can we be surprised when some young men conclude life is cheap?" Gary Bauer, *Doing Things Right* (Nashville: Word Publishing, 2001), pp. 23–24.

38. The considerable body of research evidence on this is surveyed in Elizabeth Cantor, "Gays and Lesbians as Parents and Partners: The Psychological Evidence," in *Same-Sex Marriage: The Legal and Psychological Evolution in America*, eds. Donald J. Cantor, Elizabeth Cantor, James C. Black, and Campbell D. Barrett (Middletown, CT: Wesleyan University Press, 2006), pp. 47–80.

39. Jonathan Raunch, *Gay Marriage: Why It Is Good for Gays, Good for Straights, and Good for America* (New York: Time Books, Henry Holt and Company, 2004), pp. 5–6, 81–82.

40. Myers and Scanzoni, *What God Has Joined Together*, p. 38.

41. And in practice it doesn't. Being married brings a whole coterie of financial, legal, social, and psychological advantages denied the unmarried, however long and civil their union. For a list of these, see Davina Kotulski, *Why You Should Give A Damn About Gay Marriage* (Los Angeles, Advocate Books, 2004); or R. Claire Synder, *Gay Marriage and Democracy* (Lanham, MD: Rowman & Littlefield, 2006).

42. Evan Wolfson, *Why Marriage Matters* (New York: Simon & Schuster, 2004), p. 144.

43. Press, *How the Republicans Stole Christmas*, p. 143.

44. Abortion divides churches from each other rather than dividing the religious world from the secular. For pro-choice religious views, see the Web sites of the Concerned Clergy for Choice, http://edfundpa.org/clergy/about_clergy.html, and The Religious Coalition on Reproductive Choice, www.RCRC.org, which lists the many churches affiliated with it.

45. This was 1.6 million in 1992, but 1.3 million in 2000.

46. This case has been argued again of late by Hillary Clinton, and it is defended persuasively by Bill Press, among others, in his *How the Republicans Stole Christmas*.

47. "If we are going to be pro-life, we cannot say we are against abortion and then let our children suffer in broken schools. We can't claim to be pro-life at the same time we are cutting support for Medicaid, Head Start, or the Women's, Infants and Children's Program" (from the pro-life Democratic challenger to Rick Santorum in Pennsylvania, Robert Casey, quoted in Alan Cooperman, "Senate Candidate Speaks of Life, Faith," *The Washington Post*, September 15, 2006).

48. For a fascinating discussion of evangelical attitudes to wealth, see "Does God Want You to Be Rich?" *Time*, September 18, 2006.

49. Press, *How the Republicans Stole Christmas*, p. 233.

50. Balmer, *Thy Kingdom Come*, p. 23.

51. This argument is made at length, and persuasively, in James Carville and Paul Begala *Take It Back: a Battle Plan for Democratic Victory* (New York: Simon & Schuster, 2006), pp. 62–84.

52. Although maybe St Paul was. For the relevant arguments, see Willis and Hardcastle, *Jesus Is Not a Republican*, pp. 294–306.

53. This claim in the book by David Kuo, a former official in the Faith-Based Initiatives Program based in the White House, *Tempting Faith: An Inside Story of Political Seduction* (New York: Simon & Schuster, 2006).

54. Eyal Press, "In God's Country," *The Nation*, November 20, 2006, p. 34.

55. On this, see Greeley and Hout, *The Truth About Conservative Christians*, p. 4.

56. The number of evangelicals with a favorable view of the Republican Party fell from 74 percent to 54 percent between 2004 and 2006, according to the Pew Research Center. On the "soggy center," see the exchange between James Davison Hunter and Alan Wolfe in *Is There a Culture War?* Washington, DC, Brookings Institution, 2006. On the tensions between evangelicals and Libertarians inside the Republican "big tent," see Sagar, *The Elephant in the Room*, pp. 81–105.

57. Kimball, *When Religion Becomes Evil*, pp. 154–185.

58. Ibid., p. 213.

59. Ibid., p. 208.

CHAPTER 9

1. "Postwar Findings about Iraq's WMD Programs and Links to Terrorism and How They Compare with Pre-war Assessments," Report of the Senate Select Committee on Intelligence, September 2006, p. 105.

2. Jim Loebe, "U.S. Majority Still Believe in Iraq's WMD, al-Qaeda Ties," *Common Dreams News Center*, April 22, 2004.

3. Vice President Cheney, remarks to the traveling press, December 20, 2005.

4. President Bush, when declaring the end of military operations from the deck of the USS *Abraham Lincoln,* May 1, 2003.

5. Fuller extracts of the speech can be found in David Coates and Joel Krieger, *Blair's War* (Cambridge, UK: Polity Press, 2004), pp. 31–32.

6. Perhaps even treason and betrayal? (The titles of books on this by Anne Coulter and David Limbaugh). This is a very strong and angry theme in many right-wing critiques of pre-9/11 policy: that the United States "slept" while being attacked, and that Clinton was asleep more than most. For some, that "sleeping" goes back to Teheran and the hostage crisis of 1979. For others, it begins with Beirut and the slaughter of Marines in 1983. For yet others, it starts with the killing of an American citizen on the *Achille Lauro* in 1985 or the bringing down of Pan Am 103 over Lockerbie in 1988. But whenever the story is said to begin, there is general agreement in these circles that things deteriorated dramatically in the 1990s and that the ball was dropped by the Clinton administration. The Democrats both failed to recognize the danger posed to the United States by bin Laden (in spite of being told repeatedly) and failed to kill him in 1998 when they could have done so.

7. Remarks at Whitehall Palace, November 19, 2003.

8. State of the Union Address, 2004.

9. Ibid.

10. Remarks at Whitehall Palace, November 19, 2003.

11. Ibid.

12. See, for example, Tom Tancredo, *In Mortal Danger* (Nashville, TN: WND Books, 2006), p. 185.

13. Remarks at Whitehall Palace, November 19, 2003.

14. President Bush, in his State of the Union Address, 2006.

15. This, according to a senior Palestinian politician (quoted in Mark Lawson, "The Maker of U.S. Policy," *The Guardian,* October 7, 2005). In April 2004, the president spoke of "this belief, this strong belief that freedom is not this country's gift to the world. Freedom is the Almighty's gift to every man and woman in this world. And as the greatest power on the face of the earth, we have an obligation to help the spread of freedom." Vice President Cheney made a similar argument, that "we are created in the image and likeness of God, and He has planted in our hearts a yearning to be free," in his remarks at the 2006 Vilnius Conference, May 4, 2006.

16. Speech to the American Legion, August 31, 2006.

17. This definition is Bill O'Reilly's, on townhall.com, September 7, 2006.

18. Representative Lincoln Diaz-Balart, speaking in the House of Representatives, January 30, 2005.

19. See his remarks at a rally for the troops, April 19, 2006.

20. President Bush, Address to the Nation, September 11, 2006.

21. The first and third of these by Vice President Cheney, the second by Kenneth Adelmann, recalled in Jim Rutenberg, "Washington Memo," *The New York Times*, August 6, 2006.

22. Cited by in Paul Krugman "March of Folly," *The New York Times*, July 17, 2006.

23. On Fox News, as reported in "Rumsfeld-Fox News," www.foxnews.com. *The Financial Times*, June 27, 2005.

24. NBC transcript for *NBC: Meet the Press*, June 26, 2005. www.msnbc.msn.com.

25. Defense Budget Testimony, February 4, 2004.

26. Quoted in Peter Baker, "U.S. Not Winning Ware in Iraq, Bush Says for First Time," *The Washington Post,* December 20, 2006.

27. Office of the Press Secretary, The White House, reported in Michael Fletcher, "Bushe Warns of Enduring Terror Threat," *The Washington Post*, September 6, 2006.

28. This on NBC, reported in Simon Jeffrey, "Iraq/al Qaida Remarks Misunderstood," *The Guardian*, August 31, 2004.

29. The president, speaking at Crawford, August 11, 2005.

30. Ibid.

31. Quoted in Ann Scott Tyson, "Rumsfeld Assails Critics of War Policy," *The Washington Post*, August 30, 2006.

32. According to Senator Bill Frist, quoted in Kate Zernicke, "Senate Rejects Call to begin Iraq pullback," *The New York Times*, June 23, 2006.

33. Vice President Cheney, quoted in Patrick Henley and Jennifer Medina, "Lieberman goes on the Offensive," *The New York Times*, August 11, 2006.

34. Ibid.

35. Remarks at a Luncheon for Arizona Victory 2006, August 15, 2006.

36. Quoted in Ann Scott Taylor, "Rumsfeld Assails Critics of War Policy," *The Washington Post*, August 30, 2006.

37. Maureen Dowd, "Vice Must Wash Hands Before Returning to Work," *The New York Times*, September 13, 2006.

38. See, respectively, Bill O'Reilly, *The Fight of Our Lives*, BillOreilly.com, June 22, 2006; Rush Limbaugh, "Iran is Mocking Us," *Welcome to Rush 24/7*, June 1, 2006; and Michael Savage, *Liberalism Is a Mental Disorder,* p. 52.

39. They got their prize in December 2006, as the president admitted the new need for a change of strategy in the wake of the midterm election defeat for the Republicans. Many senior Republicans believed an earlier dismissal of Rumsfeld could have prevented that defeat.

40. Representative Hoyer, quoting Thomas Friedman, in the House of Representatives, June 20, 2005.

41. This argument from the Cato Institute's report, Christopher Preble director, "Exiting Iraq: Why the U.S. Must End the Military Occupation and Renew the War Against Al Qaeda," Washington, DC, The Cato Institute, 2004.

42. Andrew Sullivan, "What I Got Wrong about the War," *Time* magazine, March 13, 2006.

43. On this, see his "Neo-conservatism has evolved into something I can no longer support," *The Guardian*, February 22, 2006, p. 27; and *America at the Crossroads* (New Haven, CT: Yale University Press, 2006).

44. The veracity of many of the claims made in the February 2003 speech was challenged in the report of the Senate Intelligence Committee released in July 2004.

45. This from David Kay, head of the Iraq Survey Group, at the end of its fruitless search for Iraqi WMD: "I was convinced and still am convinced that there were no stockpiles of weapons of mass destruction at the time of the war" (*The Guardian*, March 3, 2004). As he put it to the Senate on January 28, 2004, "Let me begin by saying, we were almost all wrong, and I include myself there." The White House discretely abandoned the search for WMD in January 2005.

46. And not just a U.S. double standard, but a U.K. one, too. The Thatcher government secretly allowed arms shipments to Iraq and lied to Parliament about them. The resulting Scott Inquiry (1996) helped pave the way for the conservative election defeat of 1997.

47. Primarily in Richard Clarke's evidence to Senate in March 2004, and in his *Against All Enemies* (New York: The Free Press, 2004).

48. See Bob Woodward, *Bush at War* (New York: Simon & Schuster, 2002), p. 49.

49. "The truth is that for reasons that have a lot to do with the U.S. government bureaucracy we settled on the one issue that everyone could agree on, which was weapons of mass destruction as the core reason" (Wolfowitz interview with *Vanity Fair*, May 30, 2003).

50. The call for military action to effect regime change in Baghdad was made in an open letter to President Clinton in January 1998 signed by, among others, Richard Armitage, John Bolton, Richard Perle, Donald Rumsfeld, and Paul Wolfowitz—all big players in the formation of foreign policy under George W. Bush.

51. See, for example, the vice president's address to the American Enterprise Institute, November 21, 2005.

52. For an extremely timely warning of this dimension of emerging U.S. foreign policy, see Eric Alterman, "Neocon Dreams, American Nightmares," *The Nation*, August 28–September 4, 2006, p. 10. The NPR Web site for September 20, 2006, carried an alarming report than many of the individuals who had staffed the Pentagon's Office of Special Planning—a major backdoor route to the White House for émigré-based intelligence in the buildup to the invasion of Iraq—were now staffing a new "Iran desk" unit in the Pentagon.

53. Cited in Richard Norton-Taylor, "A Boost for bin Laden," *The Guardian*, September 26, 2006.

54. The attempt to discredit Joseph Wilson, after he reported that Iraq was not actively seeking uranium in Niger, by outing his wife Valerie Plame as a CIA agent, brought Lewis "Scooter" Libby, Dick Cheney's chief of staff, before a grand jury in October 2005.

55. Quoted in Paul Krugman, "Reign of Error," *The New York Times*, July 28, 2006.

56. The first at a news conference, January 8, 2004; the second when interviewed by Barbara Walters of ABC News, September 2005; the third when interviewed by James Naughtie, see *The Accidental American* (London: PublicAffairs, 2004), p. 121.

57. On NBC News, *Meet the Press*, September 10, 2006.

58. "It is true that much of the [pre-war] intelligence turned out to be wrong." President Bush, quoted on cnn.com, December 14, 2005. Tony Blair conceded the same point in the House of Commons on October 13, 2004.

59. For details, see BBC News, "Bush's Iraq WMD Joke Backfires," March 26, 2006.

60. Press conference by the president, August 21, 2006.

61. Quoted in S. Ackerman and J. B. Judis, "The First Casualty," *The New Republic*, June 30, 2003.

62. There are now many official reports arguing this. The CIA's own internal think tank concluded in January 2005 that Iraq had now replaced Afghanistan as the training ground for a new generation of jihadist terrorists (see Ewen MacAskill, "Iraq Creating New Jihadists, Says CIA, "*The New York Times*, July 27, 2006).

63. The imagery is that of former Vice President Al Gore, speaking in New York in May 2004.

64. Interviewed by Sir David Frost on Al-jazeera, November 2006.

65. Zalmay Khalilzad, quoted in Julian Borger and Ewen MacAskill, "U.S. Envoy to Iraq: We Have Opened the Pandora's Box," *The Guardian*, March 8, 2006.

66. See, for example, the testimony of General John Abizaid, head of U.S. Central Command, to the Senate Armed Services Committee, August 3, 2006: "the sectarian violence is probably as bad as I've seen it. If not stopped, it is possible Iraq could move towards civil war."

67. The Iraqi Health Ministry estimated that 22,950 Iraqis died because of the war in 2006 alone. The United Nations later put the figure even higher, at 34,000. The U.K. medical journal, *The Lancet*, estimated the total war dead in Iraq by 2006 as 655,000—1 Iraqi in 40 (Dan Murphy, "Iraq Casualty Figures Open Up New Battleground," Christian Science Monitor, October 13, 2006).

68. This was the conclusion of a report commissioned by the United Kingdom's Ministry of Defence academy, leaked to the BBC, September 27, 2006.

69. The official report into the events of 7/7 made it clear that the four bombers were motivated to act by U.K. involvement in the Iraq invasion. In November 2006, MI5 reported 30 terror plots being planned, 1,600 individuals, and 200 networks under surveillance in the United Kingdom, with the United Kingdom as al-Qaeda's "number one target."

70. "... the federal government is spending more every three days to finance the war in Iraq than it has provided over the last three years to prop up the security of all 361 U.S. commercial seaports." Stephen Flynn, author of *America the Vulnerable*, cited in Terry Neal, "Iraq War Hasn't Made United States Safer, Author Says," *The Washington Post*, July 18, 2005.

71. *The New York Times*, *The Washington Post*, and the BBC all reported the existence of a National Intelligence Estimate, based on the analyses of the United States' 16 intelligence agencies, arguing that the invasion had spawned a new generation of Islamic radicalism worldwide (see the Web sites of the three sources for September 24, 2006: www.nytimes.com, www.washingtonpost.com, and www.newsbbc.com.uk).

72. "The world is beginning to doubt the moral basis of our fight against terrorism. To redefine Common Article Three [of the Geneva Conventions] would add to these doubts. Furthermore it would put our own troops at risk" (letter from Colin Powell to John McCain, September 15, 2006).

73. For a presidential briefing on the costs of U.S. double standard—soft on Israel, hard on the Palestinians—see Bob Woodward, *State of Denial* (New York: Simon & Schuster, 2006), p. 46.

74. Vice President Cheney has referred to them accurately as "enemies who dwell in the shadows and recognize neither the laws of warfare nor standards of morality" (remarks to the National Restaurant Association, September 12, 2005). The novelty of this enemy, and is particular illusiveness, is a key part of many of the vice president's speeches—and quite properly so. The dispute here is not with the characterization of the problem, but with the nature of the administration's response to it.

75. This argument is developed at length in chapters 7 and 8 of Coates and Krieger, *Blair's War*, pp. 115–155.

76. Quoted in Eric Schmitt, "Rapid Pullout from Iraq Urged by Key Democrat," *The New York Times*, November 18, 2005.

77. Lawrence Freedman, "A Region Held Hostage to Failed Policies," *The Financial Times*, August 2, 2006.

78. Geoffrey Wheatcroft, "Iraq Is a Full-Scale Military Balls-Up. Our Best Move Is to Cut and Run," *The Guardian*, June 23, 2006.

79. Most strikingly, John Mearsheimer and Stephen Walt, whose March 23, 2006, article in *The London Review of Books* brought a gale of abuse down upon them; see also Thomas Friedman, "War of Ideas: Part 4," *New York Times*, January 18, 2004.

80. Most notably, former President Clinton, in his *Financial Times* interview of September 20, 2006.

CHAPTER 10

1. "U.S. Economic Strength," Department of the Treasury, November 3, 2006.

2. George W. Bush, press conference, October 11, 2006.

3. Presidential radio address, July 15, 2006.

4. Radio interview, November 4, 2005.

5. George W. Bush, press conference, October 11, 2006.

6. Presidential radio address, October 28, 2006.

7. George W. Bush, press conference, October 11, 2006.

8. *President Bush's Agenda for Job Creation and Economic Opportunity*, delivered to the Economic Club of Chicago, January 6, 2006.

9. President Bush, speaking in Detroit, June 9, 2006.

10. Both of these White House news reports are cited, and challenged, in the Economic Policy Institute's (EPI's) "Critiquing Misleading White House statements About the Economy," *Snapshot*, May 3, 2006.

11. These, from Dinesh D'Souza, *What's So Great about America?* (Washington, DC: Regnery Publishing, Inc., 2002), pp. 192–193.

12. Dick Cheney, speaking at a luncheon for Vern Buchanan, October 6, 2006, Florida.

13. Lobbyists in Washington are currently spending about $25 million a year per politician (Gary Younge, "Like Arsenic in the Water Supply, Lobbyists Have Poisoned Washington," *The Guardian*, January 6, 2006). There are now more than 34,000 registered lobbyists in Washington, a number that has *doubled* since 2000 (for data, see Jeffrey Birnbaum, "The Road to Riches Is Called K Street," *The Washington Post*, June 22, 2005).

14. President Bush. Cited in Martin Vander Meyer, "Can Free Trade Be Fair Trade?" *New Statesman*, February 28, 2005, p. 10.

15. The details are in V. Mogensen (editor), *Worker Safety Under Siege* (New York: M.E. Sharpe, 2006).

16. Wolfgang Streeck, "Beneficial Constraints: On the Economic Limits of Rational Voluntarism," in *Contemporary Capitalism: The Embeddedness of Institutions*, eds. J. R. Hollingsworth and R. Boyer, pp. 197–219 (Cambridge, UK: Cambridge University Press, 1997).

17. For this argument, see William Lazonick, *Business Organization and the Myth of the Market Economy* (Cambridge, UK: Cambridge University Press, 1991); and David Coates, *Models of Capitalism: Growth and Stagnation in the Modern Era* (Cambridge, MA: Polity Press, 2000).

18. The mechanism here is the little-studied compensation committees. In the United States, "executive pay is, in fact, a game of leapfrog, in which every compensation committee tries to pay its CEO more than the average, with the inevitable results. . . . So are they worth it. That is a controversial question. I, for one, doubt it." (Martin Wolf, "The Rich Rewards and Poor Prospects of a New Gilded Age," *Financial Times*, April 24, 2006, p. 15).

19. On this much-forgotten but vital dimension of the U.S. postwar growth story, see D. Gordon, "Chickens Home to Roost: From Prosperity to Stagnation in the Postwar U.S. Economy," in *Understanding American Economic Decline,* eds. M. Bernstein and D.E. Adler, pp. 34–76 (Cambridge, UK: Cambridge University Press, 1994).

20. If you doubt it, read Jeremy Caplan's study of two janitors—one unionized in Pittsburgh, on $12.52 an hour, the other nonunionized in Cincinnati, on $6.50 an hour—in *Time*, June 26, 2006, pp. 56–58.

21. The key text here is actually by a leading conservative intellectual. It's *Trust* by Francis Fukuyama (New York: The Free Press, 1995).

22. See Steven Greenhouse, "How Costco Became the Anti-Wal-Mart," *New York Times*, July 17, 2005, Business Section.

23. The deficit, at $50.1 billion in 1991, was equivalent to 0.8 percent of GDP. By 2004, the deficit was $668.1 billion, and 5.7 percent of GDP. William R Cline, *The United States as a Debtor Nation* (Washington, DC: Institute for International Economics, 2005), p. 36.

24. Martin Wolf, "Do Not Believe Everything You Hear About Global Imbalances," *The Financial Times*, no date. The Cline forecast is slightly lower: A deficit equivalent to just 14 percent of GDP by 2024.

25. The biggest 1980s deficit was 1987, at 3.4 percent of GDP (Cline, *The United States as a Debtor Nation*, p. 1).

26. Paul Krugman, "CSI: Trade Deficit," *The New York Times*, April 24, 2006.

27. Quoted in Paul Bluster, "Trade Gap Hits Record for 4th Year in a Row," *The Washington Post*, February 11, 2006.

28. "Between 2000 and 2005, the U.S. economy grew by 12 percent in real terms and productivity . . . rose 17 percent. Over the same period, the median hourly wage . . . rose by only 3 percent in real terms. That compares with a 12 percent gain in the previous five years" Krishna Guha, Edward Luce, and Andrew Ward, "Anxious Middle: Why Ordinary Americans Have Missed Out on the Benefits of Growth," *The Financial Times*, November 2, 2006, p. 11).

29. Judith B. Schor, *The Overworked American* (New York: Basic Books, 1992). The EPI estimate that, in families with both parents working, hours worked

increased 11 percent overall between 1975 and 2002, with extra hours worked by wives increasing by 319 hours per year for the bottom 20 percent of earners, and by more than 500 hours a year for women in families whose earnings are the second-fifth and middle-fifth of the income distribution (EPI, *Facts and Figures: Work Hours*, Washington, DC, October 2006).

30. The figures are 1,815 hours for American workers (in 2000), 1,581 for the Swedes, and 1,444 for the Germans. In Lawrence Mishel, Jared Bernstein, and Sylvia Allegretto, *The State of Working America*, An Economic Policy Institute Book (Ithaca, NY: ILR Press, 2005), p. 415.

31. For the latest available data (2002), placing the United States *behind* Switzerland, Japan, Norway, Denmark, Austria, Sweden, Germany, and Finland, see Mishel, Bernstein, and Allegretto, *The State of Working America*, p. 384. The Japanese and Scandinavians slip slightly behind the United States if purchasing power parity (PPP) exchange rates are used, but that calculation leaves out education, child care, and health costs, which are all significantly higher in the United States. On the UN Human Development Index, which rates not only per capita income but also education levels, health care, and life expectancy, the United States dropped to eighth place in 2006.

32. Jacob S. Hacker, *The Great Risk Shift* (New York: Oxford University Press, 2006), p. 70.

33. Ibid, p. 73.

34. Cited in Edward Luce and Krishna Guha, "Seeking Shelter," *The Financial Times*, November 3, 2006, p. 13.

35. For the argument that the American Dream is increasingly unattainable for most Americans, see Jeremy Rifkin, *The European Dream: How Europe's Vision of the Future Is Quietly Eclipsing the American Dream* (London: Penguin, 2005), pp. 11–57; and Will Hutton, *A Declaration of Interdependence* (New York: W.W. Norton, 2003), pp. 130–158.

36. In 2004, average earnings for high school dropouts were less than $20,000, compared with $29,000 for high school graduates and $51,000 for college graduates. A 2006 survey conducted by business research organizations found nearly three-quarters of high school graduates deficient in basic English writing skills and more than half deficient in mathematics (cited in *The Financial Times*, October 2, 2006).

37. Jared Bernstein and L. Josh Bivens, "The Wal-Mart Debate," EPI Issue Brief No. 223, June 15, 2006, p. 2.

38. For this, see David Barboza, "China Drafts Law to Empower Unions and End Labor Abuse," *The New York Times*, October 13, 2006.

39. Mogensen, *Worker Safety under Siege*, p. xvi.

40. Not that the nonsense is all on one side on this issue. For a condemnation of George W Bush as "the King of Outsourcing," see Michael Savage, *Liberalism Is a Mental Disorder* (New York: Nelson Current, 2003), p. 91.

41. Not all of them, of course. Pat Buchanan for one has long argued against what he calls the party's "addiction to free trade." (See, for example, his "Will Free Trade Ruin America Too?" posted on his Web site, www.buchanan.org, November 6, 2001). With the U.S. trade deficit at record levels in 2006, he asked again, "what constitutes failure for a free-trade policy?" (This, in his "Our Hollow Prosperity," www.buchanan.org, February 15, 2006).

42. People who live on the same street in a typical American town often now may be in entirely different labor markets—some competing only with other skilled Americans, others competing with wage workers in countries far away. The developing world exists in the basements of many American cities just as potently as it does in Asia and Latin America.

43. The case for this is well put by Edward N. Wolff in his *What Has Happened to the Quality of Life in the Advanced Industrial Nations?* (Northampton, MA: Edward Elgar, 2004), p. 23.

44. The case is well made in Gene Sterling, "How to Reform a Winner-Takes-All Economy," *The Financial Times*, January 31, 2006; and by the Center for American Progress in their 2005 proposals to make the tax system fair and simple (see John Irons and John Podesta, "A Tax Plan for Progressives," *The American Prospect*, June 2005, pp. 52–54).

45. The case is well made in Harold Meyerson, "Not Your Father's Detroit," *The American Prospect*, April 2006, pp. 18–20.

46. The case is well put in Thomas A. Kochan, *Restoring the American Dream* (Cambridge, MA: The MIT Press, 2006), pp. 182–185.

47. The case for this is well put by Stanley Aaronovitz in *Just Around the Corner: The Paradox of the Jobless Recovery* (Philadelphia: Temple University Press, 2005), pp. 133–145.

48. The case is well made in Louis Gerstner's "Teaching At Risk," a report for the Teaching Commission, 2006.

49. The case is well made in Theda Skocpol, *The Missing Middle* (New York: W.W. Norton, 2000), pp. 156–158.

50. The case is well made in Hacker, *The Great Risk Shift*, pp. 190–191.

51. For the argument, see Kimberley Ann Elliott and Richard B. Freeman, *Can Labor Standards Improve Under Globalization?* Washington, DC: Institute for International Economics, 2003; K. Brofenbrenner, *Uneasy Terrain* (New York: Cornell University Press, 2000) pp. 57–58; and Archon Fung, Dara O'Rourke, and Charles Sabel, *Realizing Labor Standards* (Boston: Boston Review, 2001). The responses to this paper are also worth consulting.

52. On the lines of House Resolution 276, introduced by Sherrod Brown in 2003. See his *The Myths of Free Trade*, pp. 206–207. For an equivalent, see Aaronovitz, *Just Around the Corner*, pp. 147–148.

CHAPTER 11

1. R. H. Tawney, "The Choice before the Labour Party," *Political Quarterly*, volume 3 (reproduced in William A. Robson (ed), *The Political Quarterly in the Thirties*. London: Allan Lane, 1971, pp. 93–111).

2. Ibid., p. 103.

3. Ibid., pp. 107–108.

4. Matthew Yglesias, in *The American Prospect*, February 2006, p. 43. For the predominance of class over religion even among white Conservative Protestants, see Andrew Greeley and Michael Hout, *The Truth About Conservative Christians* (Chicago, University of Chicago Press, 2006), p. 40.

5. Thomas Frank, *What's the Matter with Kansas?* (New York: Henry Holt, 2004), p. 243.

6. Ibid., p. 245.

7. Ibid., p. 245.

8. On the persisting weakness of liberal think tanks—both in funding and in function—see Andy Rich, "War of Ideas," *Stanford Social Innovation Review*, Spring 2005.

9. The case has been laid out with great clarity and passion in Robert Reich's *Reason: Why Liberals Will Win the Battle for America* (New York: Vintage Books, 2004).

10. Cited in Michael Tomasky's "Party in Search of a Notion," *The American Prospect*, May 2006, p. 22.

11. Jared Bernstein, *Common Sense for a Fair Economy* (San Francisco: Berrett-Koehler Publishers, 2006).

12. Douglas Massey, *Return of the "L" Word* (Princeton, NJ: Princeton University Press, 2000).

Selected Bibliography

For a full list of sources and suggestions or further reading, go to www.liberaltoolkit .blogspot.com.

Aaronovitz, Stanley. *Just Around the Corner: The Paradox of the Jobless Recovery*. Philadelphia: Temple University Press, 2005.

Altman, Nancy. *The Battle for Social Security*. Hoboken, NJ: John Wiley, 2005.

Baker, Dean, and Mark Weisbrot. *Social Security: The Phony Crisis*. Chicago: University of Chicago Press, 1999.

Balmer, Randall. *Thy Kingdom Come*. New York: Basic Books, 2006.

Bartlett, Bruce. *Impostor: How George W. Bush Bankrupted America and Betrayed the Reagan Legacy*. New York: Doubleday, 2006.

Beck, Roy. *The Case Against Immigration*. New York: W.W. Norton, 1996.

Bernstein, Jared. *Common Sense for a Fair Economy*. San Francisco: Berrett-Koehler Publishers, 2006.

Borjas, George. *Heaven's Door: Immigration Policy and the American Economy*. Princeton, NJ: Princeton University Press, 1999.

Buchanan, Pat. *The Death of the West*. New York: Thomas Dunne Books, 2002.

————. *Where the Right Went Wrong*. New York: Thomas Dunne Books, 2004.

Cannon, Michael, and Michael Tanner. *Healthy Competition*. Washington, DC: Cato Institute, 2005.

Carville, James, and Paul Begala. *Take it Back: a Battle Plan for Democratic Victory*. New York: Simon & Schuster, 2006.

Cline, William R. *The United States as a Debtor Nation*. Washington, DC: Institute for International Economics, 2005.

Cogan, John, R. Glenn Hubbard, and Daniel P. Kessler. *Healthy, Wealthy and Wise*. Washington, DC: The AEI Press, 2005.

Danziger, Sheldon, Gary Sandefur, and Daniel Weinberg (editors). *Confronting Poverty*. Cambridge, MA: Harvard University Press, 1994.

Darby, Michael (editor). *Reducing Poverty in America*. Thousand Oaks, CA: Sage, 1996.

DeParle, Jason. *American Dream*. New York: Penguin, 2004.

D'Souza, Dinesh. *What's So Great about America*. Washington, DC: Regnery Publishing Inc., 2002.

Duignan, Peter, and Lewis Gann. *The Debate in the United States over Immigration*. Stanford, CA: Hoover Institution Press, 1998.

Ferrara, Peter J., and Michael Tanner. *A New Deal for Social Security*. Washington, DC: Cato Institute, 1998.

Forbes, Steve. *Flat Tax Revolution*. Washington, DC: Regnery Publishing Inc., 2005.

Frank, Thomas. *What's the Matter with Kansas?* New York: Henry Holt, 2004.

Galbraith, James K. *Created Unequal*. New York: The Free Press, 1998.

Greeley, Andrew, and Michael Hout. *The Truth About Conservative Christians*. Chicago: University of Chicago Press, 2006.

Hacker, Jacob. *The Great Risk Shift*. Oxford, UK: Oxford University Press, 2006.

Hays, Sharon. *Flat Broke With Children*. New York: Oxford University Press, 2003.

Hayworth, J. D. *Whatever It Takes: Illegal Immigration, Border Security and the War on Terror*. Washington, DC: Regnery Publishing Inc., 2006.

Howard, Christopher. *The Welfare State Nobody Knows*. Princeton, NJ: Princeton University Press, 2007.

Hunter, James Davison, and Alan Wolfe. *Is There A Culture War?* Washington, DC: Brookings Institution, 2006.

Huntington, Samuel. *Who Are We? The Challenge to America's National Identity*. New York: Simon & Schuster, 2004.

Hutton, Will. *A Declaration of Independence*. New York: W.W. Norton, 2003.

Kimball, Charles. *When Religion Becomes Evil*. San Francisco: HarperCollins, 2002.

Kochan, Thomas A. *Restoring the American Dream*. Cambridge, MA: MIT Press, 2006.

Kotlikoff, Laurence, and Scott Burns. *The Coming Generational Storm*. Cambridge, MA: MIT Press, 2004.

Lakoff, George. *Don't Think of an Elephant: Know Your Values and Frame the Debate*. River Junction, VT: Chelsea Green Publishing, 2004.

Lardner, James, and David A. Smith (editors). *Inequality Matters*. New York: The Free Press, 2005.

Lindsay, James, and Aubrey Singer. *Changing Faces: Immigrants and Diversity in the Twenty-First Century*. Washington, DC: Brookings Institution, 2003.

Massey, Douglas. *Return of the "L" Word*. Princeton, NJ: Princeton University Press, 2000.

McGovern, George. *Social Security and the Golden Age*. Golden, CO: Fulcrum Publishing, 2005.

Mishel, Lawrence, Jared Bernstein, and Sylvia Allegretto. *The State of Working America*. Ithaca, NY: ILR Press, 2005.

Mogensen, Vernon (editor). *Worker Safety under Siege*. New York: M. E. Sharpe, 2006.

Morone, James, and Lawrence Jacobs (editors). *Healthy, Wealthy and Fair*. New York: Oxford University Press, 2004.

Murray, Charles. *Losing Ground*. New York: Basic Books, 1984.

———. *In Our Hands*. Washington, DC: The AEI Press, 2006.

Myers, David, and Letha Dawson Scanzoni. *What God Has Put Together: The Christian Case For Gay Marriage*. New York: HarperCollins, 2005.

Nunberg, Geoffrey. *Talking Right*. New York: Public Affairs, 2006.

OECD (Organisation for Econcomic Co-operation and Development). *Towards High Performing Health Systems*. Paris: OECD, 2004.

O'Reilly, Bill. *Culture Warrior*. New York: Broadway Books, 2006.

Philips, Kevin. *American Theocracy*. New York: Viking, 2006.

Pierson, Paul (editor). *The New Politics of the Welfare State*. Oxford, UK: Oxford University Press, 2001.

Pontusson, Jonas. *Inequality and Prosperity*. New York: The Century Foundation Press, 2005.

Preble, Christopher (director). *Exiting Iraq: Why the US Must End the Military Occupation and Renew the War Against Al Qaeda*. Washington, DC: Cato Institute, 2004.

Press, Bill. *How the Republicans Stole Christmas*. New York: Doubleday, 2005.

Rainwater, Lee, and Timothy Smeeding. *Poor Kids in a Rich Country*. New York: Russell Sage Foundation, 2003.

Raunch, Jonathan. *Gay Marriage: Why It Is Good for Gays, Good for Straights, and Good for America*. New York: Time Books/Henry Holt and Company, 2004.

Reich, Robert. *Reason: Why Liberals Will Win the Battle for America*. New York: Vintage Books, 2004.

Rifkin, Jeremy. *The European Dream: How Europe's Vision of the Future is Quietly Eclipsing the American Dream*. London: Penguin, 2005.

Ryscavage, Paul. *Income Inequality in America: An Analysis of Trends*. New York: M. E. Sharpe, 1999.

Sager, Ryan. *The Elephant in the Room*. Hoboken, NJ: John Wiley, 2006.

Savage, Michael. *Liberalism is a Mental Disorder*. New York: Nelson Current, 2003.

Schwarz, John, and Thomas Volgy. *The Forgotten Americans: Thirty Million Working Poor in the Land of Opportunity*. New York: W.W. Norton, 1993.

Shipler, David. *The Working Poor: Invisible in America*. New York: Alfred A. Knoff, 2004.

Skocpol, Theda. *The Missing Middle*. New York: W.W. Norton, 2000.

Tancredo, Tom. *In Mortal Danger*. Nashville, TN: WND Books, 2006.

Tanner, Michael. *The End of Welfare*. Washington, DC: Cato Institute, 1996.

Wakefield, Dan. *The Hijacking of Jesus*. New York: Nation Books, 2006.

Wellington Haase, Leif. *A New Deal for Health*. New York: The Century Foundation Press, 2005.

Willis, Clint, and Nate Hardcastle (editors). *Jesus is Not a Republican*. New York: Thunder's Mouth Press, 2005.

Wolff, Edward N. *Top Heavy: The Increasing Inequality of Wealth in America and What Can Be Done About It*. New York: The New Press, 2002.

———. *What Has Happened to the Quality of Life in the Advanced Industrial Nations?* Northampton, MA: Edward Elgar, 2004.

Wolfson, Evan. *Why Marriage Matters*. New York: Simon & Schuster, 2004.

Woodward, Bob. *Bush at War*. New York: Simon & Schuster, 2003.

———. *Plan of Attack*. New York: Simon & Schuster, 2004.

———. *State of Denial*. New York: Simon & Schuster, 2006.

Index

About the Author

DAVID COATES is Worrell Professor of Anglo-American Studies at Wake Forest University. He was previously Professor and Director of the International Center for Labor Studies at the University of Manchester. He has written extensively on contemporary political economy, the war on terrorism, and the politics of labor. His previous books include *Prolonged Labour: The Slow Birth of New Labour Britain* (2005), *Blair's War* (2004) with Joel Krieger, and *Models of Capitalism* (2000).